IMAGES
of America

SAMPSON COUNTY

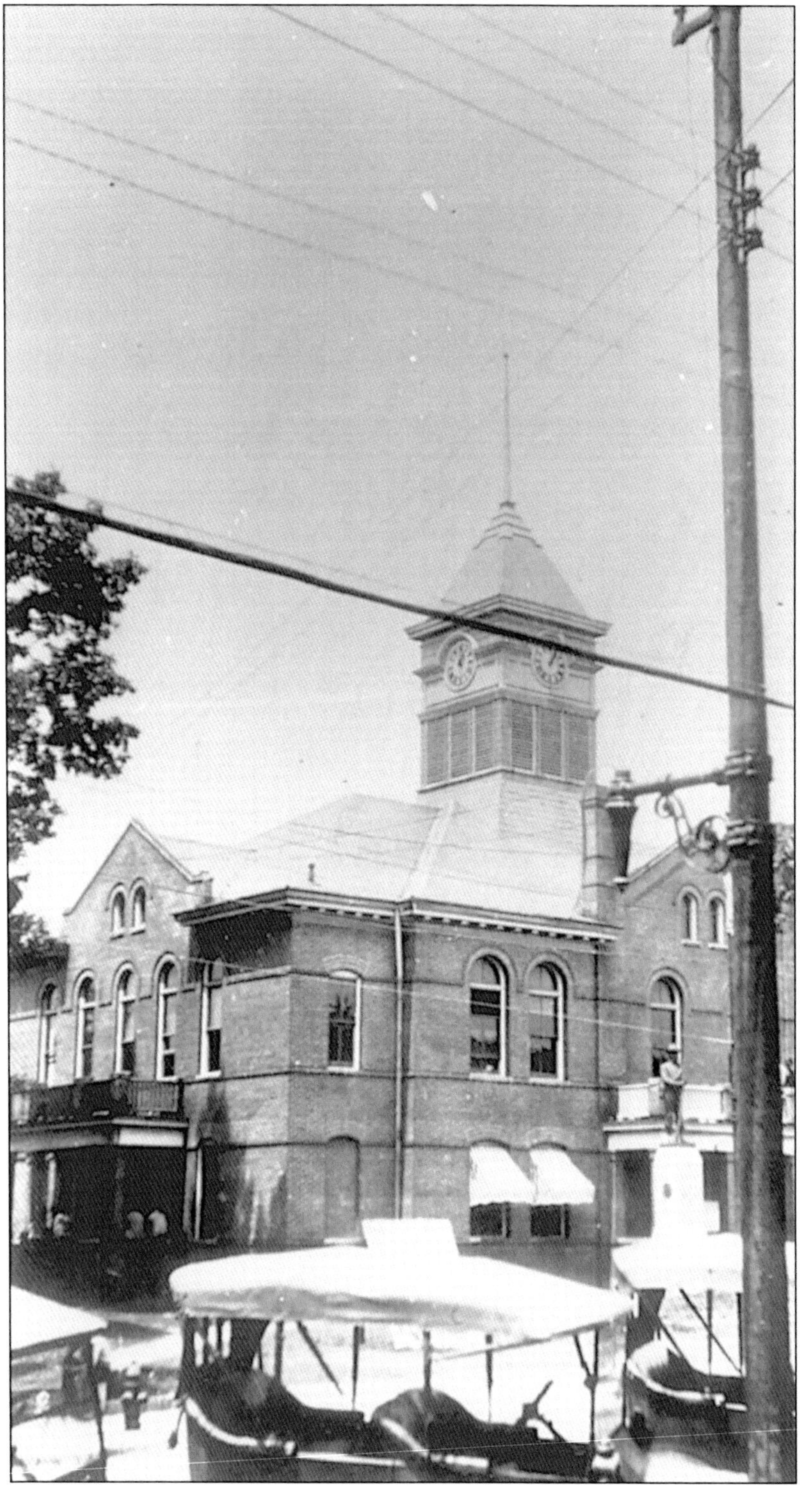

SAMPSON COUNTY COURTHOUSE, C. 1920, BEFORE THE WINGS WERE ADDED IN THE LATE 1930S. (Courtesy of North Carolina Division of Archives and History.)

IMAGES
of America

SAMPSON COUNTY

Sampson County History Museum
Kent Wrench, Editor

ARCADIA
PUBLISHING

ISBN 978-0-7385-0274-8

Published by Arcadia Publishing
Charleston, South Carolina

Printed in the United States of America

Library of Congress Catalog Card Number: 2007941527

For all general information contact Arcadia Publishing at:
Telephone 843-853-2070
Fax 843-853-0044
E-Mail sales@arcadiapublishing.com
For customer service and orders:
Toll-Free 1-888-313-2665

Visit us on the Internet at www.arcadiapublishing.com

Contents

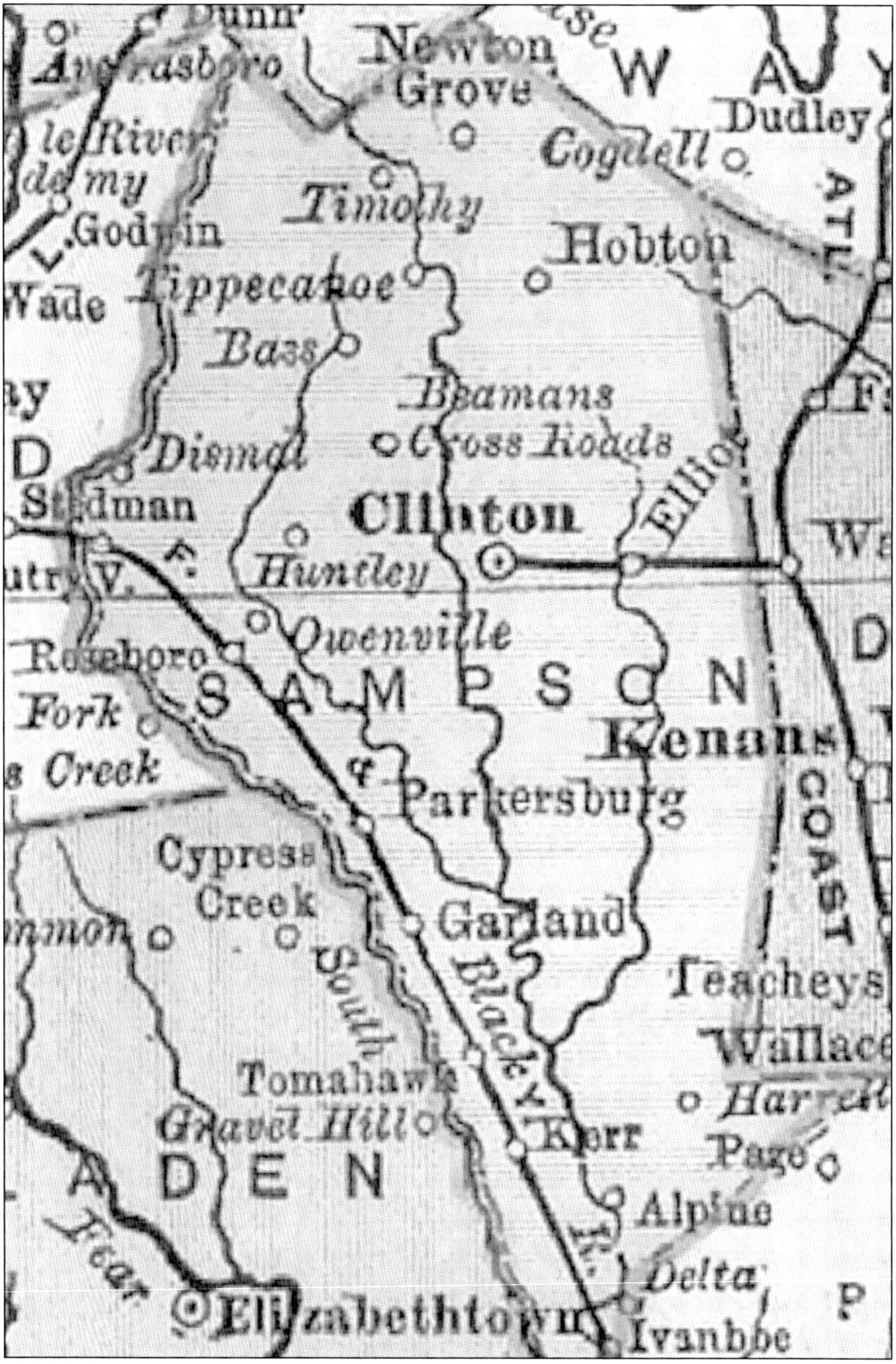

A Map of Sampson County.

INTRODUCTION

Sampson County is the daughter of Duplin, a granddaughter of New Hanover, and a great-granddaughter of Craven County. She came into existence in the following manner: Craven was created in 1712, New Hanover in 1729 by a division of Craven, Duplin in 1749 from a portion of New Hanover, and Sampson in 1784 by a division of Duplin. The boundaries of the county shifted several times, and in 1872, the present boundaries were established. Sampson was named for Richard Sampson, our first state senator.

The settlers came as early as 1740 to the area that became Sampson County and were of Scotch-Irish, English, French, and Swiss descent. Some Native Americans remained in the bounds of Sampson. African Americans came in a state of servitude to the larger plantations in the early days of our county. From the time of the first settlement to the present, agriculture has been the mainstay of the economy in Sampson County.

Sampson, the largest county in the state, established its own hewn-log courthouse with a jail and stocks attached by the fall of 1784. The courthouse was on a 5-acre plot of land that the old Fayetteville–New Berne stage road crossed. The town in which the courthouse stood was first called Rhodes' Cross Roads. When a post office was established there in 1801, the town's name was changed to Sampson Courthouse, and later, to Clinton in 1819.

What were the inhabitants of early Sampson like? Generally speaking, the citizens were rude and uncultivated in their manners. Many could not read a chapter from the Bible or write their name legibly. Dancing, gambling, horseracing, and whiskey drinking were common practices of the people, at least until the circuit-riding preachers set them straight. We have certainly progressed in sociality and civilization since those early beginnings.

Religion has shaped the character of the people of this county from its beginning. The Presbyterians and Baptists were here before Sampson even existed as a county, and the Methodist circuit preacher was just a few hoof beats away. A few common schools were conducted in the same meetinghouses that were used for religious purposes in pre–Civil War days. The Bible and textbooks were side by side on the schoolmaster's desk in the one-room schoolhouses that dotted the countryside.

Sampson was but a young county and already many of its inhabitants were moving to greener pastures in Georgia, Alabama, Tennessee, and other destinations. Some reasons for this migration were worn-out soil, mud-rutted roads, and a lack of bridges. The raw itch to see this new country was another reason for migration. Sampson County actually lost population during periods of the early nineteenth century.

Sampson County has a total area of 616,320 acres, and its elevation ranges from about 60 feet above sea level in the southern part of the county to about 200 feet in the northern part. The county is located in the Coastal Plains. All but a few thousand acres are in the Cape Fear River Basin and are drained by two principal tributaries of the Cape Fear River, namely, the Black River and the South River. The Mingo Swamp and the South River divide the western edge of Sampson from Cumberland and Harnett Counties.

The Little Coharie Creek, the Great Coharie Creek, and the Six Run Creek come together to form the Black River in lower Sampson. Steamboats came up to Clear Run and even Lisbon in times of high water in the nineteenth century. These watercourses, along with the South River, became the waterway to the Wilmington port for our ancestors. When the winter and spring freshets (high water) arrived, the year-long harvest from the longleaf pine was floated to market.

Sampson County lies in the center of the longleaf pine belt. Woodlands are and have always been an important part of the county's economy. North Carolina led all the states and Sampson County led all other counties in the production of tar, pitch, and turpentine for most of the nineteenth century. Those virgin forests of longleaf pines provided a majestic landscape throughout the county prior to the interference of European settlers.

During the course of Sampson's relatively short history, we have had the birth and death of towns, including Lisbon, the first town. Owensville was also laid to rest. Villages experienced growth spurts with the coming of the railroad only to wither later as the train whistle faded. The railroad initially came to the county when the Warsaw Clinton spur was opened in the mid-1880s. A few years later, the Cape Fear and Yadkin Valley Railroad entered the county at Autryville, ran parallel with the South River, and exited the county at Ivanhoe on its way to Wilmington.

Sampson County farmers have followed the ox, horse, mule, and eventually employed the tractor to till the soil in order to feed family and neighbor alike. Early agricultural products included rice, corn, cotton, and sweet potatoes. Sheep, geese, hogs, and cows freely foraged over the countryside. Also, from its earliest days, Sampson County was known as the "huckleberry county" by our neighbors.

During the early twentieth century, cotton and tobacco replaced tar, pitch, and turpentine as the cash crop of the county. Combines, harvesters, pickers, and all types of mechanical equipment have replaced the grub hoe, broad ax, ox cart, water mill, cotton sack, and many of the stooped backs of past generations.

Your town or village, your church or school, the home place, the huckleberry bush, the stately longleaf pine, or whatever your most pleasant memory might be, represents Sampson County. We have received a heavenly charge "to tend it by the sweat of our brow and to work it until we returned unto its soil." Many of Sampson County's citizens have finished their work here and their bodies have been returned to its soil.

"A picture is worth a thousand words," and by that measure, the following images speak volumes. It is in the spirit of an appreciation for our history that these many images from the bygone days of our Sampson County home are presented.

One

THE COUNTY SEAT

Our county seat was first called Rhodes' Cross Roads. It was named Clinton Courthouse in 1801, when a post office was established. The courthouse was built on 5 acres of land purchased from Richard Clinton for 30¢ per acre. The courthouse, a simple structure of hewn logs, with a jail and stocks attached, was most likely built by the fall of 1784 and served as the courthouse for 34 years. In 1818 the second courthouse was built and served until 1904.

The first Sampson County Court was held in the eighth year of our independence, and in the year of our Lord one thousand seven hundred and eighty-four, promptly at 9 o'clock on June 21. The following excerpts come from the earliest court minutes: "James Thomson prays license to keep a tavern on the courthouse lot . . . license granted. The overseers of the poor certified to this court that a tax had been laid for the support of the poor; six pence on each pole and six pence on every three hundred acres of land. Next, Jesse Bratcher summoned on a charged of begetting a bastard child on the body of Sarah Goodman . . . a bond of 200 pounds was filed."

Lots were sold from the original 5 acres in 1818, and "Clinton Town" was first mentioned in court records. Our county seat has evolved from these primitive days to what we see presently. This chapter sketches the changing views of our county seat.

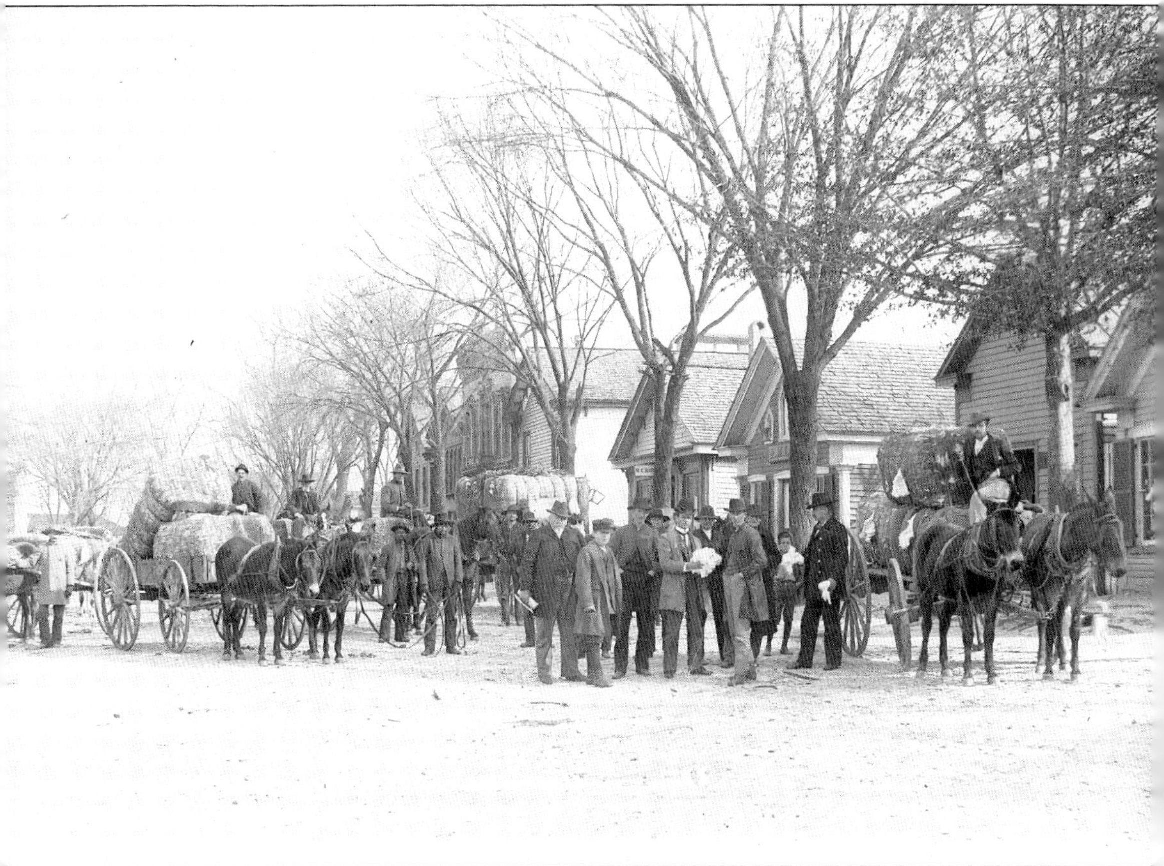

MAIN STREET CLINTON AS IT APPEARED IN THE EARLY 1880S. The courthouse square was serving as the auction block for a cotton sale on this cold day. Many of the wood buildings pictured were burned in the fire of 1894. (Courtesy of Sampson County History Museum, Inc.)

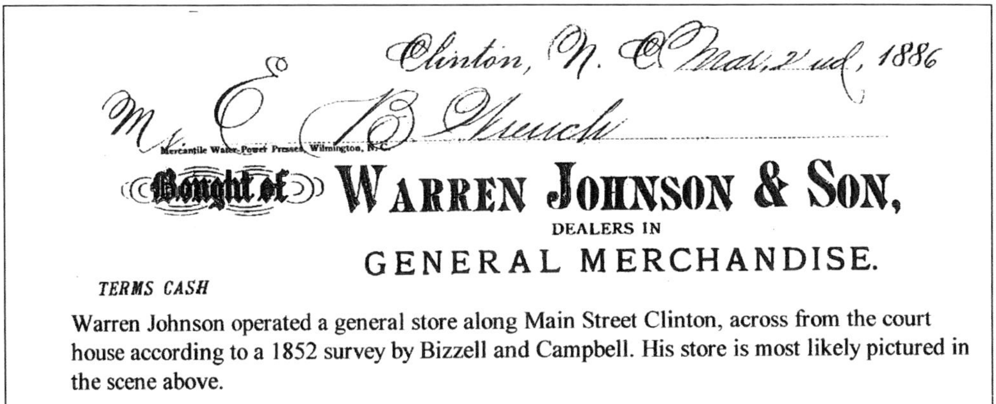

Clinton, N. C. Mar. 2nd, 1886

Mr. E. B. Wrench

Mercantile Water-Power Presses, Wilmington, N.C.

Bought of WARREN JOHNSON & SON,

DEALERS IN

GENERAL MERCHANDISE.

TERMS CASH

Warren Johnson operated a general store along Main Street Clinton, across from the court house according to a 1852 survey by Bizzell and Campbell. His store is most likely pictured in the scene above.

WARREN JOHNSON & SON'S LOGO FROM 1886. The store was on Main Street and was one of the earliest establishments in the town. The fire of 1894 caused $50 in damages to this store, while others were destroyed. (Courtesy of Troy Wrench.)

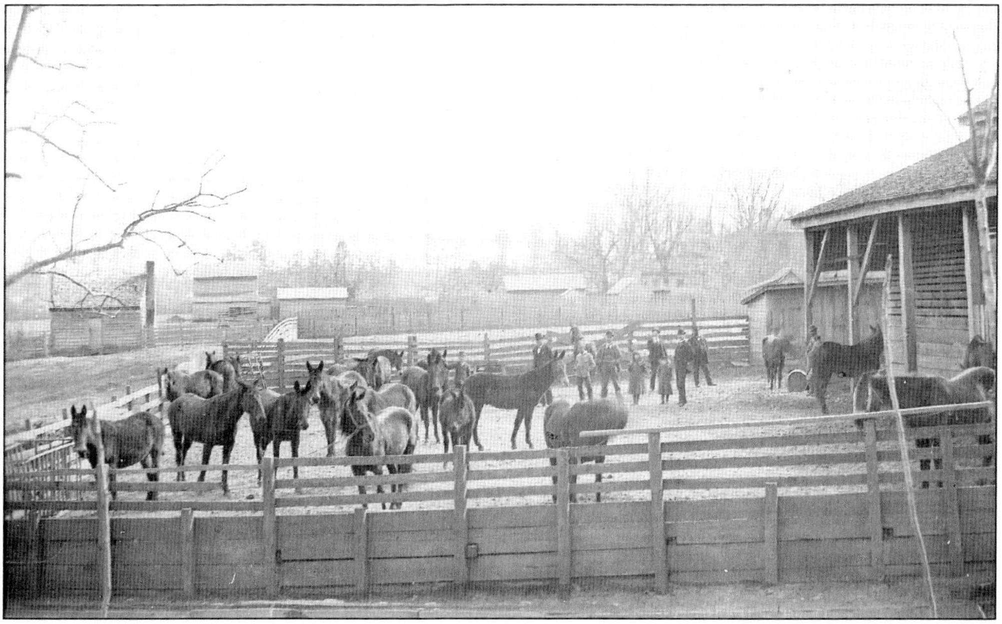

LIVERY STABLE. This stable was quartering mules and horses within the town limits of Clinton in 1882. A survey map of Clinton in that year lists Boykin's Livery Stable and Ferrell Brothers' Livery Stables. Both were on Elm Street, which later became Lisbon Street. Boykin's stable was one block from the courthouse. (Courtesy of Sampson County History Museum, Inc.)

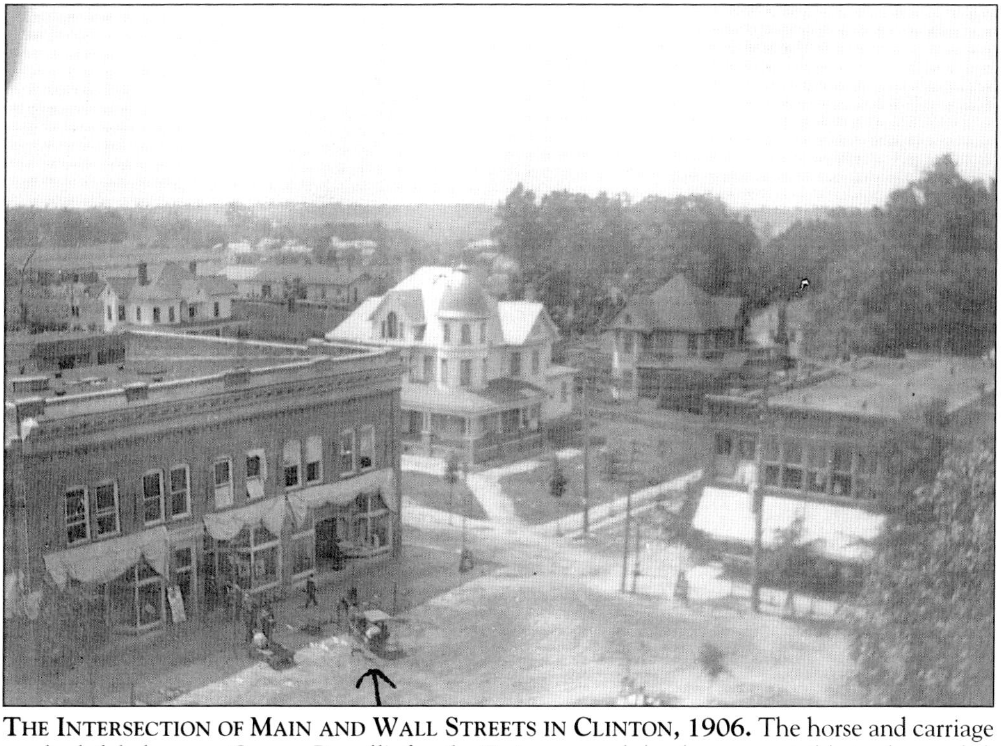

THE INTERSECTION OF MAIN AND WALL STREETS IN CLINTON, 1906. The horse and carriage on the left belongs to George Powell's family. Train cars and the depot are visible in the top left of this picture. (Courtesy of Sampson County History Museum Inc.)

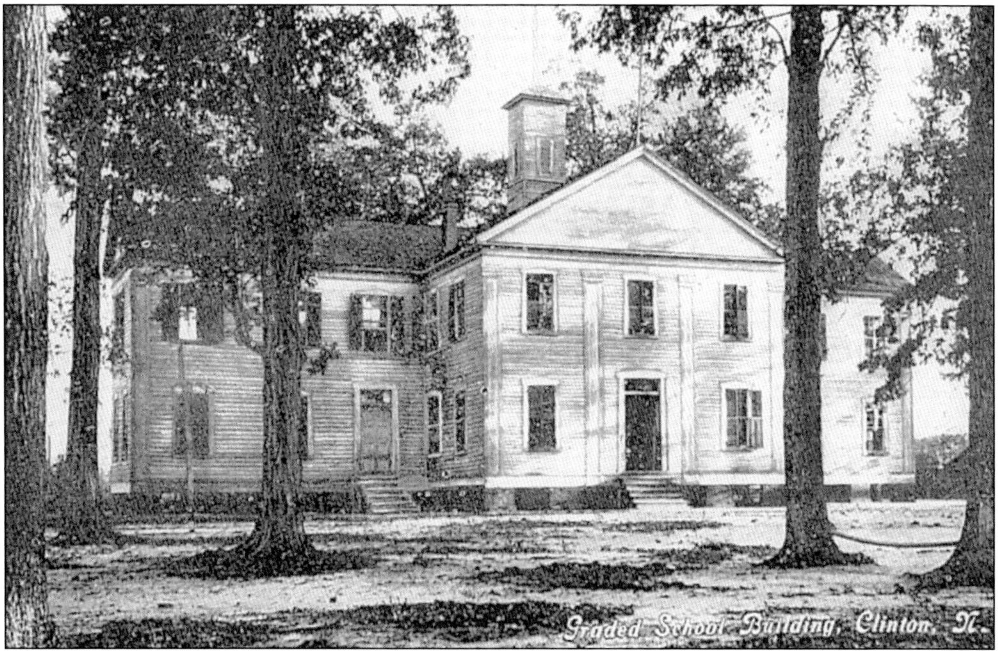

THE CLINTON GRADED SCHOOL BUILDING, 1909. This structure was built in 1826 and was originally known as the Clinton Academy. (Courtesy of Jerry R. Roughton.)

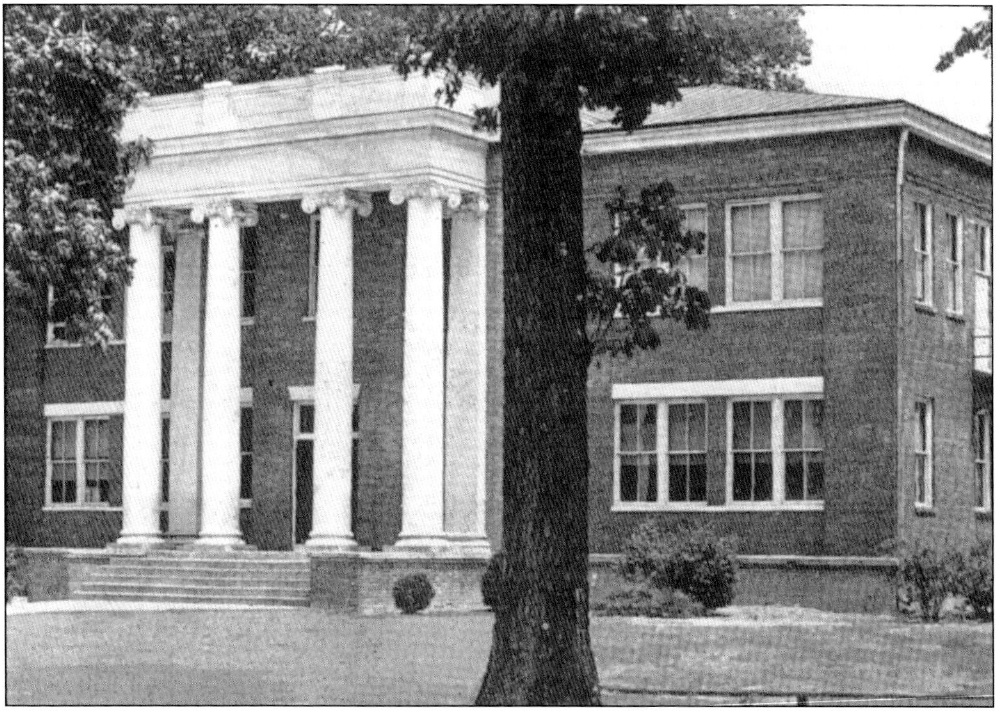

SCHOOL BUILDING, 1930. The site on which the College Street School stands has been devoted to education since 1826. Originally, the Clinton Academy and then the Clinton Female Institute, the school became a public institution in 1900. In 1954, it was named the College Street School. (Courtesy of Sampson County History Museum, Inc.)

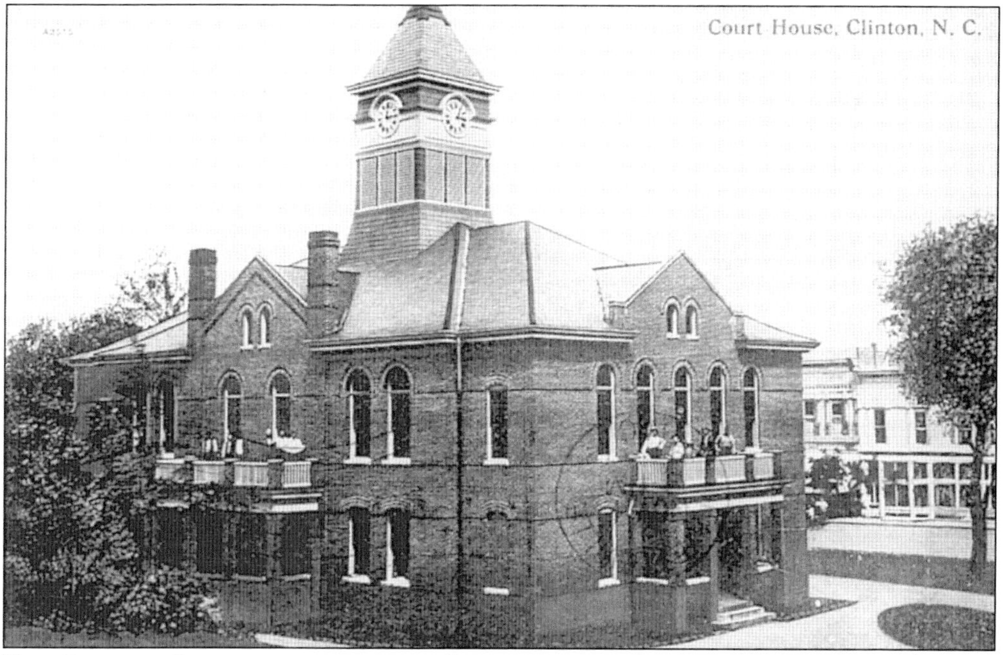

THE CLINTON COURTHOUSE IN 1912. This structure was built in 1904 at a cost of $30,000 and was completely remodeled in 1938–1939 at a cost of $100,000. (Courtesy of Jerry R. Roughton.)

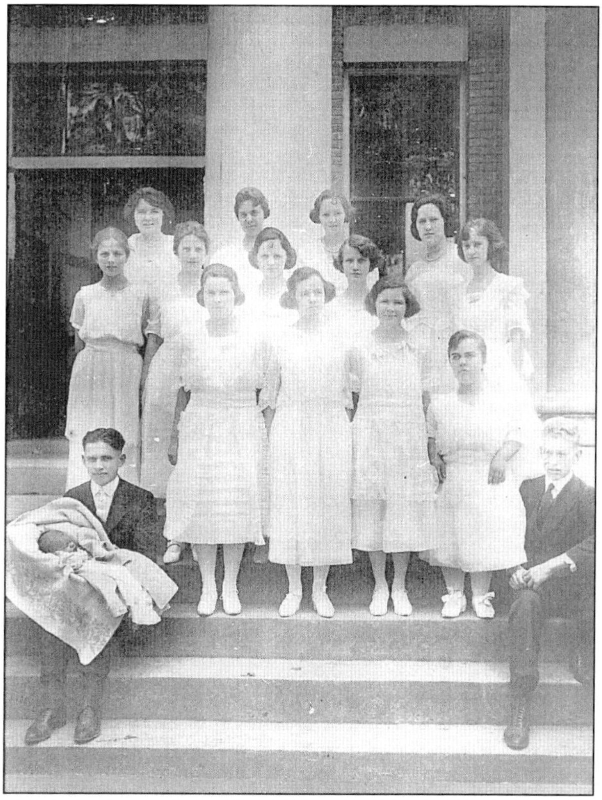

THE 1920 GRADUATING CLASS OF THE CLINTON HIGH SCHOOL. Many men had been away at war during this period in Sampson County's history. (Courtesy of Clarence E. McLamb Jr.)

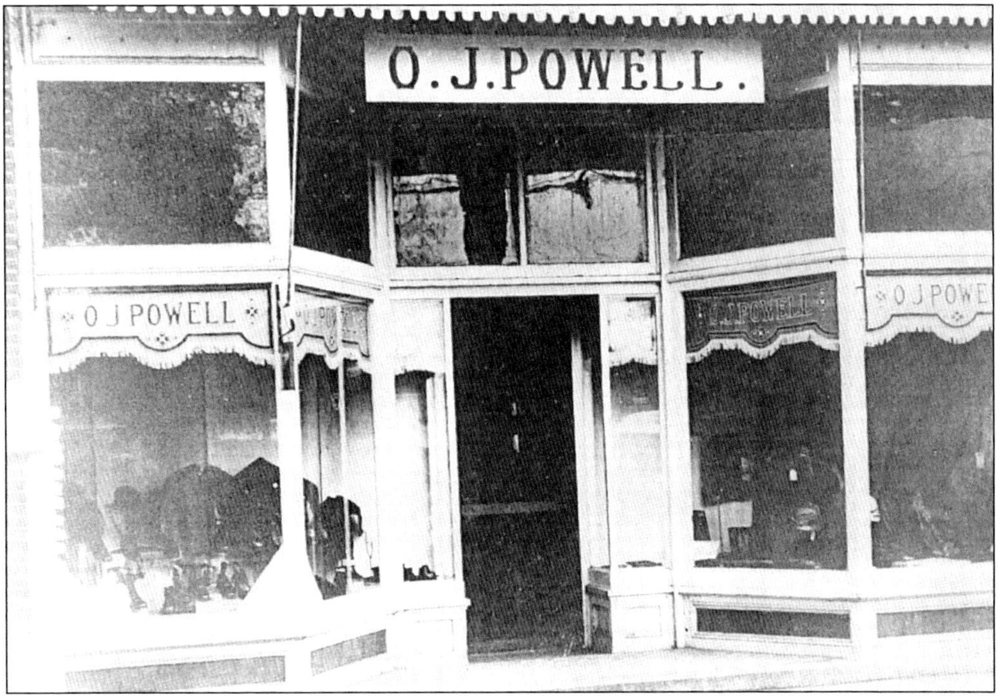

The O.J. Powell Store as It Appeared in 1912. (Courtesy of Sampson County History Museum, Inc.)

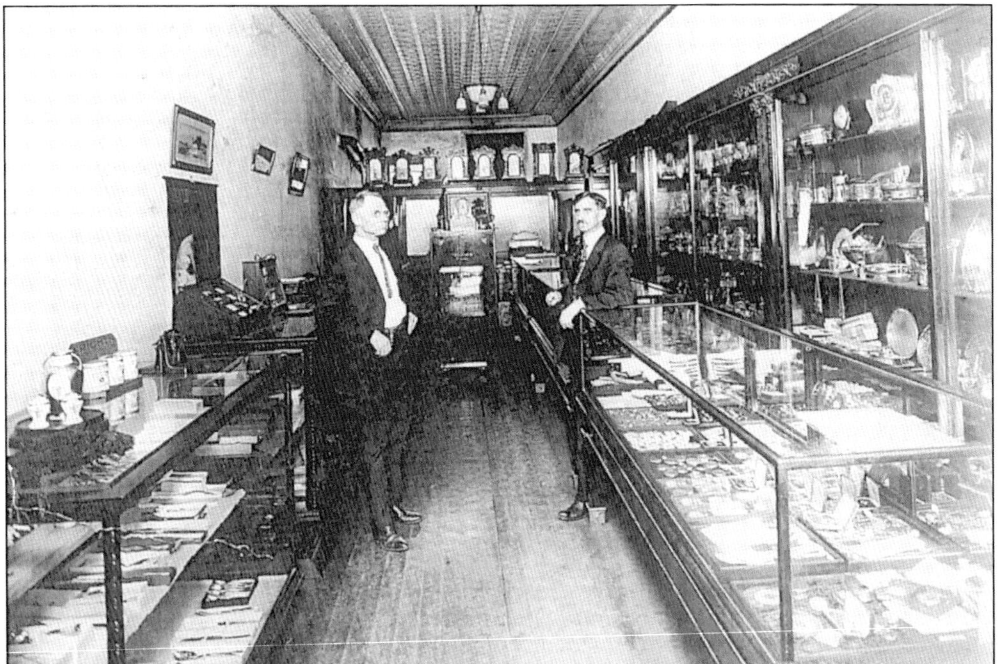
A 1917 Interior View of Rawl's Jewelry Store. The store was established in 1888. (Courtesy of Sampson County History Museum, Inc.)

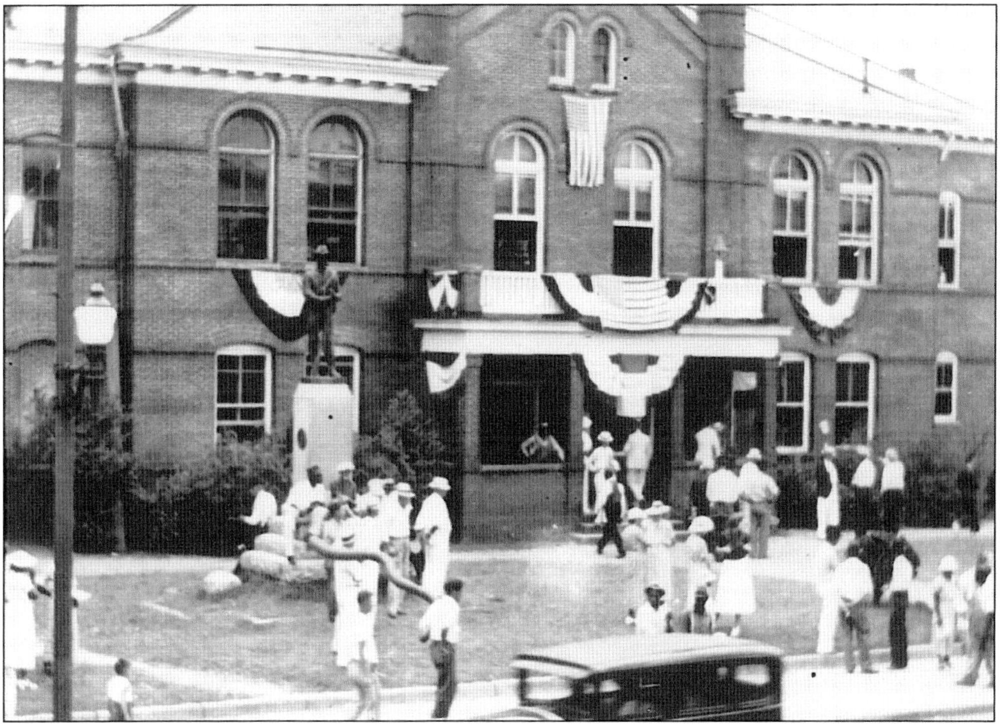

A FOURTH OF JULY CELEBRATION ON THE COURTHOUSE SQUARE, 1934. (Courtesy of Sampson County History Museum, Inc.)

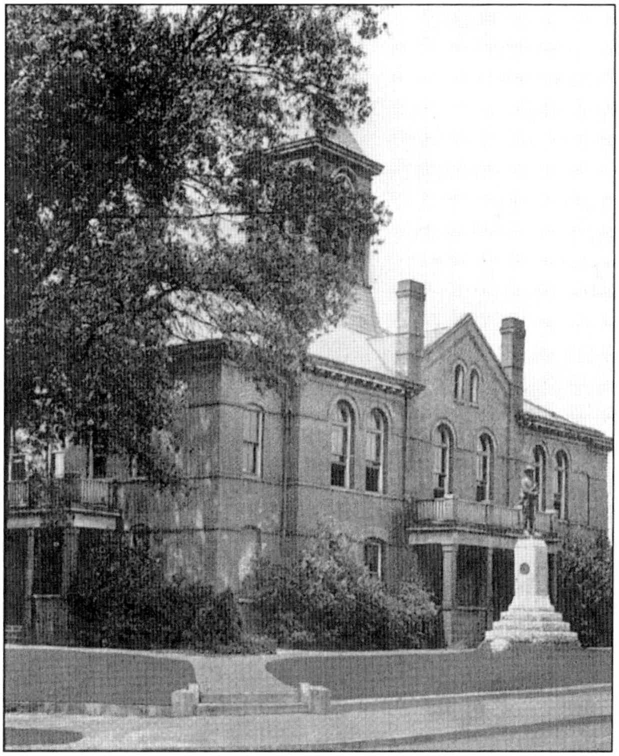

THE COURTHOUSE AS IT APPEARED IN 1934. (Courtesy of Sampson County History Museum, Inc.)

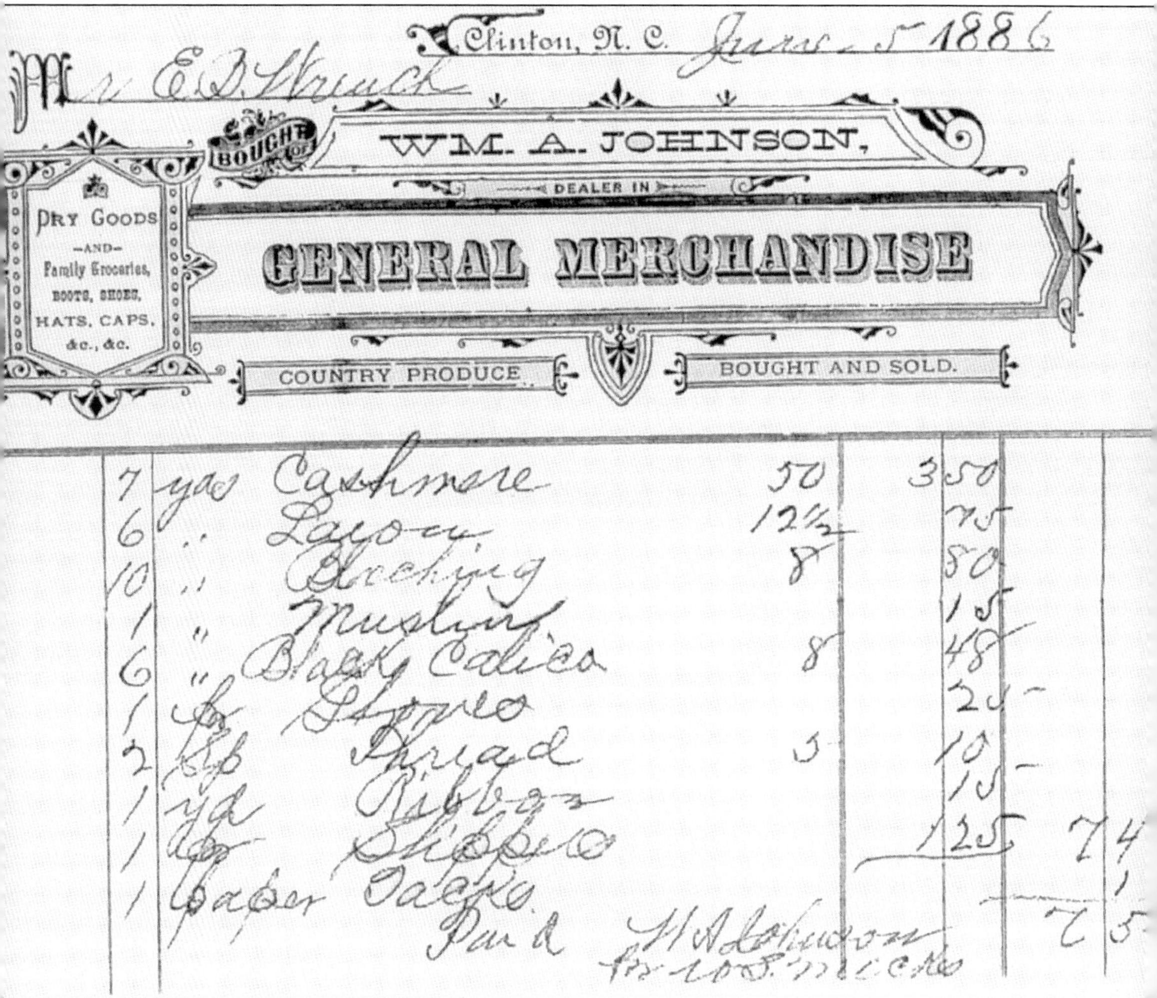

Clinton, N. C. June 5 1886

Mr E. B. Wrench

Bought of WM. A. JOHNSON,

Dealer in GENERAL MERCHANDISE

Dry Goods —and— Family Groceries, Boots, Shoes, Hats, Caps, &c., &c.

Country Produce Bought and Sold.

Qty	Item	Price	Amount	Total
7 yds	Cashmere	50	3 50	
6 "	Lawn	12½	75	
10 "	Bleaching	8	80	
1 "	Muslin		15	
6 "	Black Calico	8	48	
1 pr	Gloves		25	
2	Thread	5	10	
1 yd	Ribbon		15	
1 pr	Slippers		1 25	7 4[illegible]
1	Paper Tacks			1
				7 5[illegible]

Paid W A Johnson per [illegible]

WILLIAM A. JOHNSON GENERAL MERCHANDISE. Egbert Wrench traveled 17 miles by horse and buggy from western Sampson to the county seat to trade with William A. Johnson in 1886. (Courtesy of Troy Wrench.)

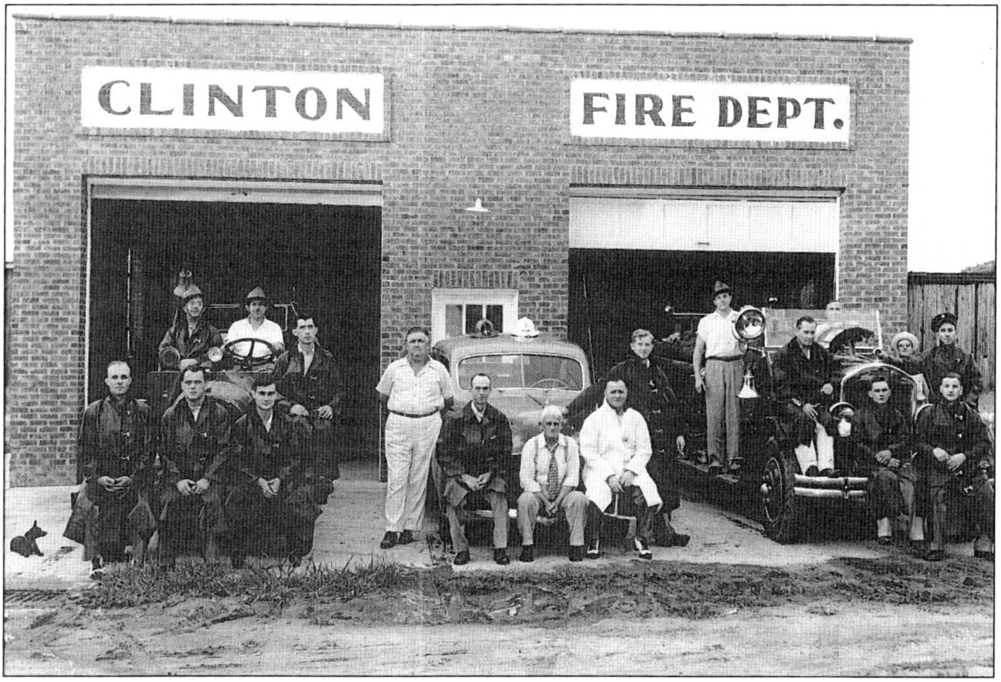

CLINTON'S FIREFIGHTERS, 1948. From left to right are Elizah Barefoot, Ash Britt, Hamp Britt, Herman Bunch, Herbert Ingram, Fred Johnson, David Jones, James (Rooster) Lee, Bernice McLaurin, Joe Melton, Charles Lee Pope, Max Price, Paul Shippe, Charles Warren, Hebron Warren, and Marson Warren. (Courtesy of Sampson County History Museum, Inc.)

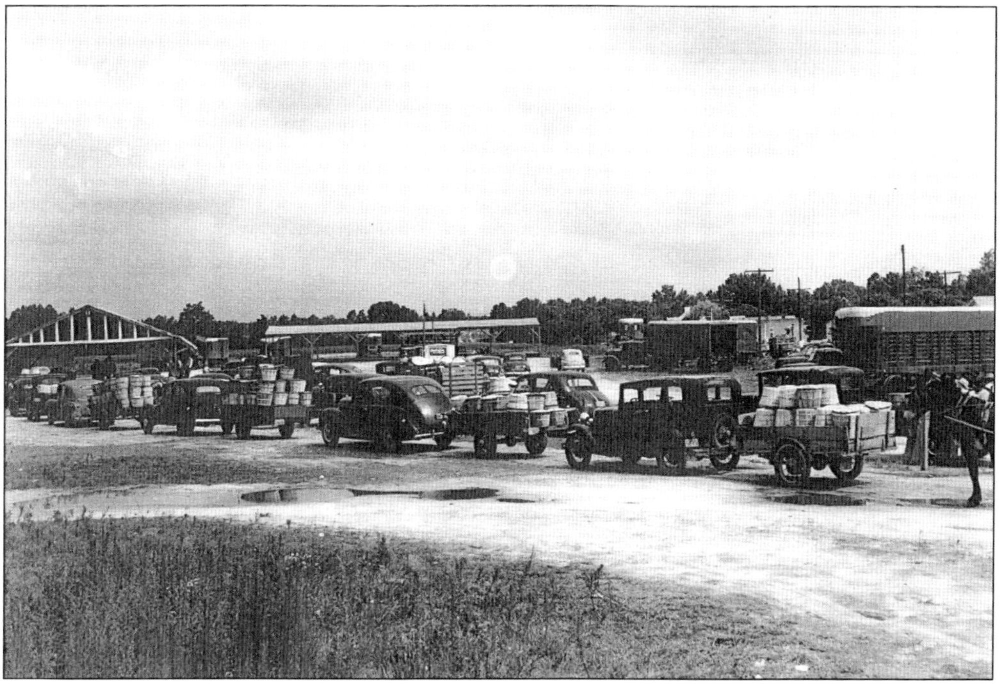

THE OPENING DAY OF CLINTON'S NEW PRODUCE MARKET. (Courtesy of Sampson County History Museum, Inc.)

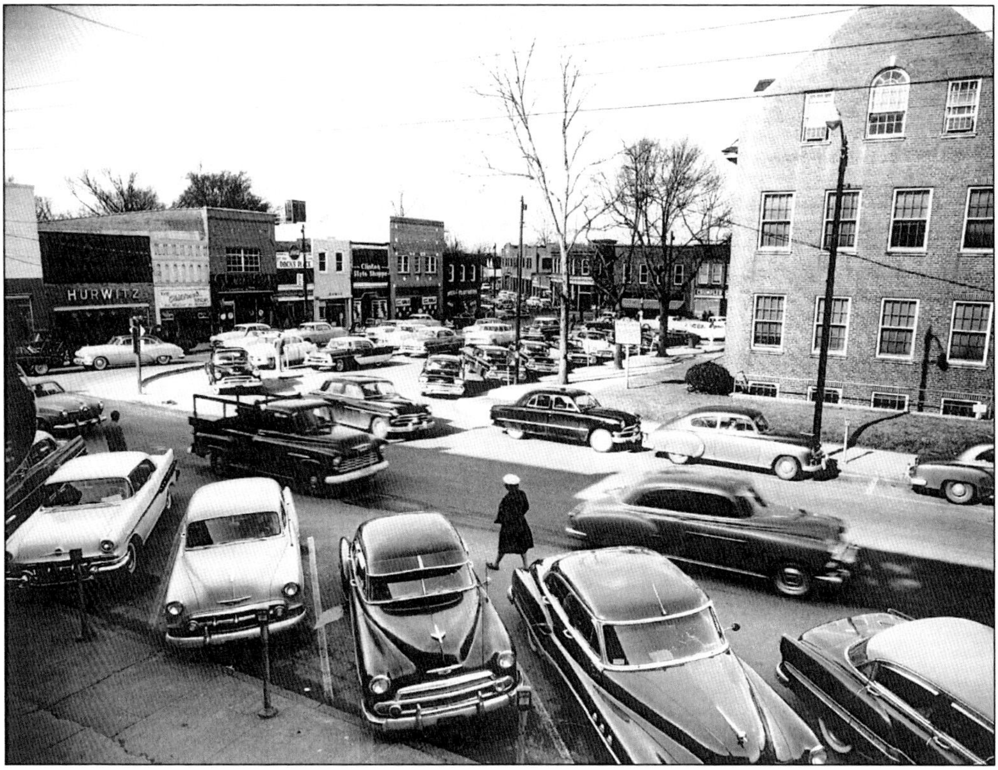

A Mid-1950s View of Main and Wall Streets in Clinton. Sampson County's forefathers of the 1800s wouldn't believe their eyes if they saw the county seat of the 1950s with parking meters replacing the hitching post. (Courtesy of Clinton Area Chamber of Commerce.)

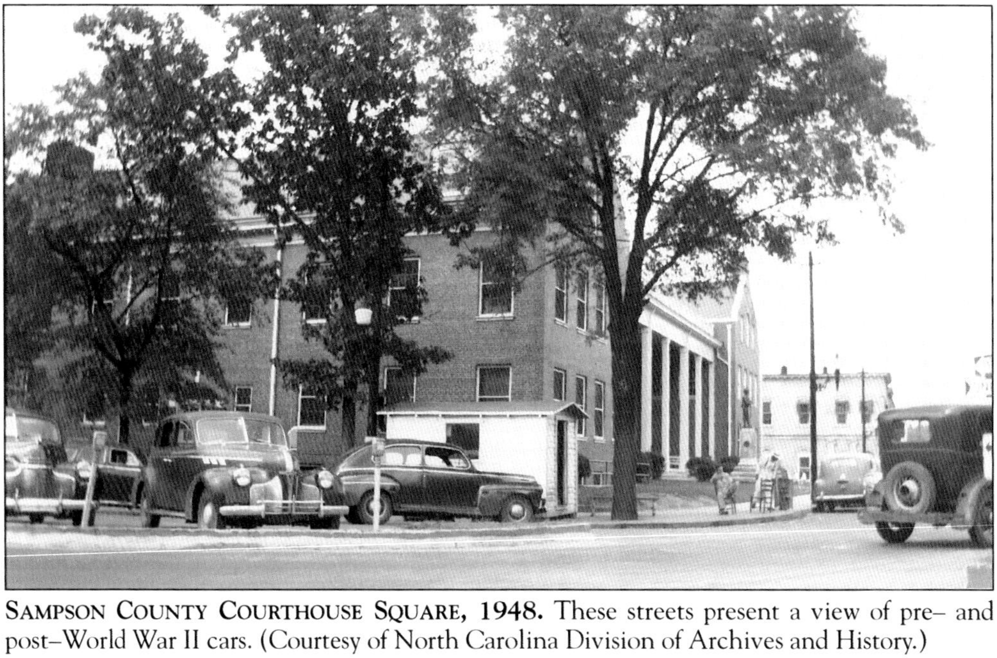

Sampson County Courthouse Square, 1948. These streets present a view of pre– and post–World War II cars. (Courtesy of North Carolina Division of Archives and History.)

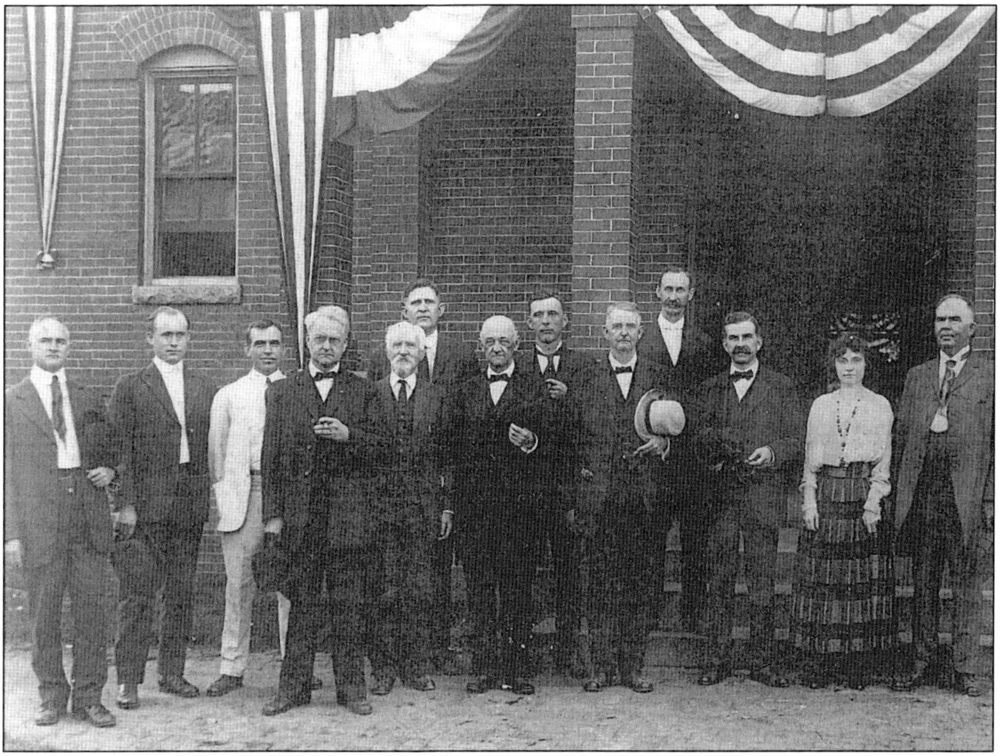

ATTORNEYS AND COURT OFFICIALS IN FRONT OF THE SAMPSON COUNTY COURTHOUSE. Pictured, from left to right, are Cyrus M. Faircloth, Harrison Fisher, Archie McLean Graham, Henry Grady, John Kerr, Richard Herring, Judge Lyon, B.H. Crumpler, Henry Faison, W.F. Sessoms, George Butler, Carrie Speight, and John Fowler. (Courtesy of Sampson County History Museum, Inc.)

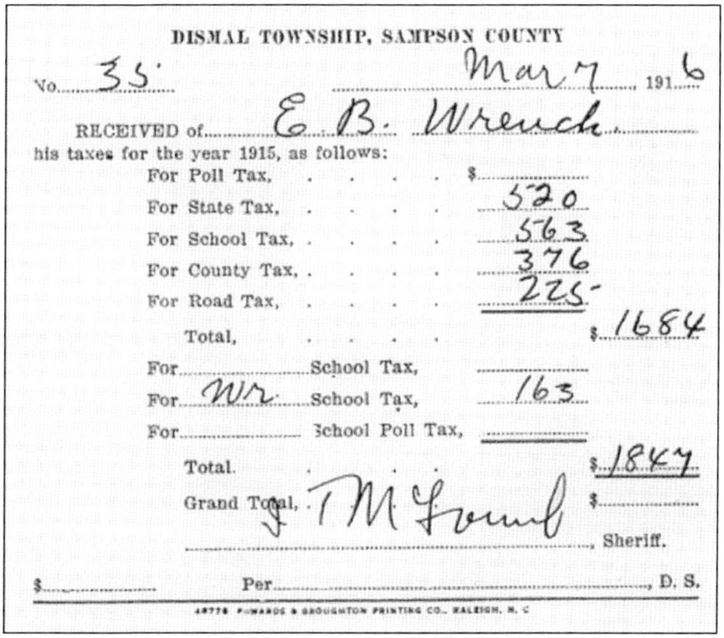

DISMAL TOWNSHIP, SAMPSON COUNTY

No. 35 Mar 7 1916

RECEIVED of E. B. Wrench

his taxes for the year 1915, as follows:

For Poll Tax,	$
For State Tax,	520
For School Tax,	563
For County Tax,	376
For Road Tax,	225
Total,	$ 1684
For ...... School Tax,	
For Wr School Tax,	163
For ...... School Poll Tax,	
Total.	$ 1847
Grand Total,	$

J T M Lamb, Sheriff.

$ ...... Per ...... D. S.

48778 EDWARDS & BROUGHTON PRINTING CO., RALEIGH, N. C

A 1916 TAX BILL. This bill is a reminder that some things in the county seat never change.

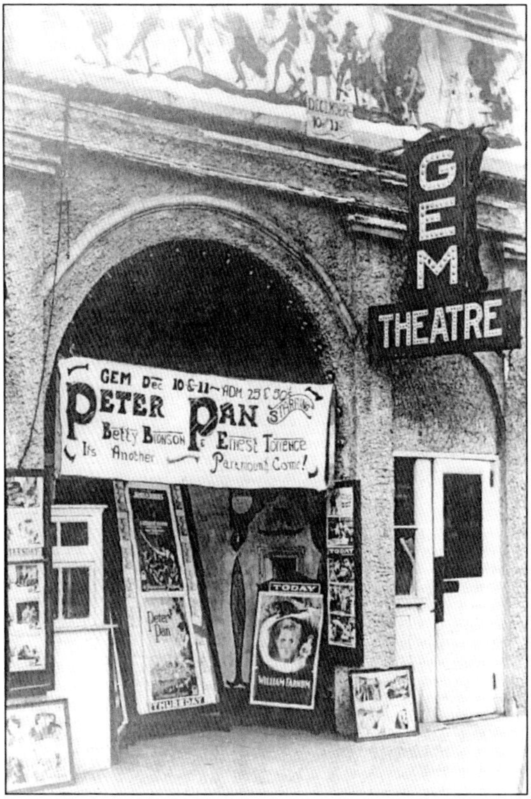

THE OLD GEM THEATRE IN CLINTON. (Courtesy of Sampson County History Museum, Inc.)

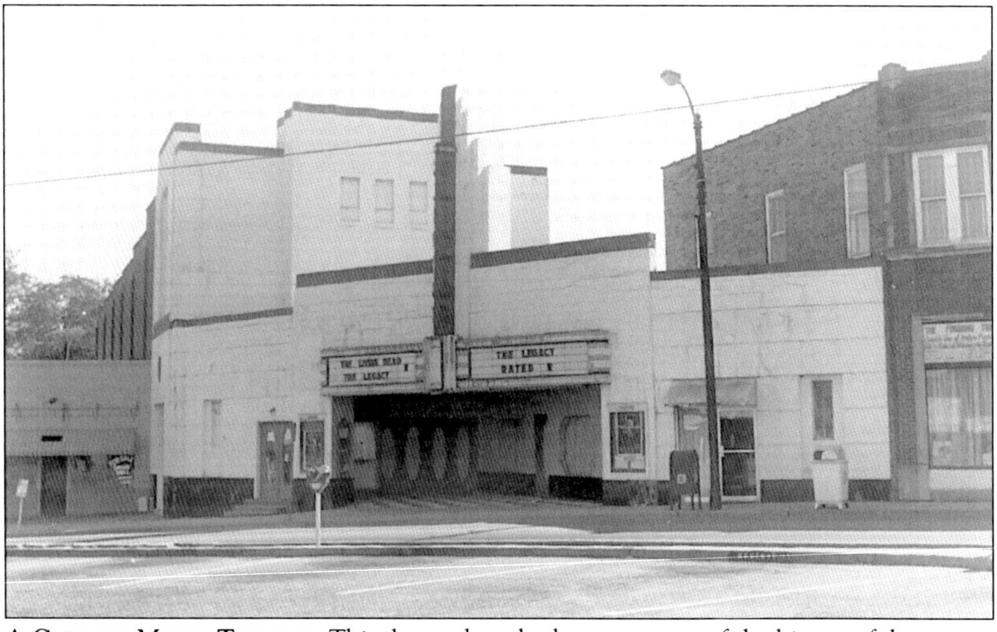

A CLINTON MOVIE THEATER. This theater has also become a part of the history of the county seat. (Courtesy of North Carolina Division of Archives and History.)

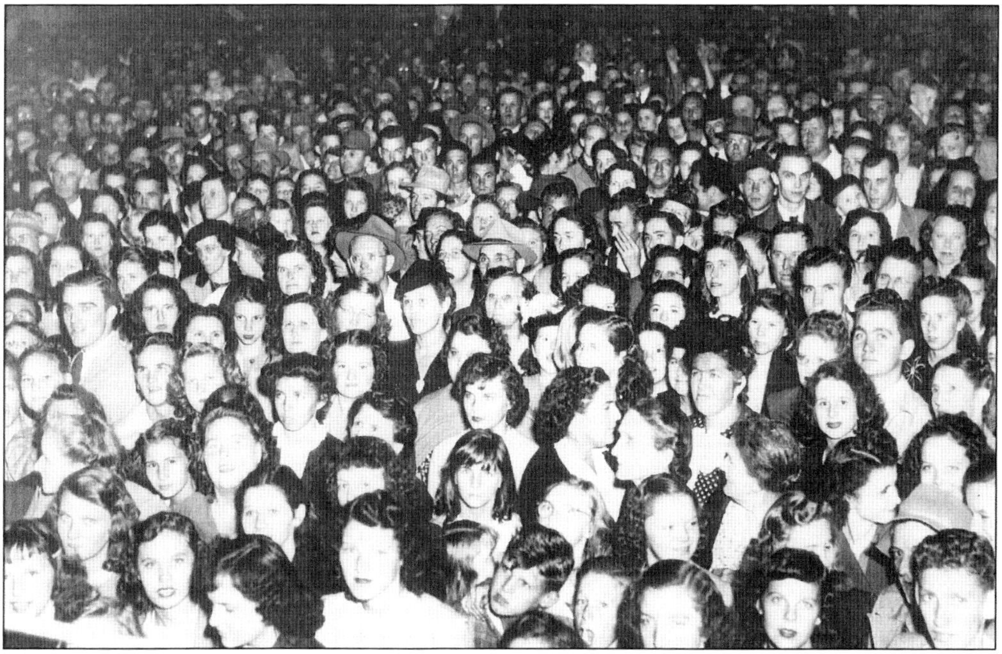

FARMERS' DAY CELEBRATION, 1947. The many faces of Sampson County enjoy the big street dance on the last day of the Farmers' Day Celebration in 1947. (Courtesy of Sampson County History Museum, Inc.)

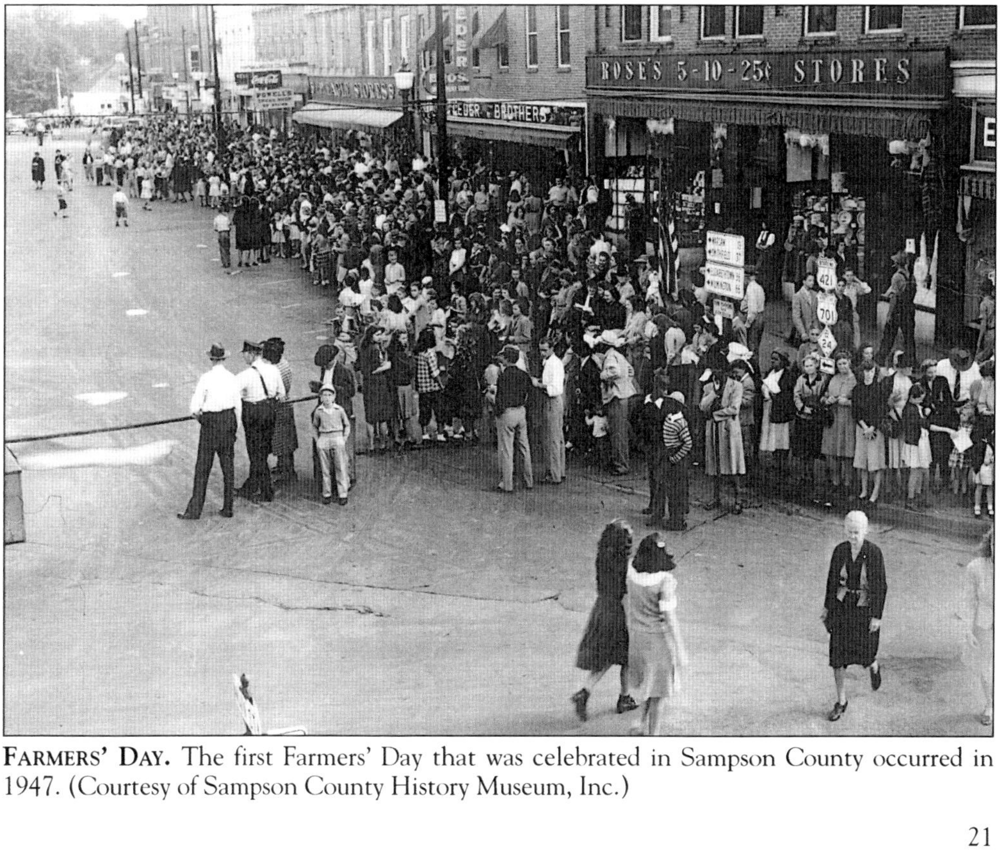

FARMERS' DAY. The first Farmers' Day that was celebrated in Sampson County occurred in 1947. (Courtesy of Sampson County History Museum, Inc.)

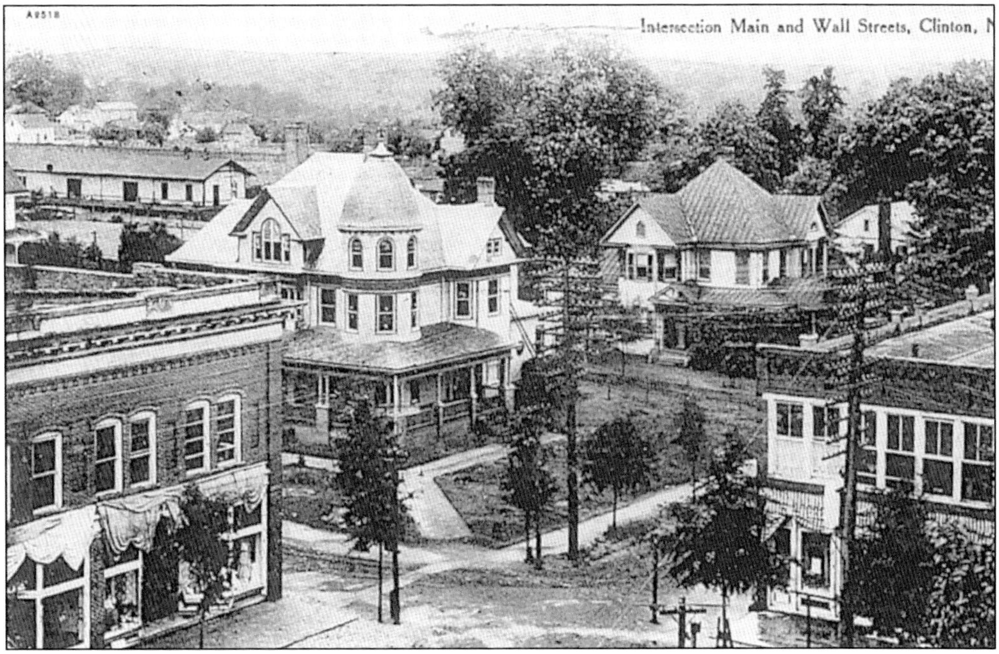

A VIEW OF THE INTERSECTION OF MAIN AND WALL STREETS, 1909. (Courtesy of Jerry R. Roughton.)

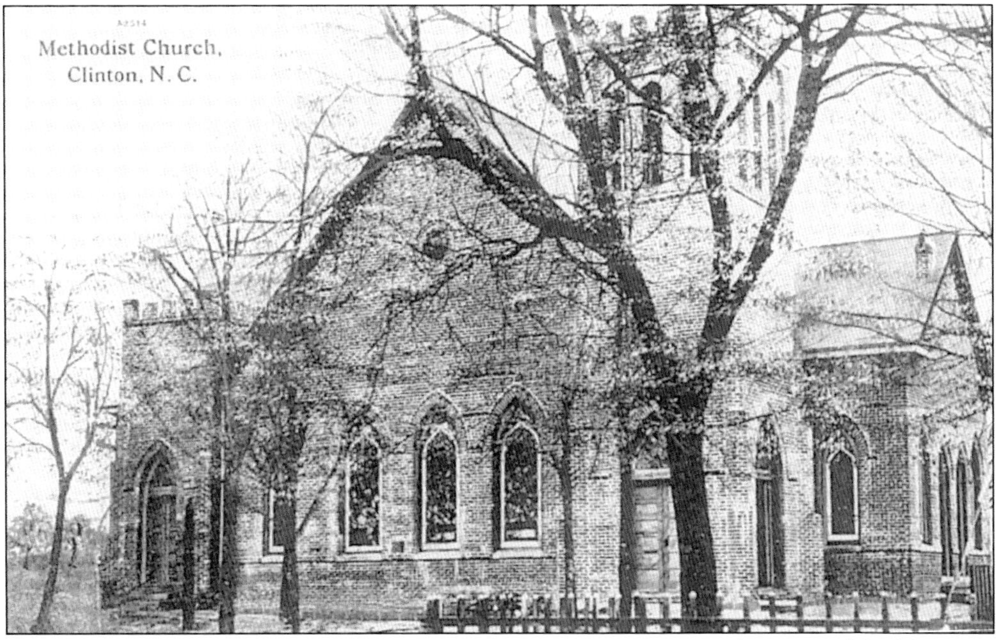

THE CLINTON METHODIST CHURCH AS IT APPEARED IN 1913. The original building was destroyed by fire in 1890 and was rebuilt the same year. On the second Sunday in February 1908, fire again reduced the building to ashes, and a new building was again completed within the year. (Courtesy of Jerry R. Roughton.)

Two

Tar, Pitch, Turpentine, and Timber

Smoldering lightwood from the tar kilns and gathering resin from pine trees was dirty, sticky work. After a long day's work, the laborers would find the heels of their feet black from tar, hence the nickname "Tar Heels" for the residents of the state known as the "Land of the Longleaf Pine."

North Carolina led the world in the production of naval store products from about 1720 until 1870. Sampson County led all other counties many of those years. Fortunes were made in the bountiful longleaf pine forest. The near total destruction of those forests denied future generations the opportunity to see their awesome beauty.

Census taker Edward Vail, in 1850, commented about the turpentine industry in southern Sampson County as follows: "The turpentine and timber business of the county has been followed about 30–35 years until the business is very much depreciated and the trees are mainly wore out. The natural growth of the county is pine. The principal occupation is making turpentine, tar and timber."

By the early 1900s, the trees were mostly bled dry of their resin and the end of the original "Tar Heels" was within sight. This chapter takes us back to Sampson's all but forgotten longleaf pine forest and the smell of fresh pine resin.

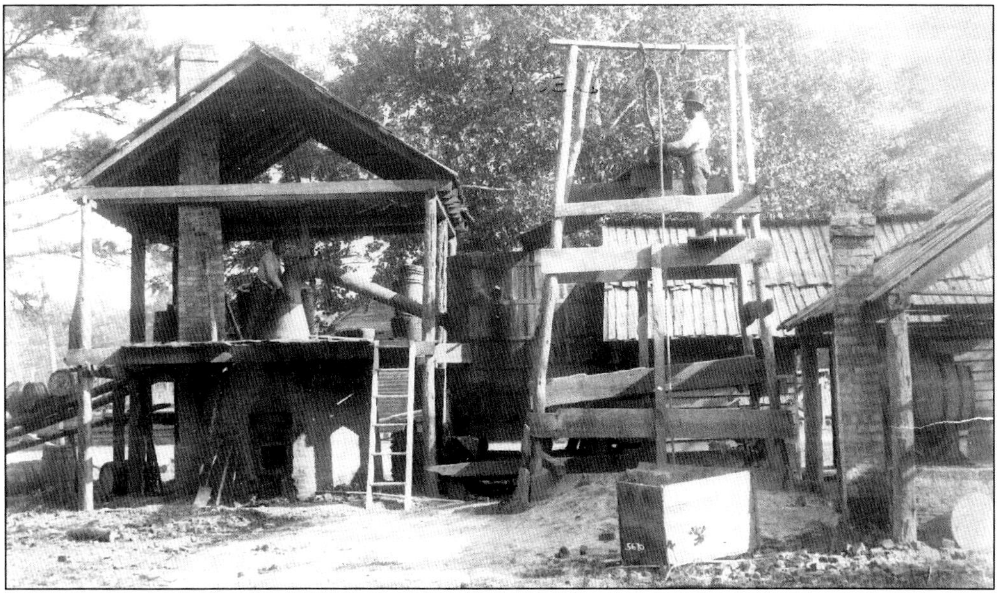

COLONEL J.R. BEAMAN'S TURPENTINE WORKS IN HERRING TOWNSHIP, SEPTEMBER 1890. Fortunes were built on the resin from the pine tree. (Courtesy of North Carolina Division of Archives and History.)

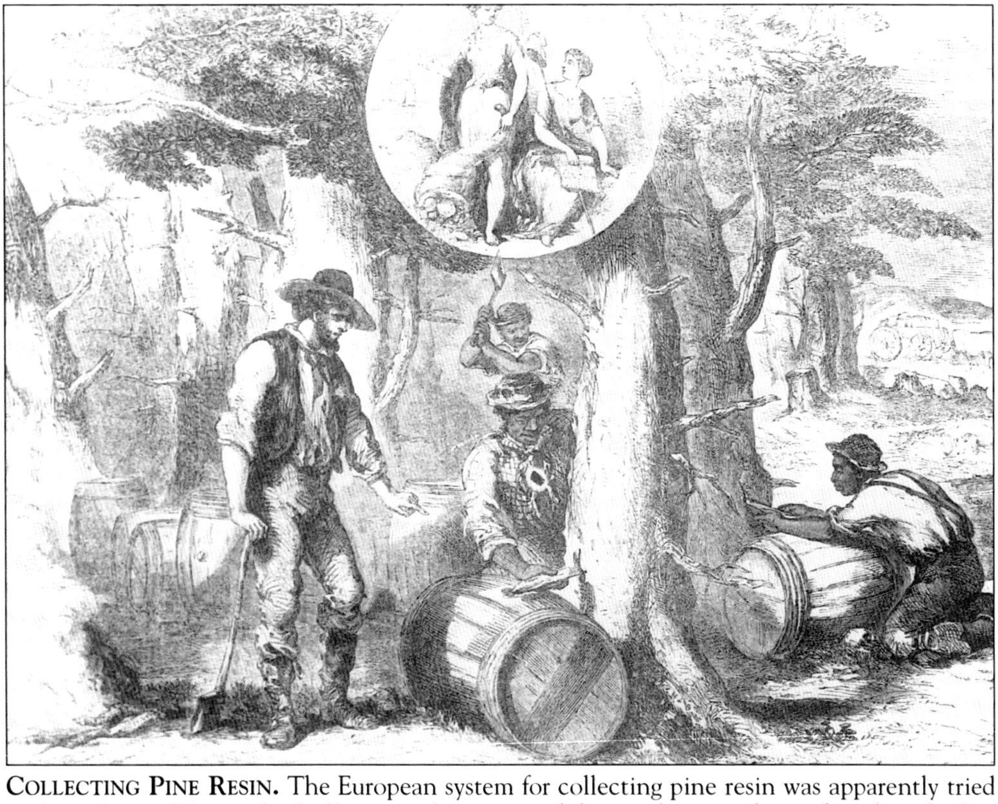

COLLECTING PINE RESIN. The European system for collecting pine resin was apparently tried in the colonies. The method of boxing, chipping, and dipping became the preferred method in the North Carolina colony. (Courtesy of North Carolina Division of Archives and History.)

A Sampson County Scene, 1890. Two hacks, or chips, were made on the tree in a "V" pattern to induce sap flow. The "V"-shaped hacks acted as gutters to channel the resin to the center of the box face on its way to the box at the base of the tree. Note the short-handled shove, or chipping tool. (Courtesy of North Carolina Division of Archives and History.)

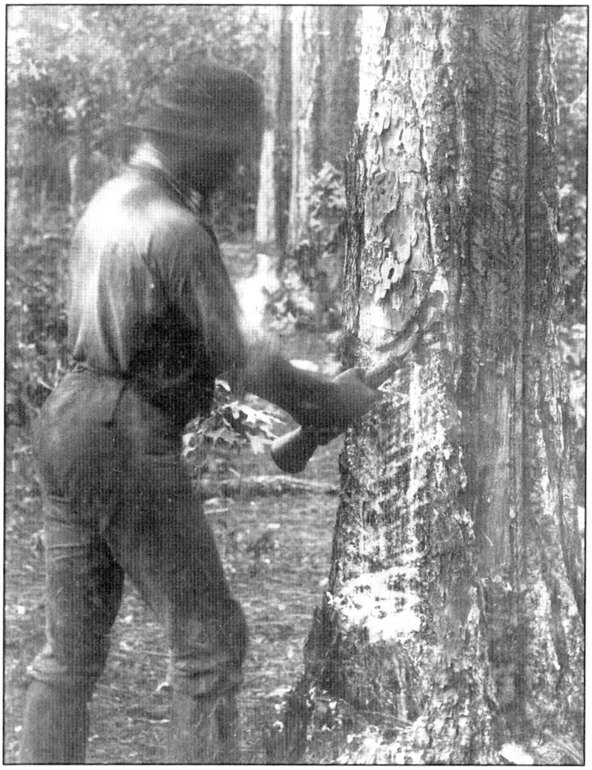

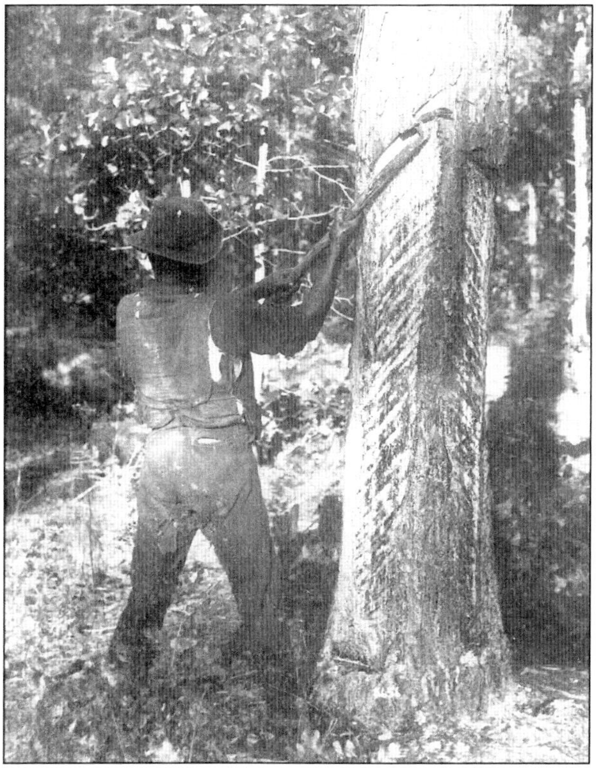

A Puller. This Sampson worker is using a puller (an extended handle) to chip this tree. After about the fourth year of working a tree, the face extended upward beyond the reach of the normal tool. After six years or more, the box face could be 12 or more feet up the tree trunk. It would soon become unprofitable to work the tree. (Courtesy of North Carolina Division of Archives and History.)

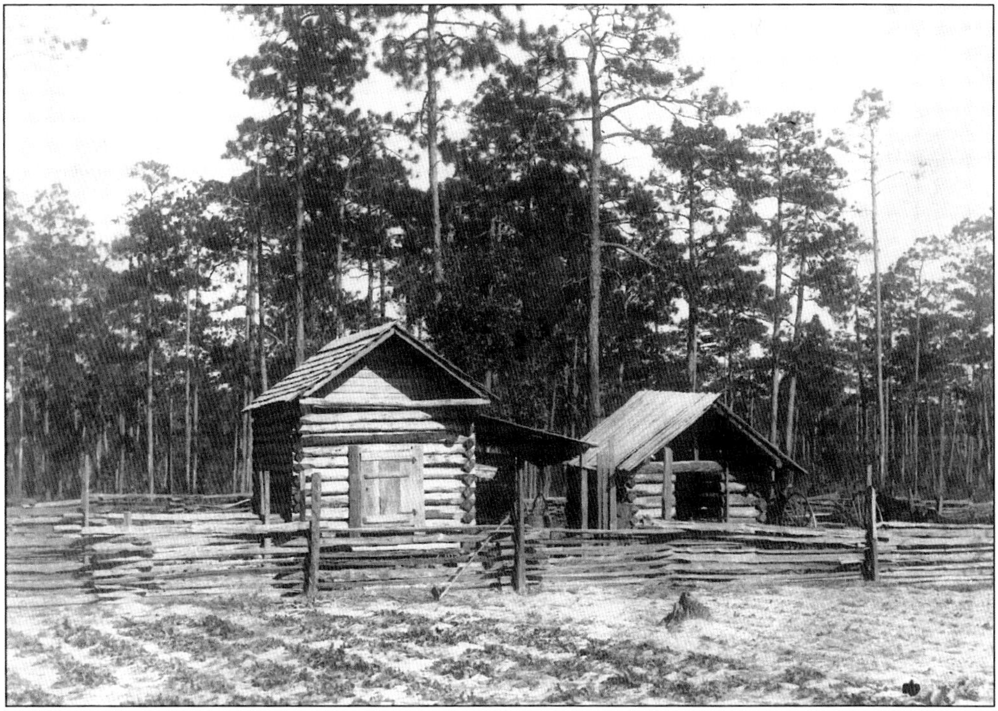

A TURPENTINE FOREST BEHIND AN OPERATIVE'S CORN CRIB AND OX STABLE IN SAMPSON COUNTY, 1889. (Courtesy of North Carolina Division of Archives and History.)

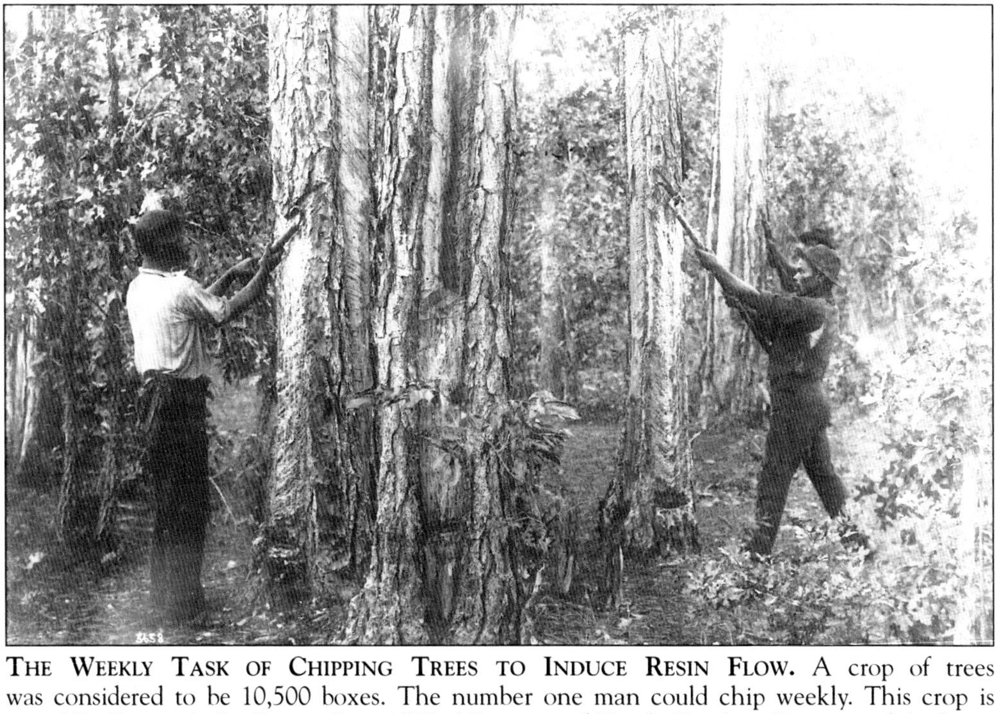

THE WEEKLY TASK OF CHIPPING TREES TO INDUCE RESIN FLOW. A crop of trees was considered to be 10,500 boxes. The number one man could chip weekly. This crop is near J.R. Beaman's Six Run still in 1890. (Courtesy of North Carolina Division of Archives and History.)

SAMPSON COUNTY'S ISAAC BOYKIN. Boykin is seen here dipping, or gathering, the soft turpentine or resin from the boxes near J.R. Beaman's Six Run place in September 1890. The boxes were dipped monthly. (Courtesy of North Carolina Division of Archives and History.)

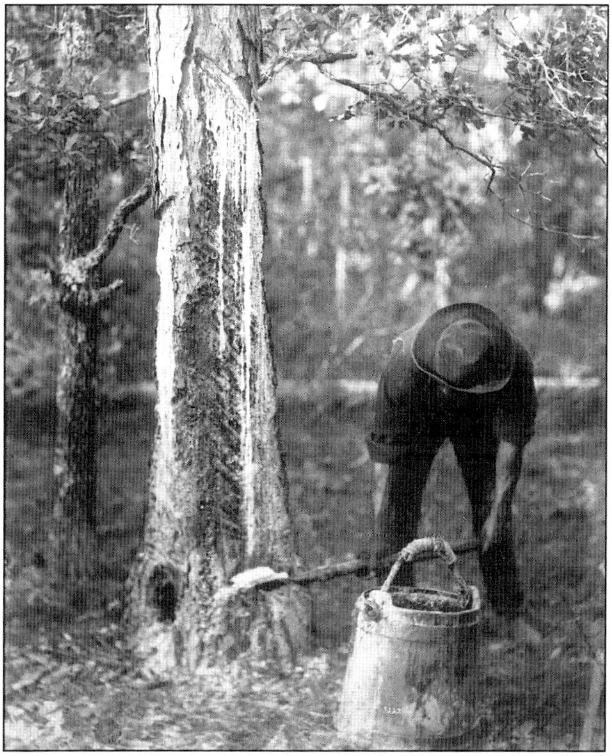

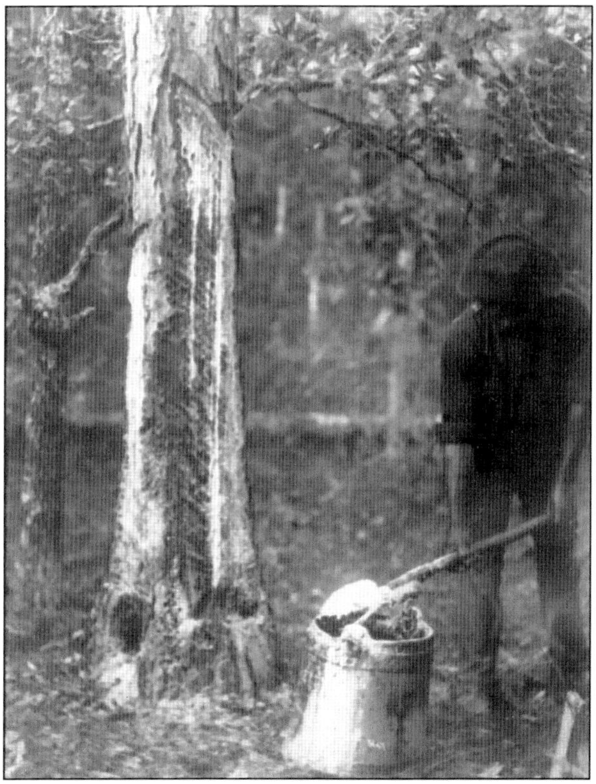

ISAAC BOYKIN DIPPING SOFT TURPENTINE OR RESIN, 1890. The gum was collected from the boxes seven or eight times a season, which lasted from early spring until late fall. A tree was normally double boxed, and two faces were worked during the same season. When a turpentine orchard became unproductive, it was abandoned. If the trees recovered and grew larger, sometimes they were triple boxed. (Courtesy of North Carolina Division of Archives and History.)

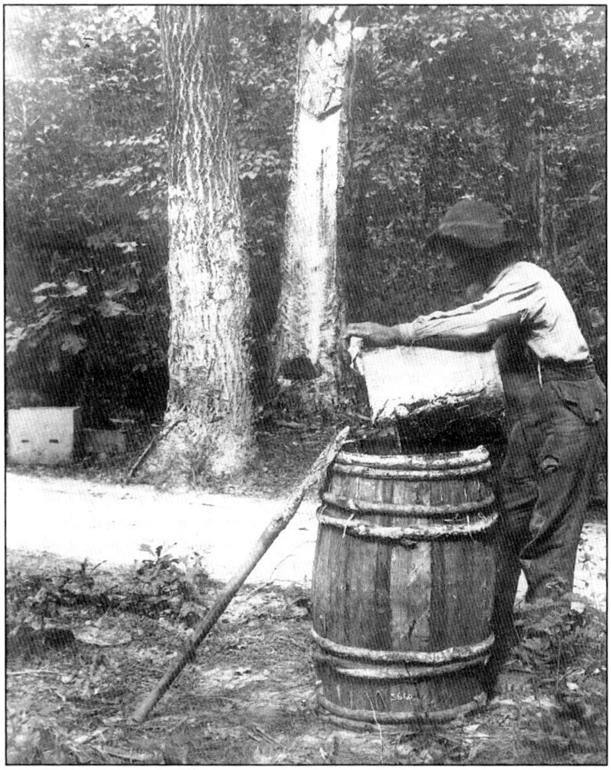

ISAAC IZZELL AT WORK. Izzell is pouring soft turpentine into a barrel in the piney woods of Sampson County in the year 1890. The barrel gave rise to a separate industry of cooperage, or barrel making. A man could produce eight or ten barrels daily and earn up to 25¢ for each barrel. (Courtesy of North Carolina Division of Archives and History.)

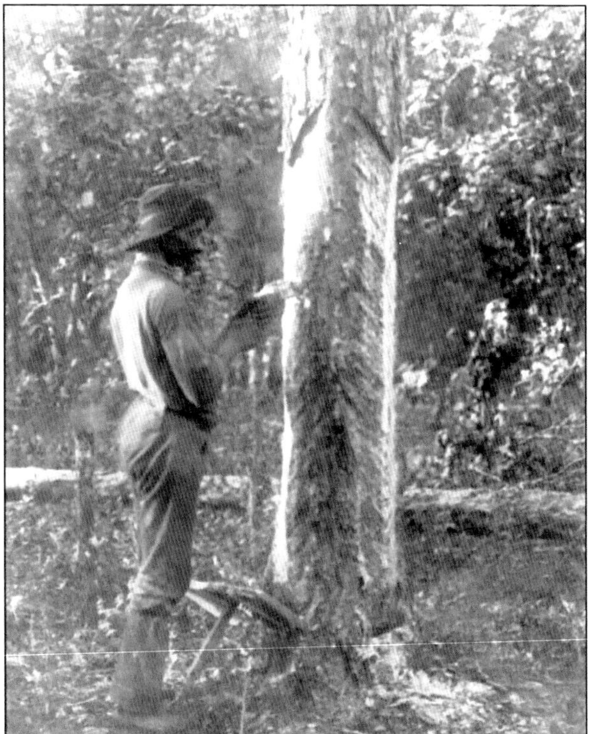

SCRAPPING HARD TURPENTINE IN SAMPSON COUNTY, 1890. The hard turpentine is collected in the pan at the base of the tree. Some turpentine hardens and needs to be scrapped from the tree; this hard turpentine is inferior to soft. (Courtesy of North Carolina Division of Archives and History.)

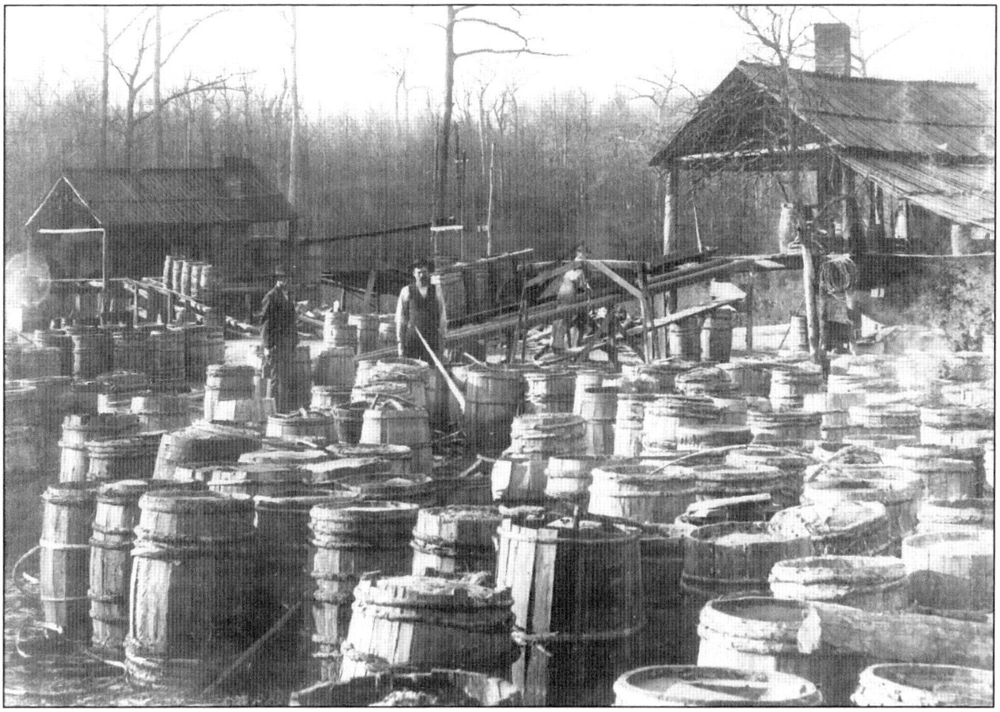

CAPTAIN JAMES L. AUTRY'S STILL YARD ALONG THE SOUTH RIVER'S STARLING BRIDGE IN SAMPSON COUNTY, 1890. (Courtesy of North Carolina Division of Archives and History.)

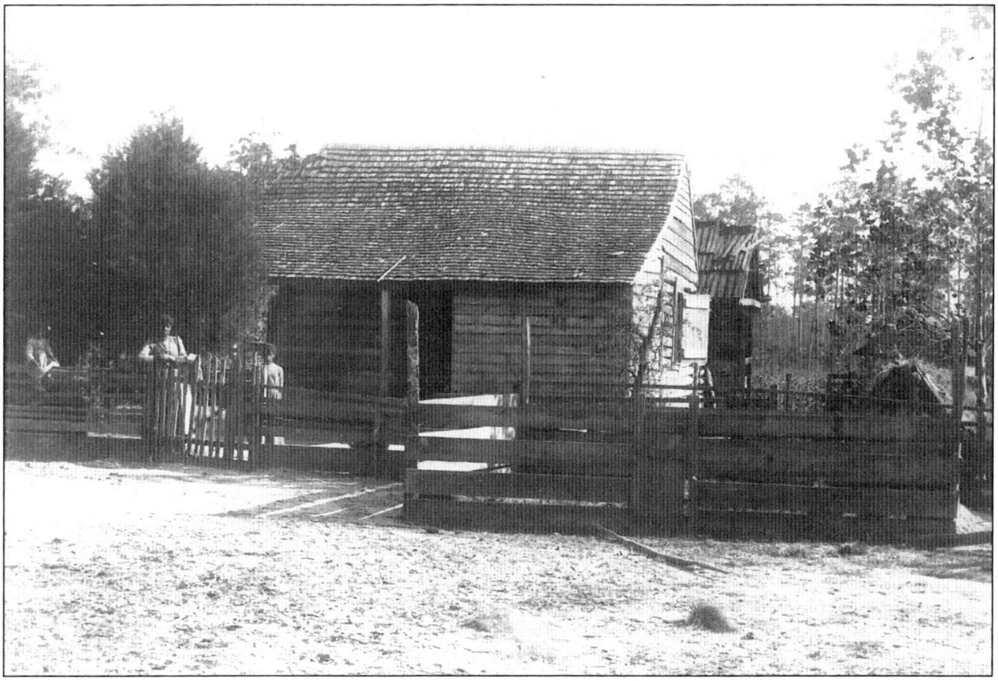

THE HOME OF A SAMPSON COUNTY TURPENTINE OPERATIVE, 1890. Many tracts of timber were leased out to operators, or they were sharecropped. (Courtesy of North Carolina Division of Archives and History.)

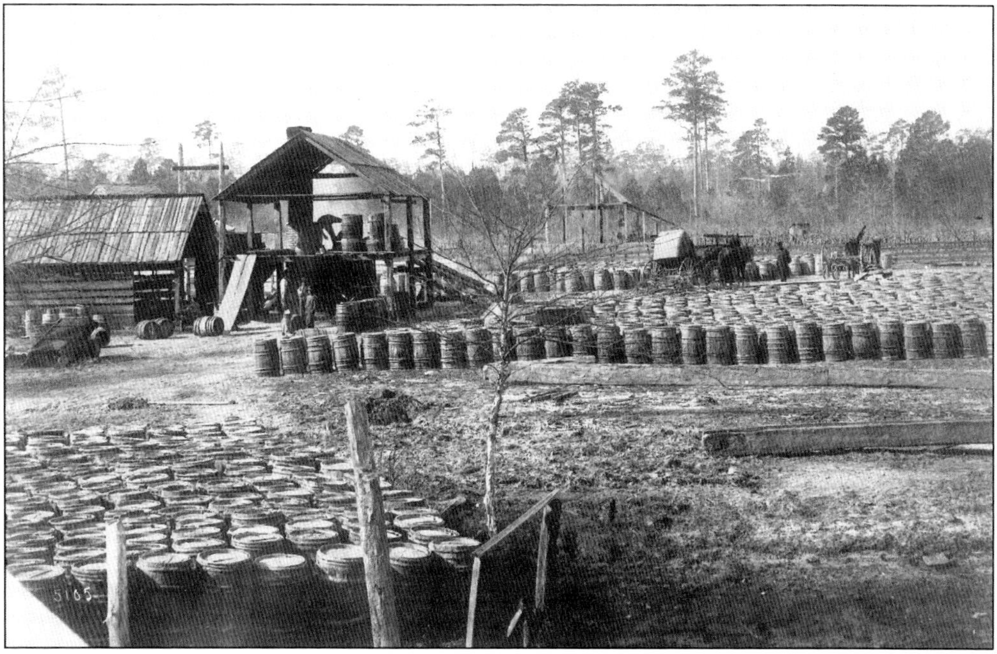

H.B. Culbreth and Brothers Still Yard at Boykin's Bridge in Sampson County, 1889. The processed turpentine was floated to Wilmington by raft or boat. (Courtesy of North Carolina Division of Archives and History.)

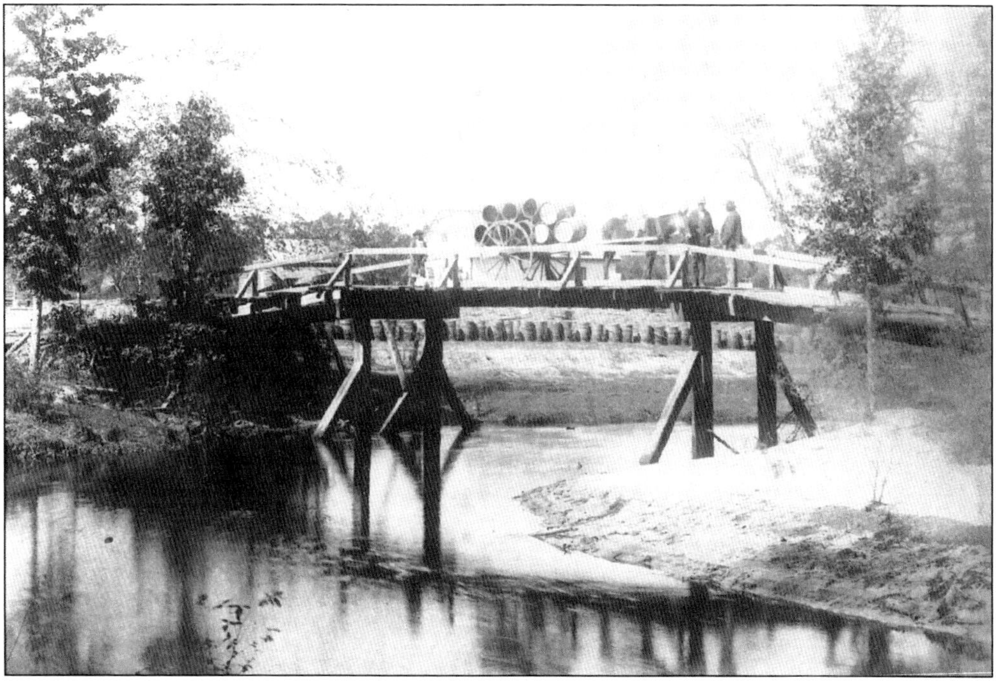

A Turpentine Cart on Boykin's Bridge. The arch in the bridge is designed to allow the clear passage of rafts and their cargo of naval store products. The still yard can be viewed on the opposite bank of the Big Coharie Creek. (Courtesy of North Carolina Division of Archives and History.)

LARKIN WRENCH. Wrench's weathered face is the result of working the longleaf pine forest for most of the 82 years of life, which began in 1819 and ended in 1902. Wrench floated many timber rafts loaded with turpentine and tar down the Little Coharie Creek into the port of Wilmington. (Courtesy of Troy Wrench.)

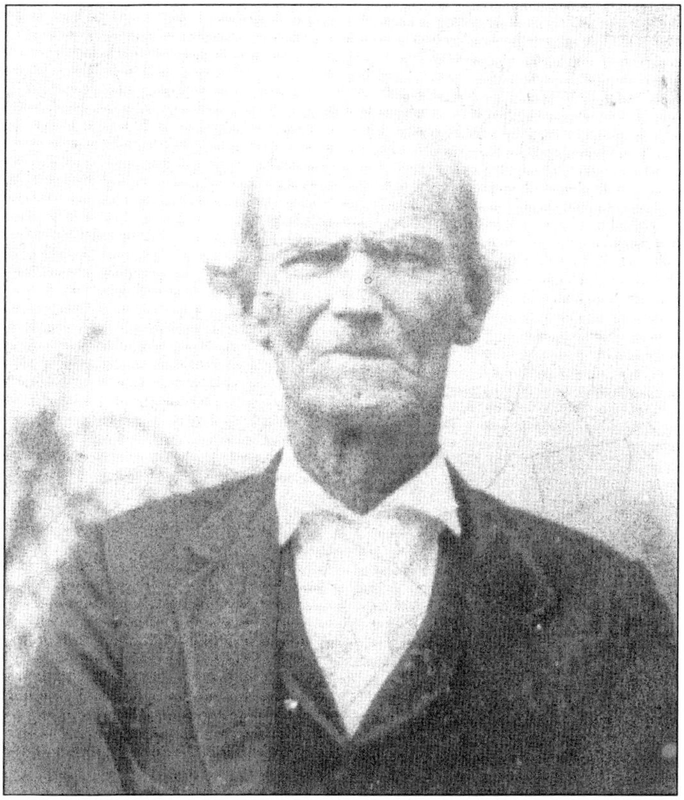

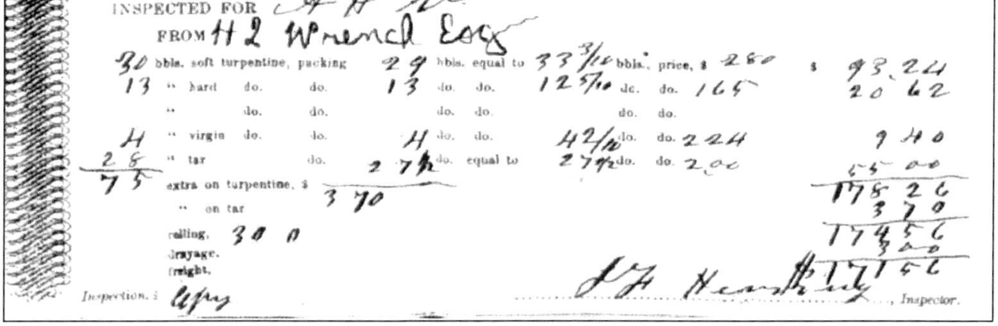

INSPECTOR'S CERTIFICATE.—WILMINGTON, N. C., Feb 17, 1860

INSPECTED FOR A H

FROM H L Wrench Esq

30	bbls. soft turpentine, packing	29	bbls. equal to 33 3/10 bbls.	price, $ 2 80	$ 93.24
13	" hard do. do.	13	do. do. 12 5/10 do.	do. 1 65	20 62
	" do. do.		do. do.	do. do.	
4	" virgin do. do.	4	do. do. 4 2/10 do.	do. 2 24	9 40
28	" tar do.	27 1/2	do. equal to 27 1/2 do.	do. 2 00	55 00
75	extra on turpentine, $	3 70			178 26
	" on tar				3 70
	rolling, 3 0 0				174 56
	drayage,				3 00
	freight,				171 56

Inspection,

J. H. Hemphill, Inspector.

A CERTIFICATE DOCUMENTING A SHIPMENT OF NAVAL STORE PRODUCTS. The products indicated here were floated down the Little Coharie Creek from the Hall's Store community to Wilmington in 1860. This shipment consisted of 30 barrels of soft turpentine, 13 barrels of hard turpentine, 4 barrels of virgin turpentine, and 28 barrels of tar for a total of 75 barrels of naval stores. The total receipt was $171.56. (Courtesy of Troy Wrench.)

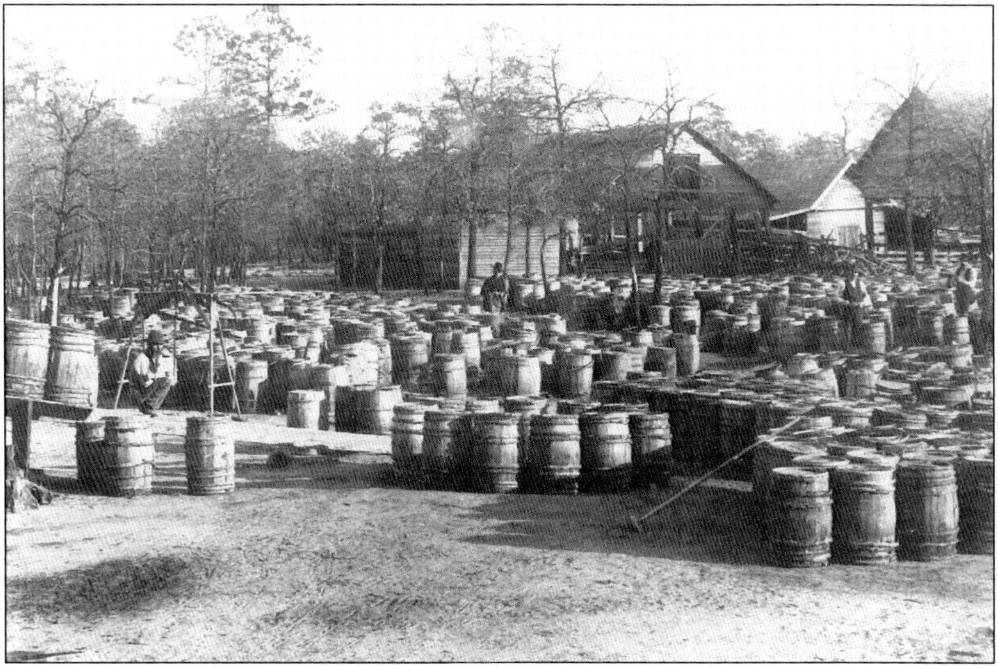

DISTILLING TURPENTINE AT CAPTAIN JAMES L. AUTRY'S STILL YARD, 1891. Captain Autry's yard was located at Clement in Sampson County. (Courtesy of North Carolina Division of Archives and History.)

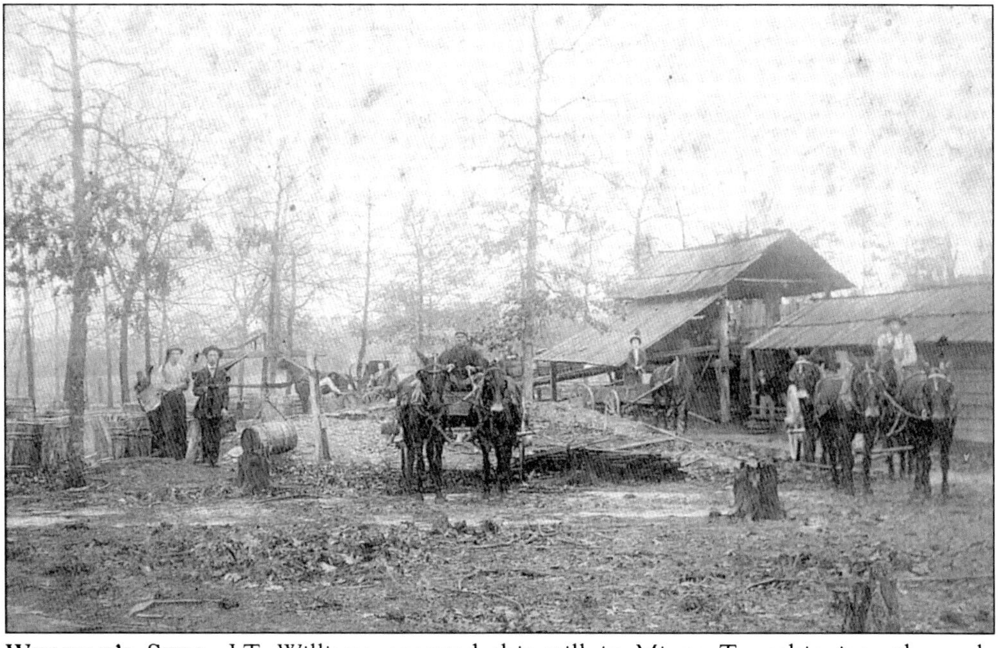

WILLIAMS'S STILL. J.T. Williams operated this still in Mingo Township into the early twentieth century. Part-time turpentine farmers traded resin for merchandise at the company store. The finished naval store products were hauled to the rail depot at Godwin, North Carolina, by mule and wagon and were then shipped to the Tolar Hart Co. in New York. (Courtesy of Tom Jackson.)

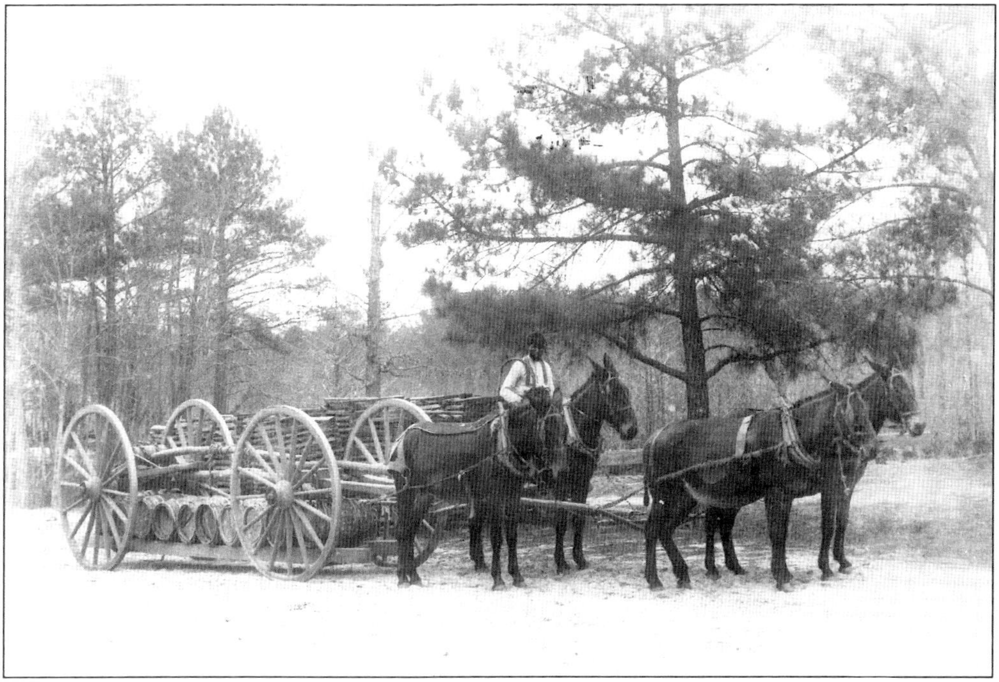

AMOS J. JOHNSON'S TEAM. This team is hauling still rosin to Six Run Creek from the Taylor's Bridge still in 1891. The barrels are suspended from a log cart. (Courtesy of North Carolina Division of Archives and History.)

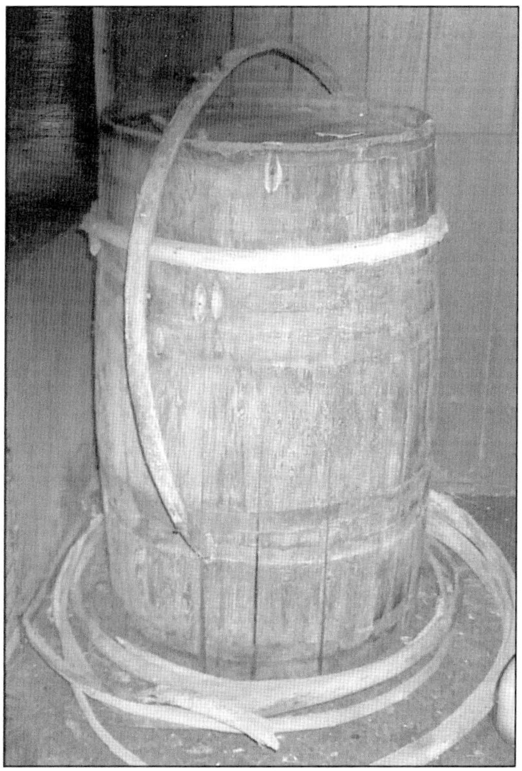

WOODEN BARRELS. Barrels were completely handmade in the early days of the naval store industry. The barrel hoops were made by splitting white oak saplings, but Father Time caused these hoops to separate from the barrel. (Courtesy of John Howell.)

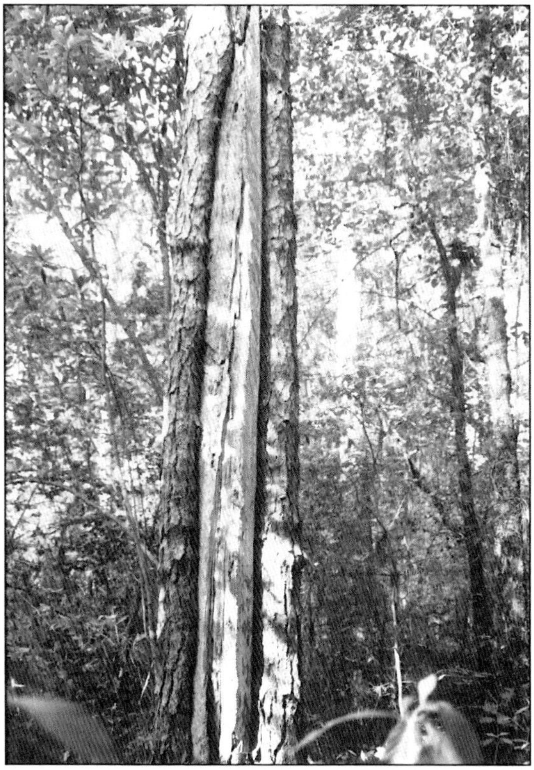

A 175-YEAR-OLD TREE. This tree was most likely boxed in the nineteenth century but has since recovered from the wounds inflicted by the boxing ax and the chipper's shove. This is a rare tract of timber since most tracts were harvested for lumber or the tar kiln after being worked for turpentine. (Courtesy of Graham Jackson.)

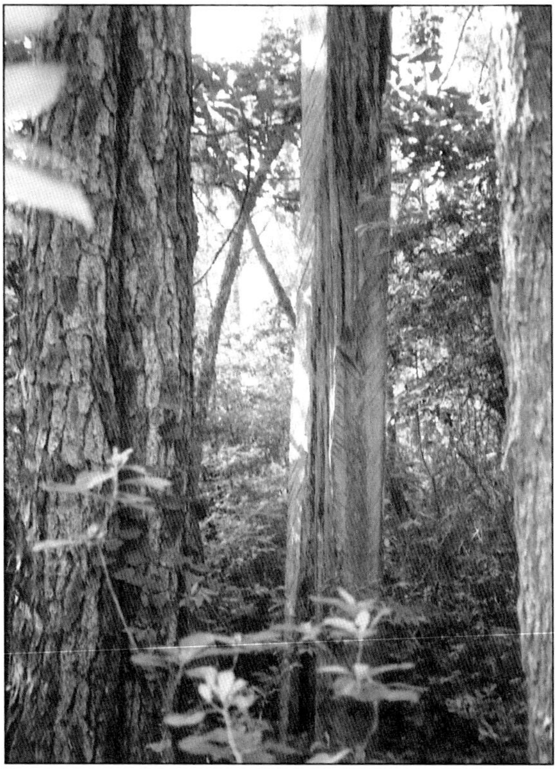

LONGLEAF PINES. The center tree is a longleaf pine that died years ago from the wounds inflicted by double boxing for many years. The heart portion is preserved by the remaining resin that has caused the tree to change into "lighterd" (backwoods talk for "lightwood"). Many trees such as this were split for rail fences or burned in the tar kiln to extract the remaining resin in the form of tar. The workers bare feet tracked through the spilled tar and resin, causing sticky, dirty heels, hence the state's nickname "Tar Heels." (Courtesy of Graham Jackson.)

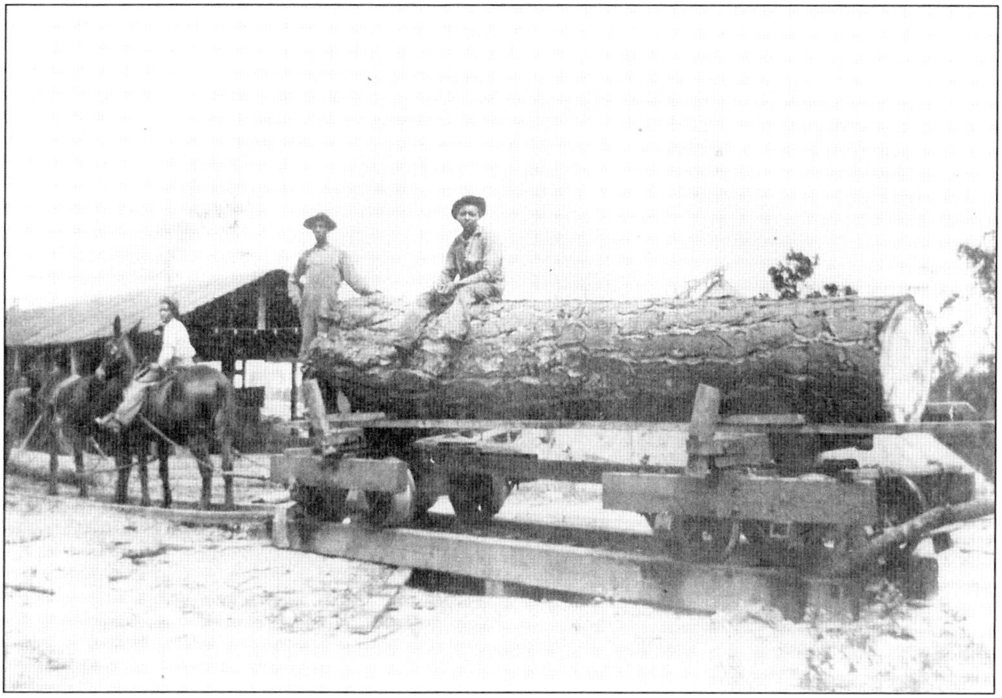

A LONGLEAF PINE POSITIONED FOR THE SAW CARRIAGE. By the early twentieth century, the naval store industry was winding down and the cross-cut saw was overtaking the turpentine chipper. Brown Brothers moved into the Ivanhoe section of the county, *c.* 1910, with their huge sawmill. (Courtesy of Sampson County History Museum, Inc.)

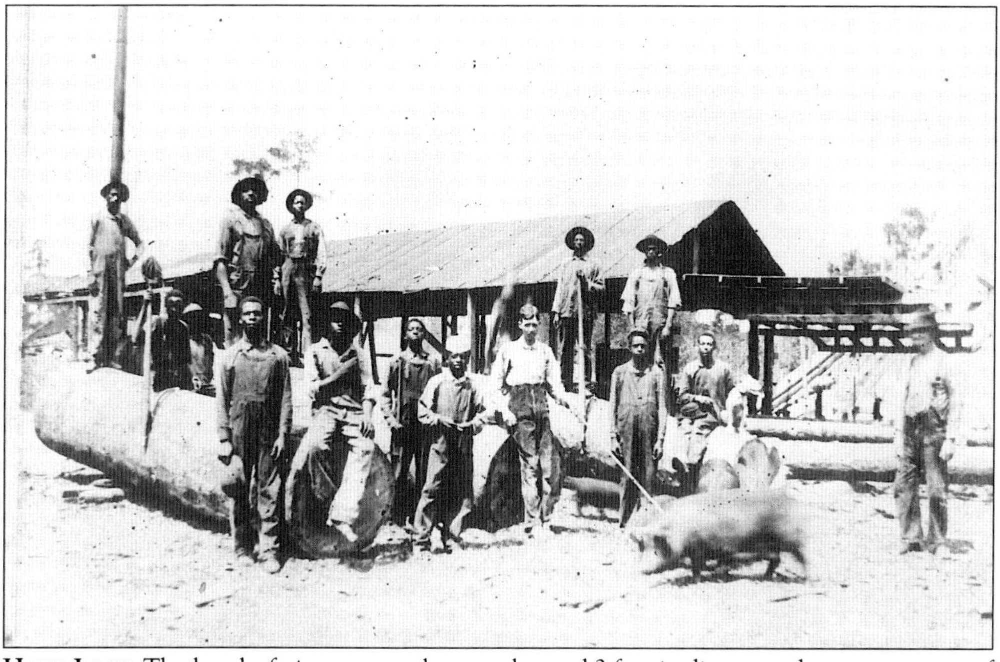

HUGE LOGS. The longleaf pine tree rarely grows beyond 3 feet in diameter, the measurement of the logs pictured here. (Courtesy of Sampson County History Museum, Inc.)

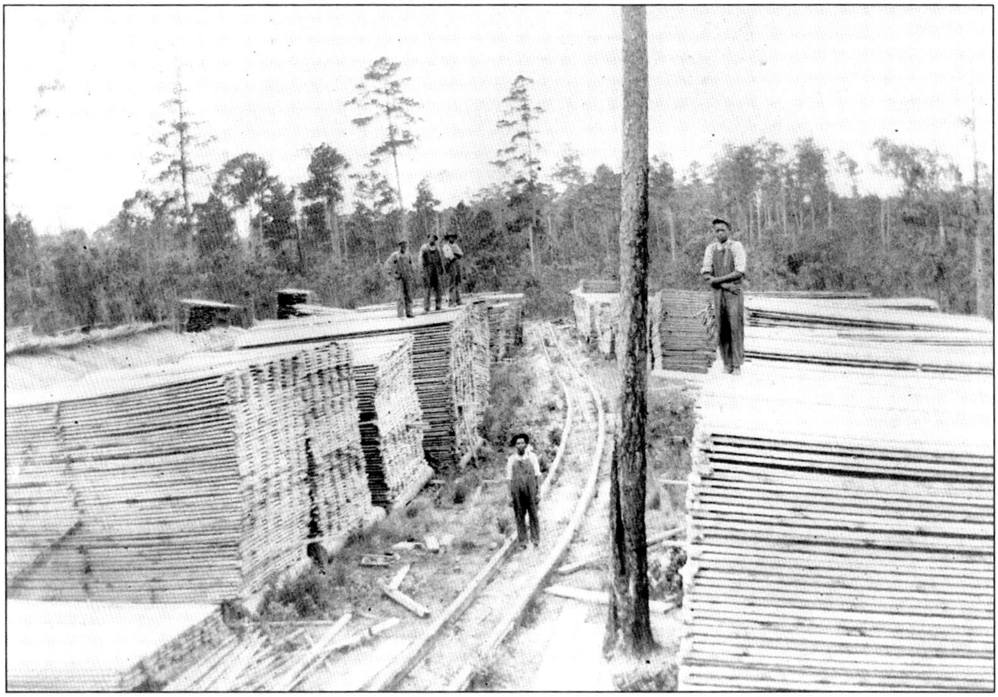

STACKS OF CHOICE LUMBER WAITING FOR SHIPMENT VIA THE RAILROAD. The narrow-gauge tram tracks pictured were used to bring logs to the mill from distant tracts of timber. (Courtesy of Sampson County History Museum, Inc.)

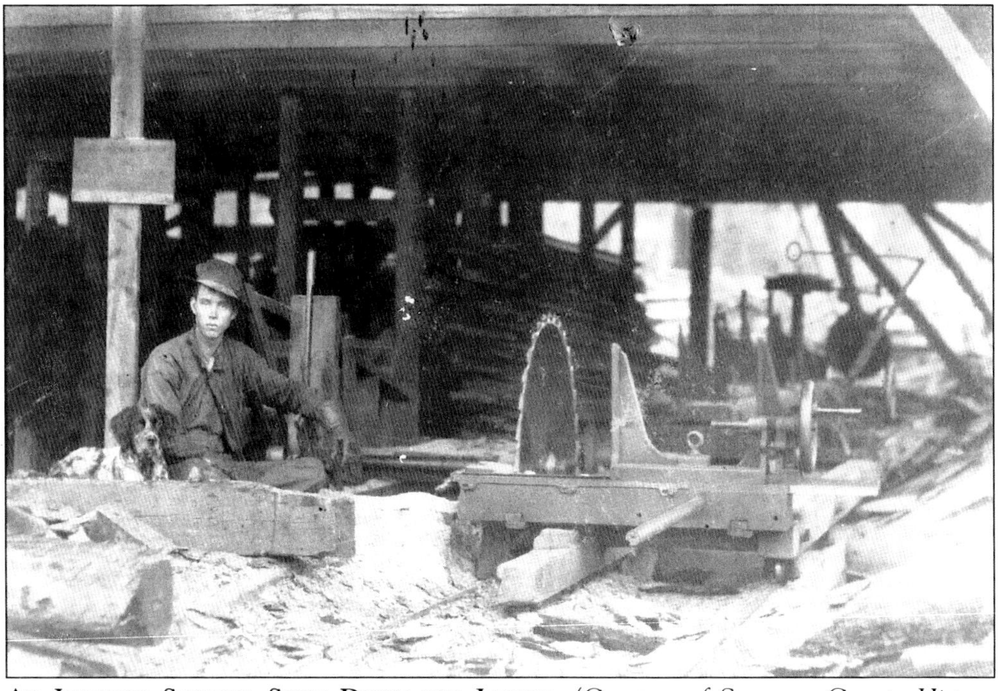

AN IVANHOE SAWMILL SHUT DOWN FOR LUNCH. (Courtesy of Sampson County History Museum, Inc.)

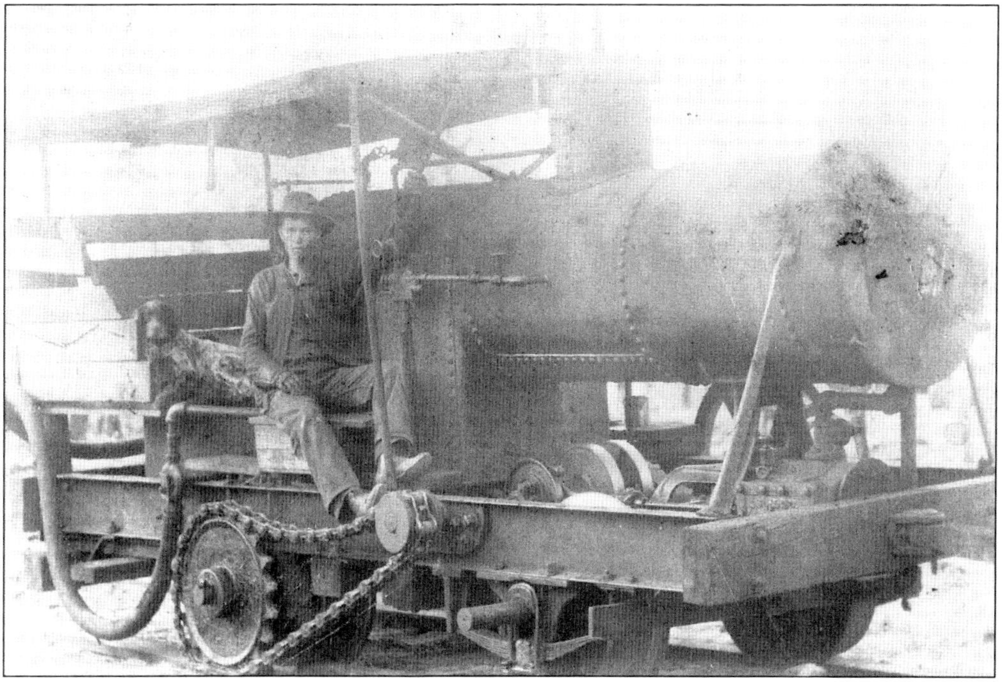

A Tram Engine, c. 1910. Part of the Browns' operation in Ivanhoe, this "dummy train," as they were referred to, was about one-tenth the size of a regular train. (Courtesy of Sampson County History Museum, Inc.)

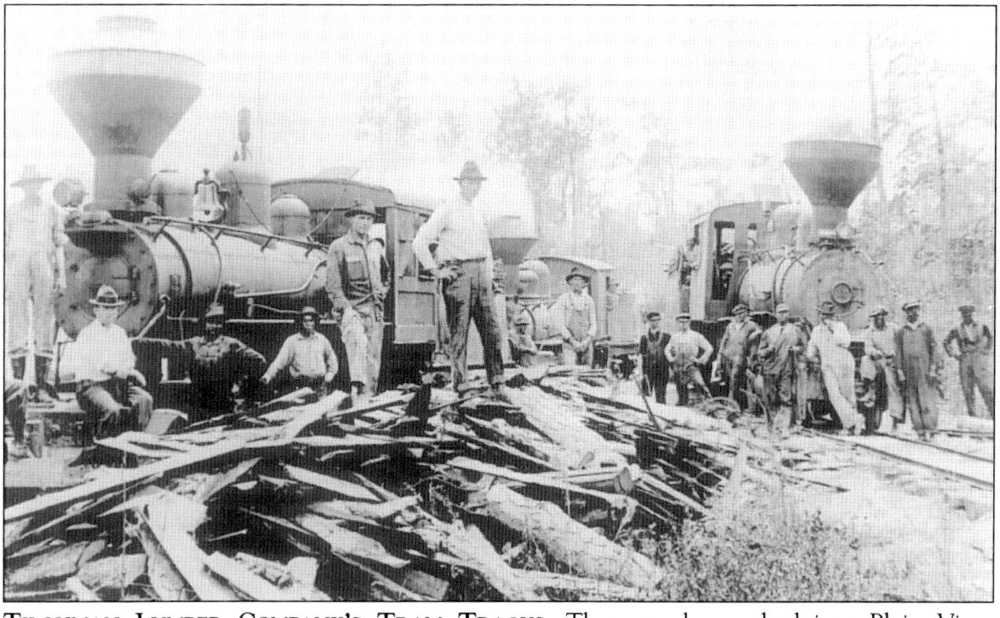

Tilghman Lumber Company's Tram Tracks. These tracks reached into Plain View, Westbrook, Herring, Mingo, Dismal, Honeycutt, Belvoir, and Newton Grove Townships. Freight back-hauls were delivered to points in Sampson, and logs were hauled back to Dunn. A car was also fitted with seats and carried rural Sampson folks to and from Dunn. (Courtesy of Granville Tilghman.)

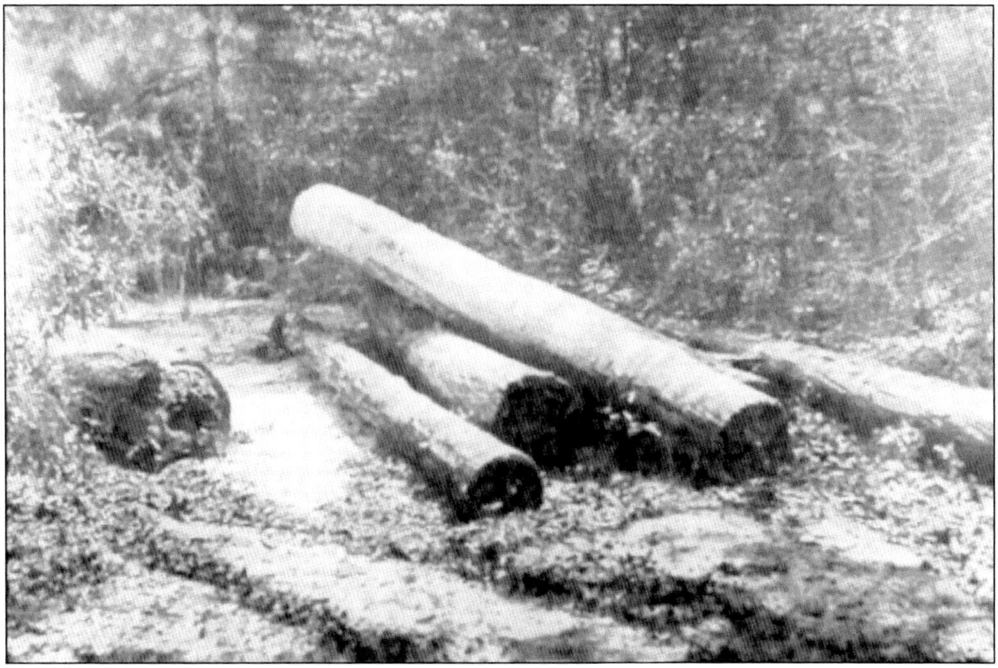

ONE-HUNDRED-YEAR-OLD LOGS DRAGGED FROM THE SOUTH RIVER. Occasionally, logs would become separated from the rafts and eventually sink to the river's bottom. Today, quality timber is being harvested from river bottoms in parts of the country.

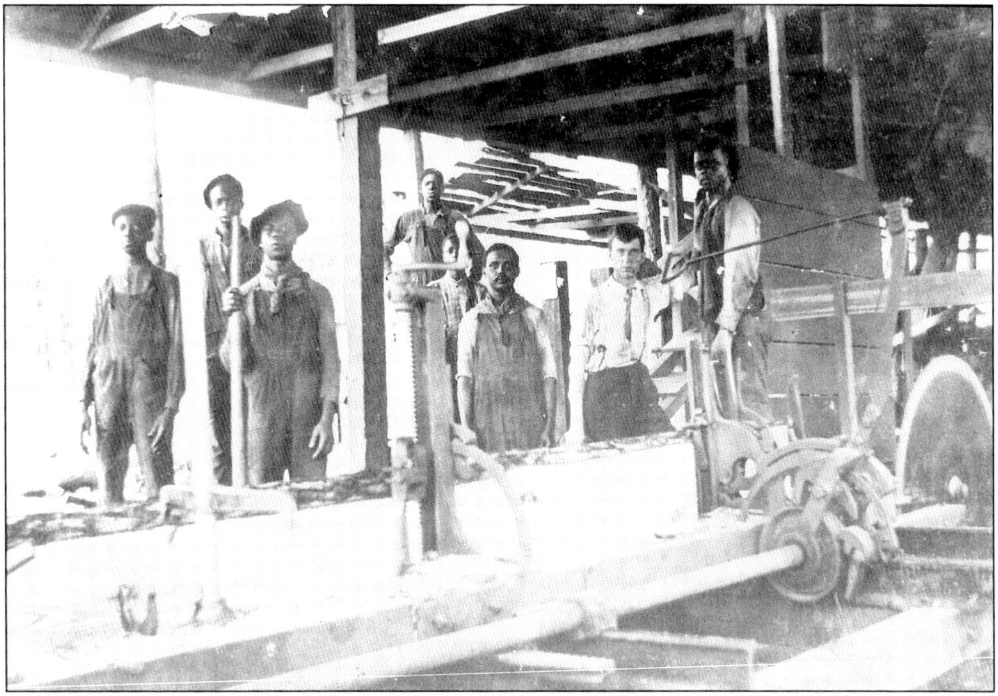

THE NAVAL STORE. The naval store industry had flourished and declined. The sawmill promised a brief period of prosperity, but when the longleaf pine trees were gone, the people moved away. (Courtesy of Sampson County History Museum, Inc.)

Three

Old-Time Schools

Our earliest schools were born out of ignorance and hard times. The schools were a child of the church. The teacher-preacher man cared for the church and school in pioneering days. Sampson was almost devoid of any educational opportunities in the earliest days of its history. Before the War Between the States, only a fraction of our citizens received a formal education.

The early rural schoolhouse was first a "log structure" and later "a weather-boarded box" with two or three windows on each side, furnished with a few wooden benches, and a stove in the middle of the room or a fireplace in one end of the building. The rod of correction was always within the teacher's reach. Schoolbooks were family heirlooms and continued in use as long as they held together. A young scholar would bring a copy to school, which had been used by some family member of the preceding generation. The value placed on books is expressed by the scribbled rhymes found in early school books: "If this book should chance to roam / Box its ears and send it home. / This book was bought for good intent / Pray bring it home when it is lent." A likely list of early schoolbooks was the following: *Reed & Kellogg's Grammar*, *Sanford's Arithmetic*, *Maury's Geography*, *Holme's Reader*, *Holme's History*, and *Webster's Speller*.

Many early schools were financed by subscription, which was paid by the parents of the student, and later the students were supported by special school taxes and local funds. Many rural schoolteachers inspired county girls and boys to reach for dreams beyond their rural upbringing.

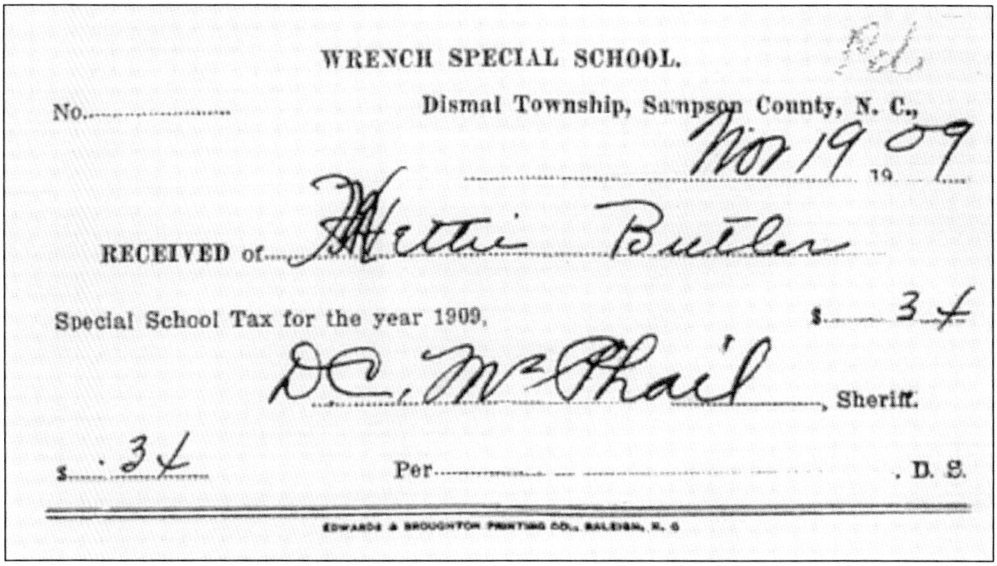

WRENCH SPECIAL SCHOOL. Pd

No.......... Dismal Township, Sampson County, N. C., Nov 19 1909

RECEIVED of Hettie Butler

Special School Tax for the year 1909, $ .34

D.C. McPhail, Sheriff.

$ .34 Per .... D. S.

EDWARDS & BROUGHTON PRINTING CO., RALEIGH, N. C

WRENCH SPECIAL SCHOOL TAX. Early rural schools were financed by the local citizens through special taxes. Hettie Butler was unmarried and had no children, yet she paid 34¢ in taxes to support the Wrench School. The more than 100 rural schools, at this time, were supported by a similar system.

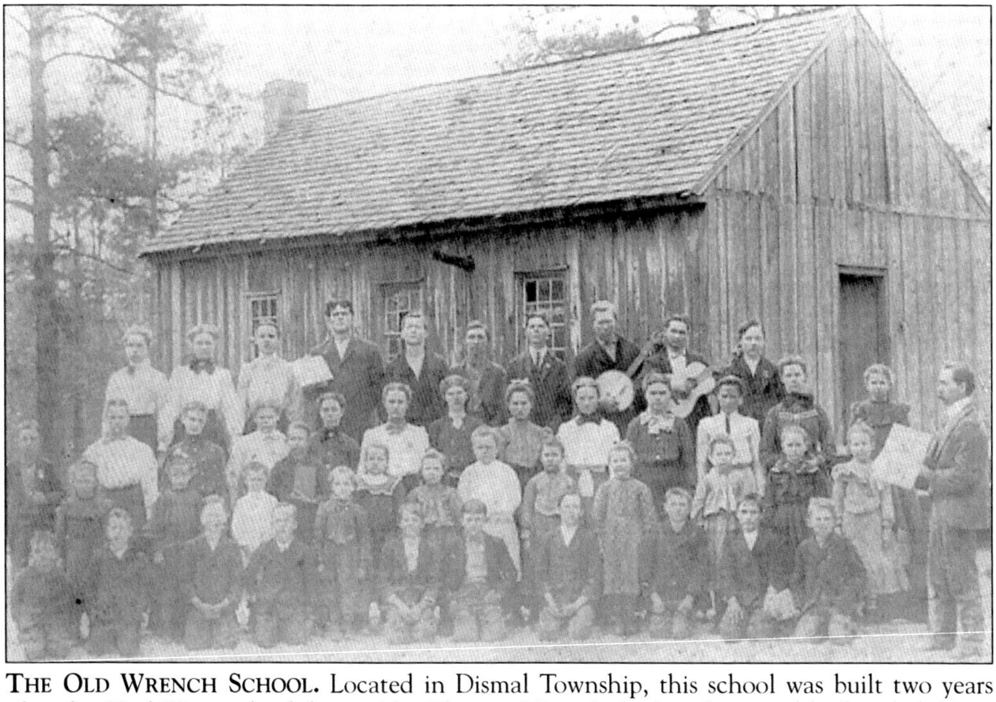

THE OLD WRENCH SCHOOL. Located in Dismal Township, this school was built two years after the Civil War on land donated by Thomas Wrench. Before this, neighborhood children attended school in the local Baptist meetinghouse. (Courtesy of Graham Jackson.)

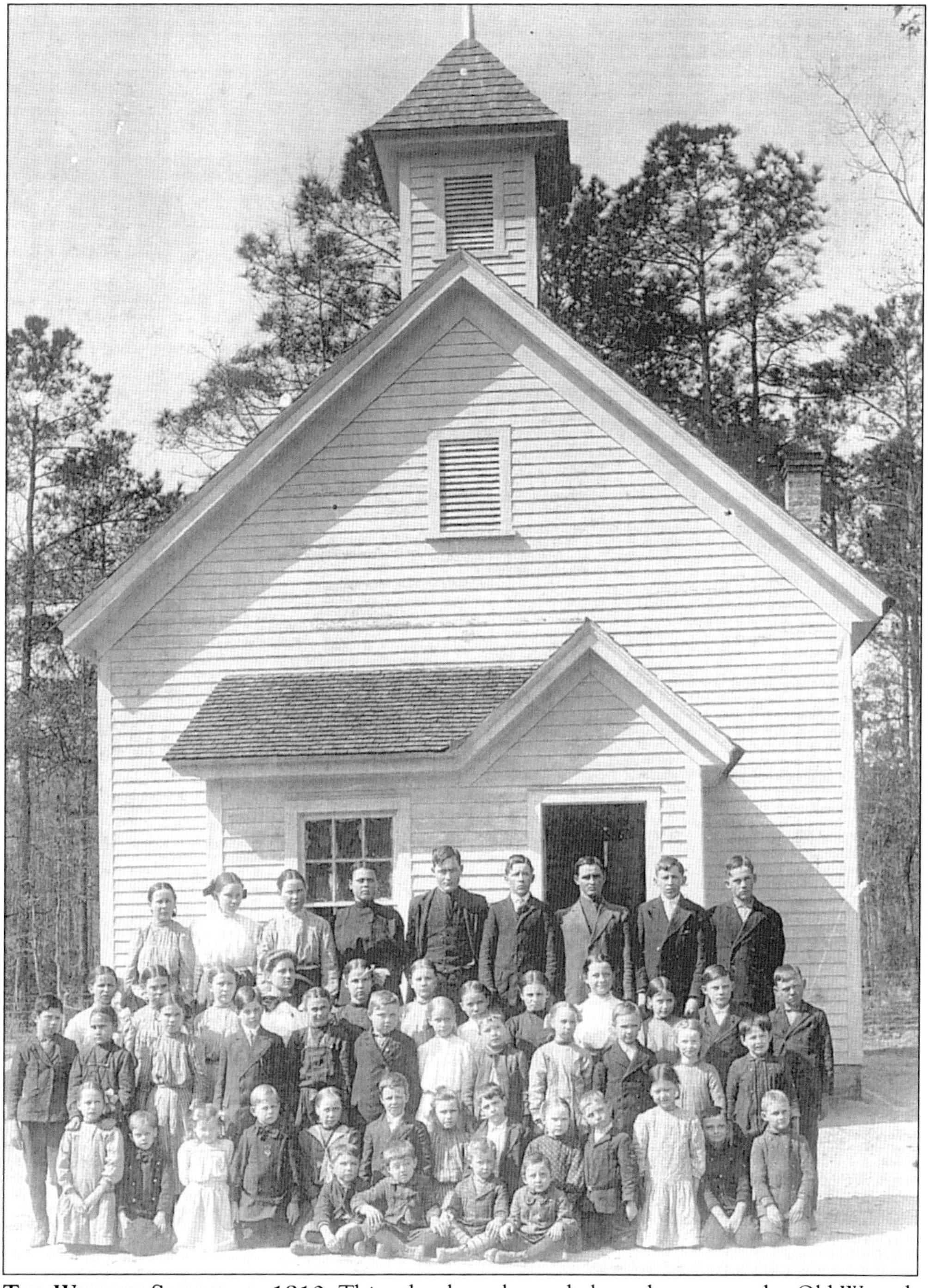

THE WRENCH SCHOOL, C. 1910. This school was located along the present-day Old Wrench School Road in Dismal Township. The 1909 school address was Route #1, Box 34 in Cooper, North Carolina. This was the third recorded school building in the community and operated until 1926, when Clement High School replaced the many one-room school districts. (Courtesy of Graham Jackson.)

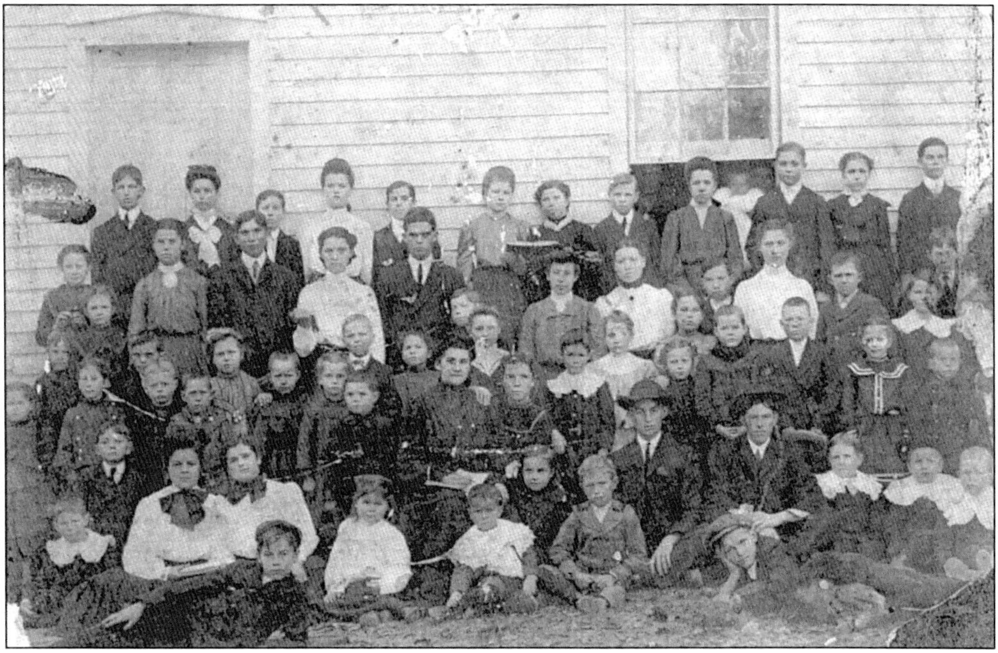

THE ST. PAUL'S SCHOOL NEAR HOBBTON, 1890S. The St. Paul's F.W. Baptist Church meets at this site today. Some of the surnames of neighborhood students attending the school include Hobbs, Bass, Warwick, Hudson, Wilson, Giddeon, and others. (Courtesy of Joyce Bass Binkley.)

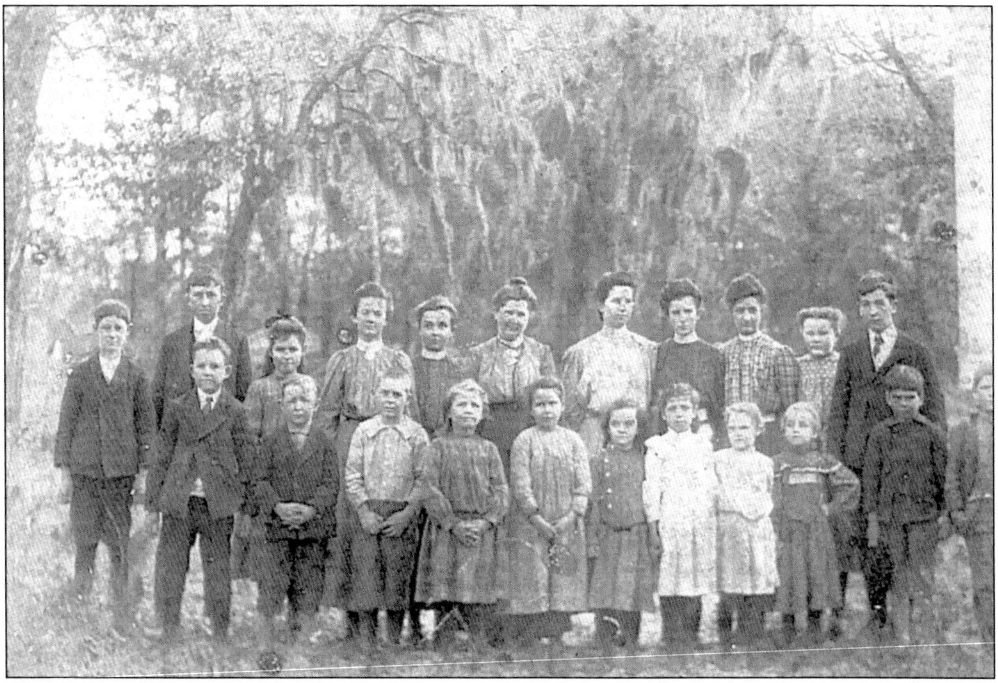

THE SLOAN SCHOOL. In the Garland vicinity, this school was located in Dr. David Solan's old office building on the property of William Solan. Some of the students' surnames were Solan, Johnson, McDuffie, Murphy, Colvin, and others. (Courtesy of Charles and Laura Murphy.)

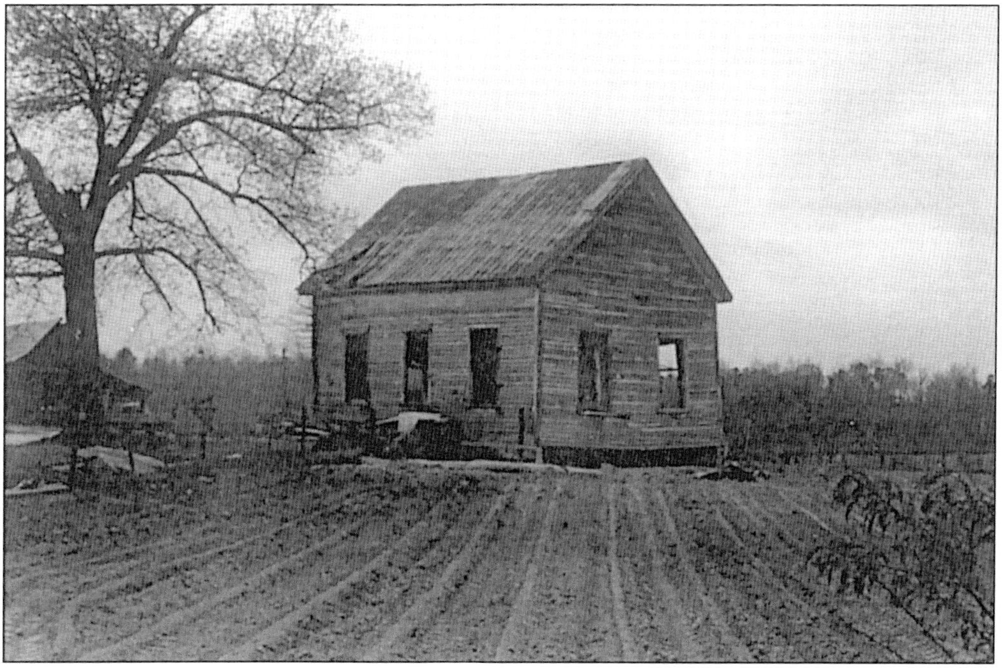

THE SHILOH CHURCH AND SCHOOL. On July 18, 1910, the Croatan Indians in Dismal Township, near South River, organized the Shiloh Indian School Clan. Mattie B. Cummings taught at the school for $10 per month and her board. The school was supported by private subscription of a few cents a day per student. This ghostly building served as the Shiloh Church and School. (Courtesy of Eva Maynor.)

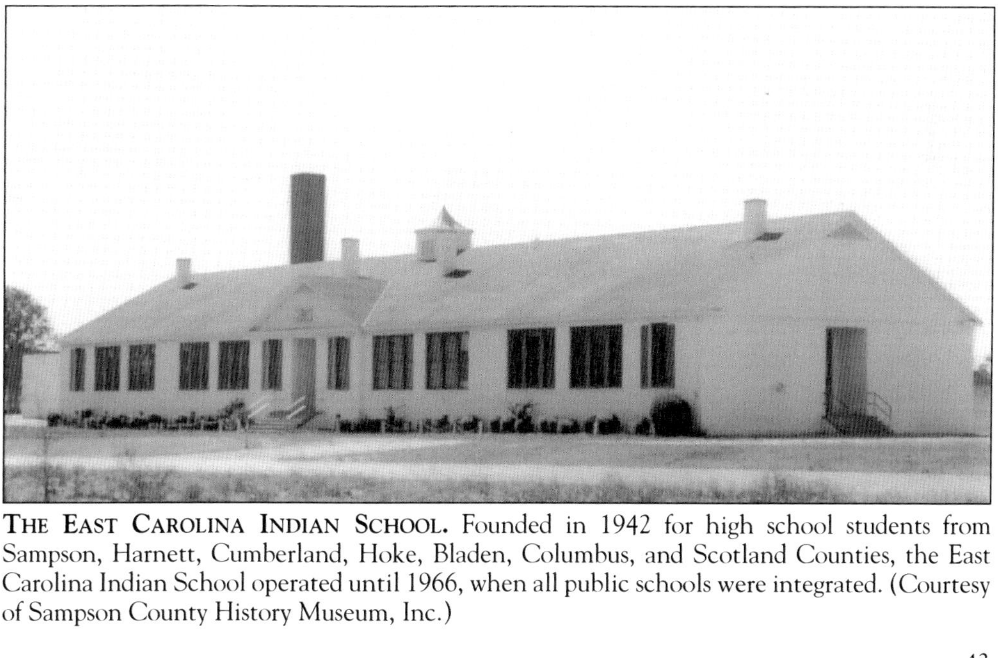

THE EAST CAROLINA INDIAN SCHOOL. Founded in 1942 for high school students from Sampson, Harnett, Cumberland, Hoke, Bladen, Columbus, and Scotland Counties, the East Carolina Indian School operated until 1966, when all public schools were integrated. (Courtesy of Sampson County History Museum, Inc.)

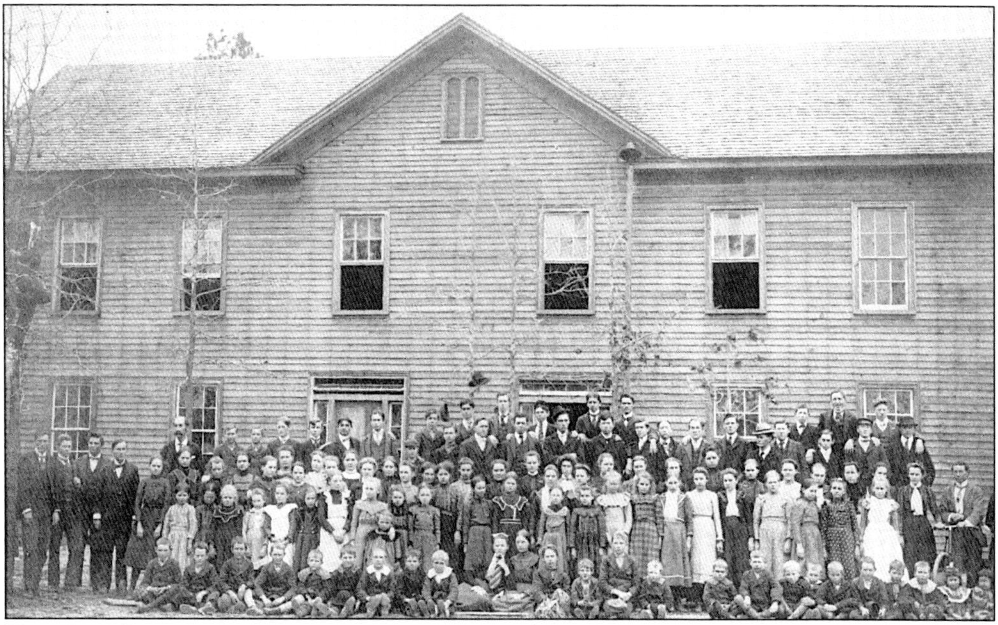

THE OLD SALEM ACADEMY, C. 1901. Organized on January 1, 1875, Salem Academy had Isham Royal as its first principal. Pictured here, a few decades later, are Professor J.J. Gardner, principal; Professor Edward Tucker; and Ralph Fisher, music teacher. The building burned in the 1920s. (Courtesy of Jerry R. Roughton.)

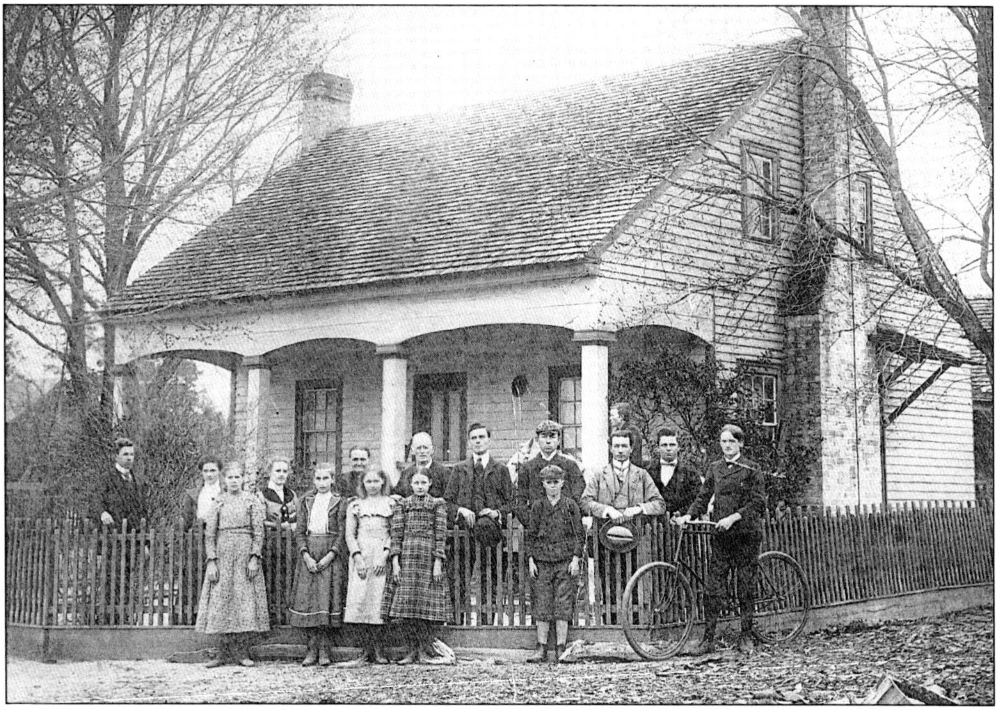

MR. AND MRS. MOLTON ROYAL AND STUDENTS. Molton Royal and his wife gave land for the Salem Academy in Salemburg, and they are posed here with students who boarded in their home for a fee of $4.50 per month. (Courtesy of C.A. Royal.)

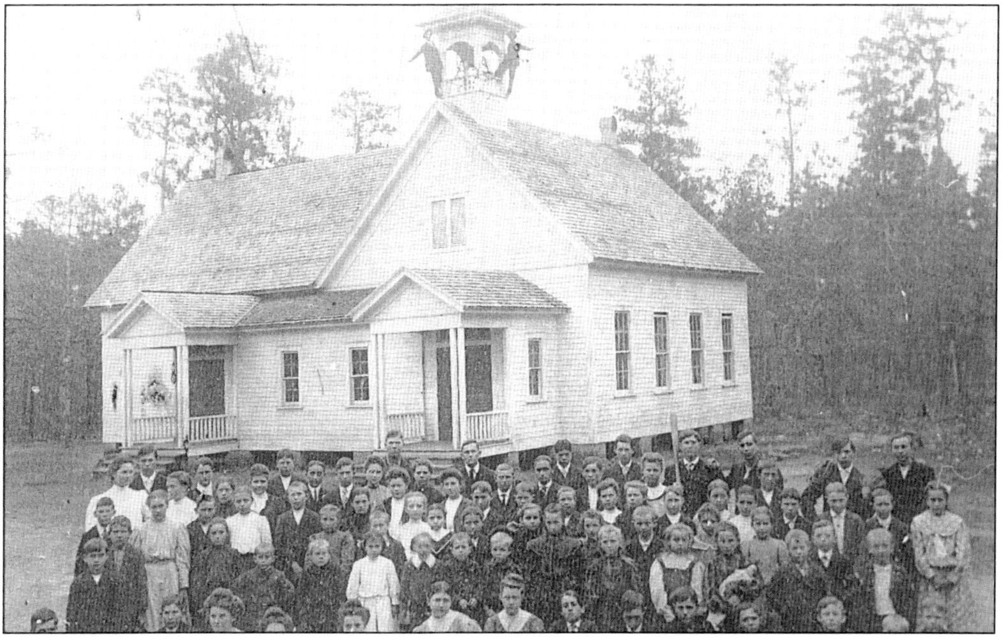

ROANOKE SCHOOL, EAST OF MIDWAY ON ROANOKE ROAD, C. 1908. A school term was three to four months, and a teacher's salary was $120 for the term during this early period. (Courtesy of Clarence E. McLamb Jr.)

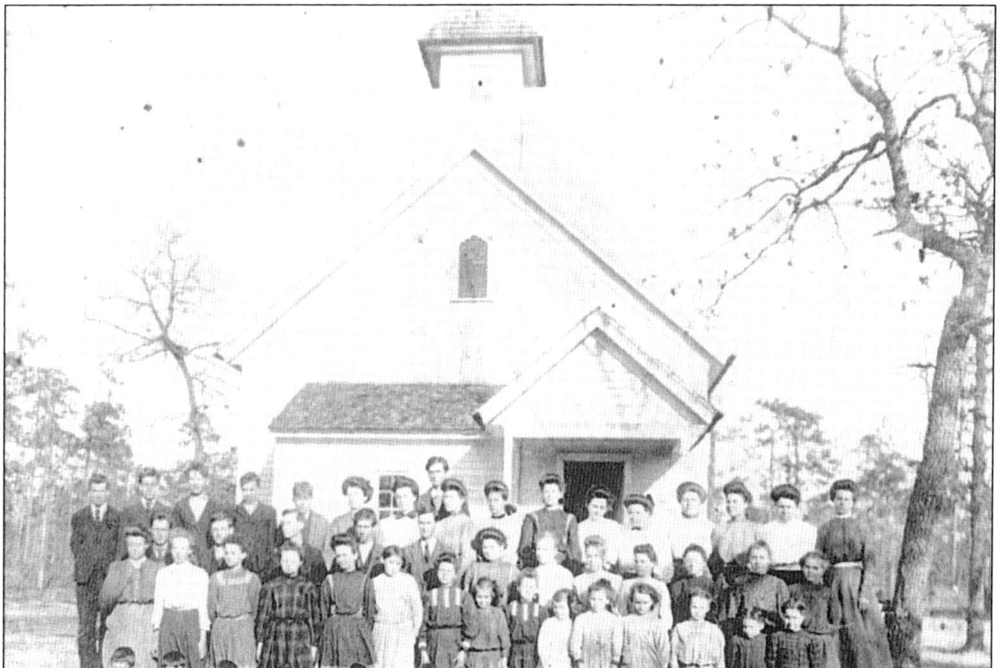

MINGO SCHOOL, C. 1910. In 1884, Reverend William Bland of Hawley's Store was the principal of Mingo High School. In that same year, there were 39 white public schools and 31 African-American public schools in Sampson County. This school burned in the 1920s, and the students were transferred to Spring Branch School. (Courtesy of Clarence E. McLamb Jr.)

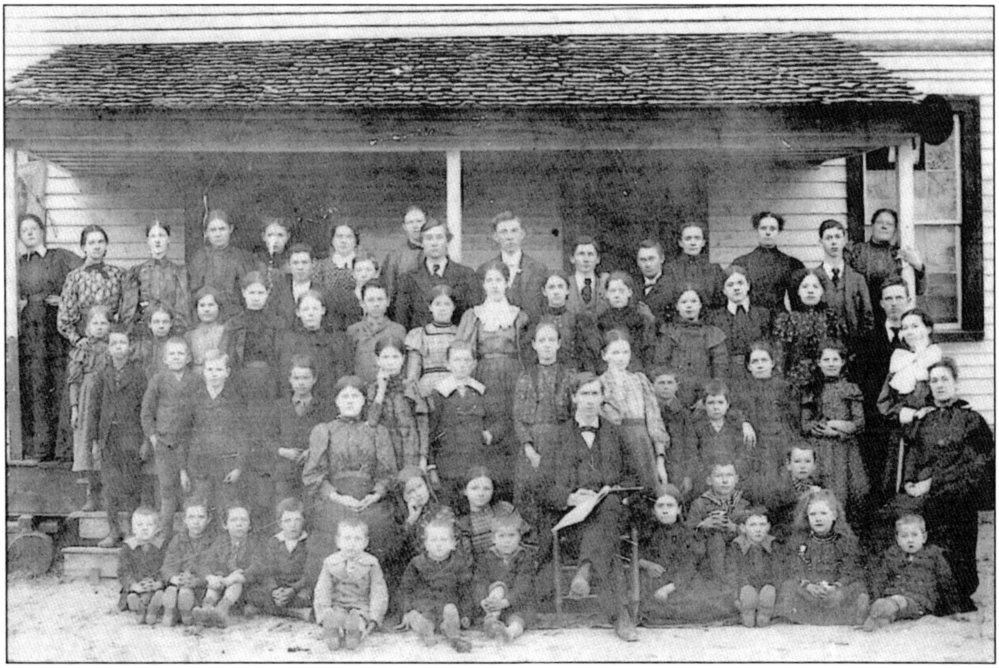

Belvoir One-Room Schoolhouse on Five Bridge Road near McGee Church. The early school districts were approximately 6 square miles. Prior to 1920, only seven grades were taught in the common schools. (Courtesy of Sampson County History Museum, Inc.)

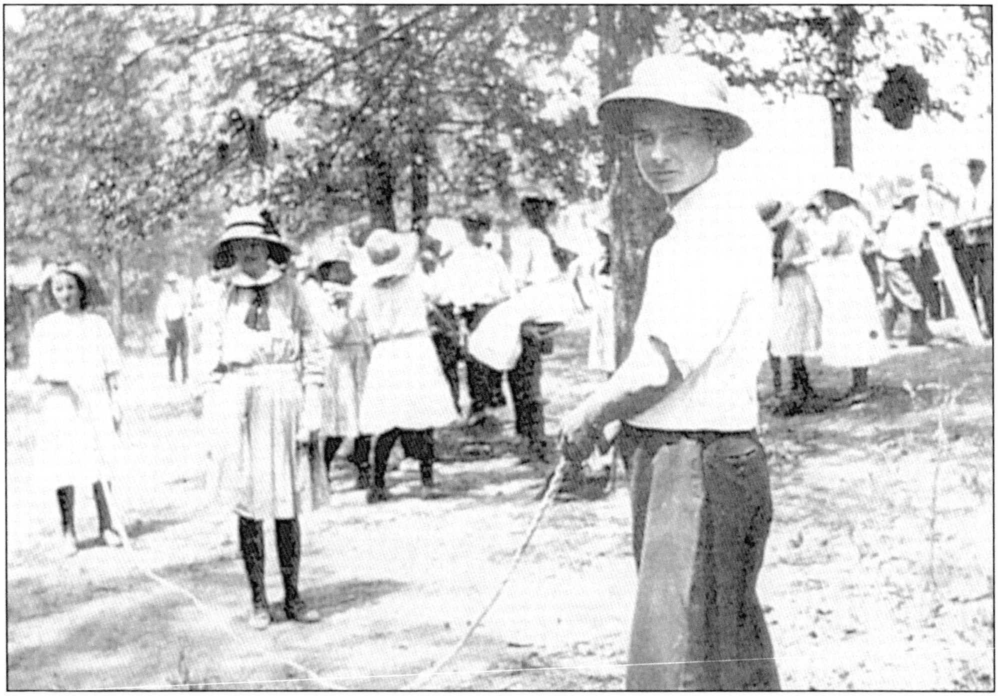

Recess in the Pine Forest Schoolyard, c. Early Twentieth Century. This small neighborhood school was replaced by Mingo and Herring High Schools in 1926. (Courtesy of Tom Jackson.)

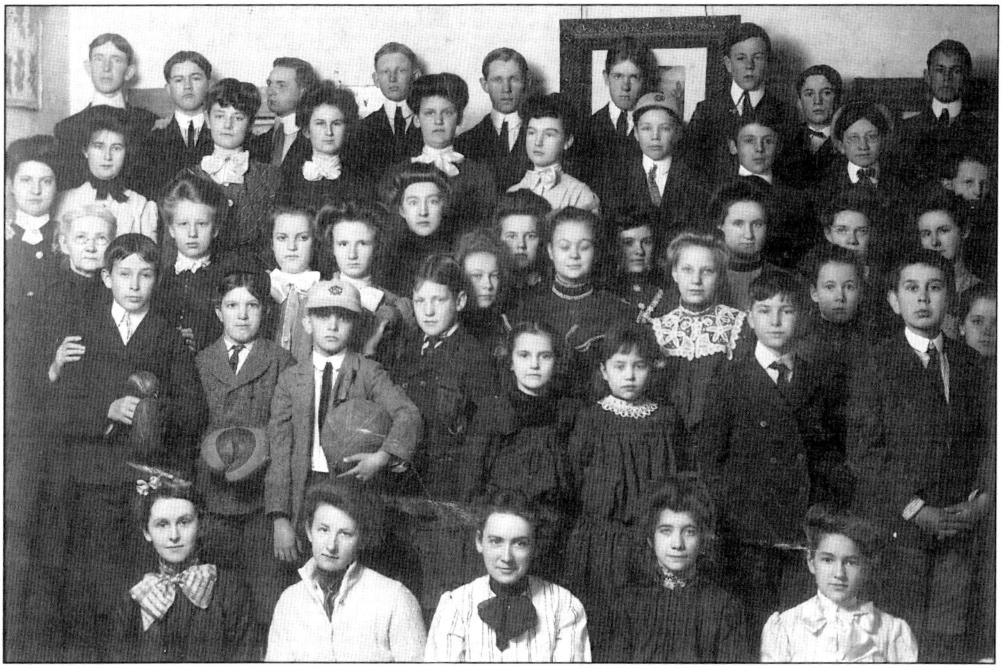

THE COHARIE HIGH SCHOOL, OR MRS. WRIGHT'S PRIVATE SCHOOL. Founded in 1888 for the purpose of teaching Mrs. Wright's own nine children, this school was conducted in the Wright home and admitted neighborhood students. Later, other teachers were employed, and facilities for boarding students were added. Tuition was $4.50 monthly. (Courtesy of Charles and Laura Murphy.)

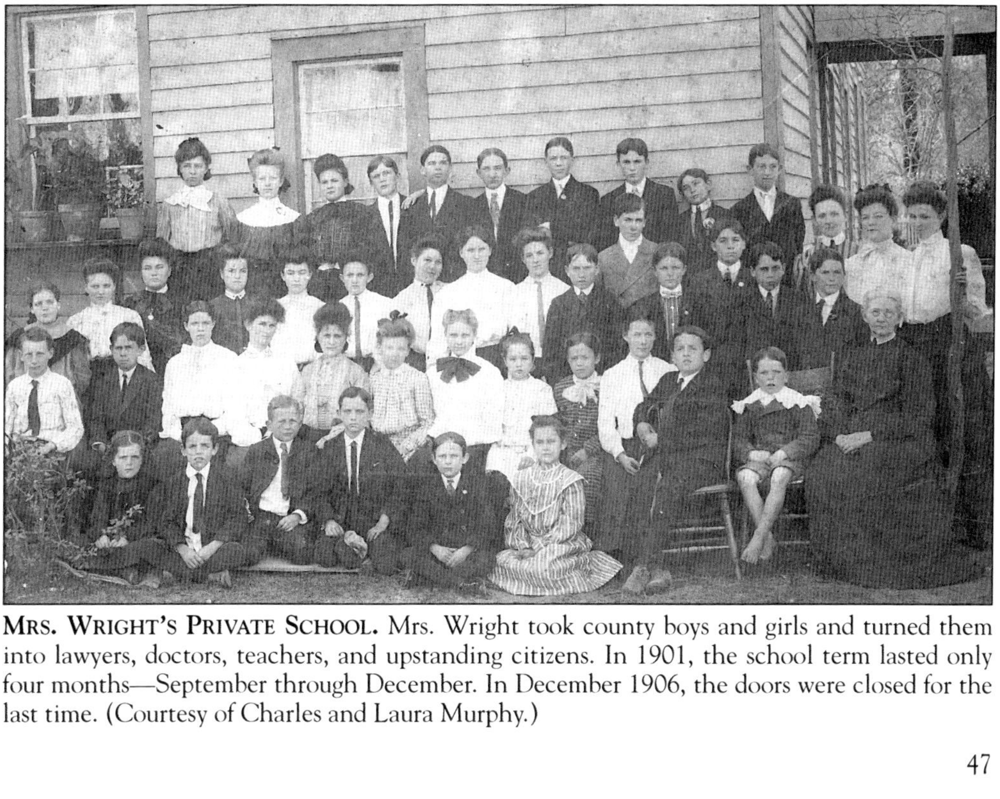

MRS. WRIGHT'S PRIVATE SCHOOL. Mrs. Wright took county boys and girls and turned them into lawyers, doctors, teachers, and upstanding citizens. In 1901, the school term lasted only four months—September through December. In December 1906, the doors were closed for the last time. (Courtesy of Charles and Laura Murphy.)

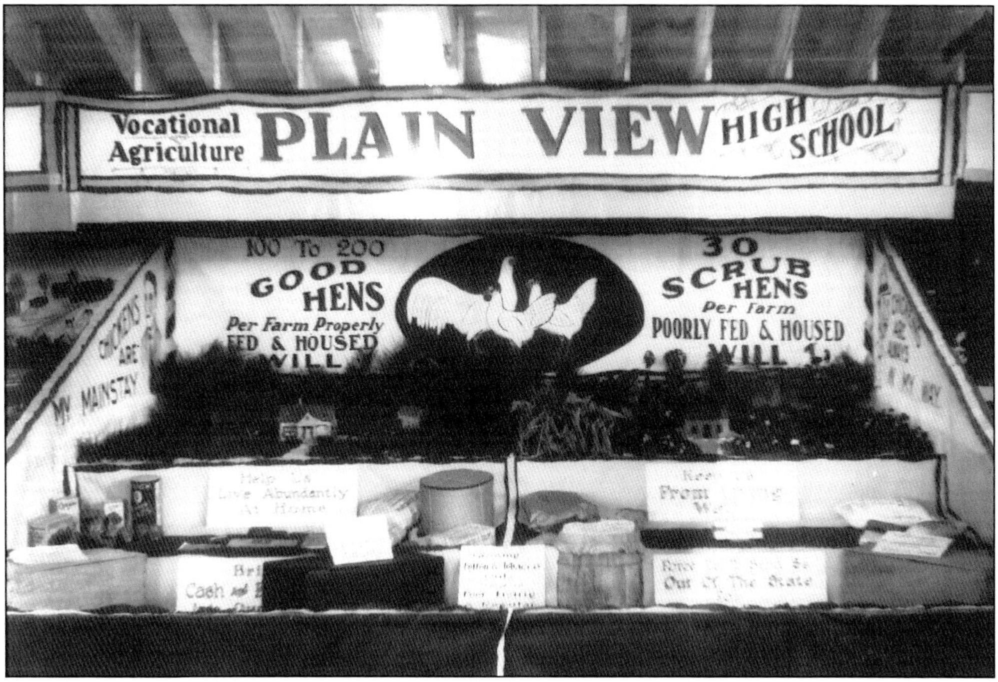

PARTICIPATING IN THE FAIR. Agricultural exhibits were entered in the 1931 County Fair by Plain View, Clement, Franklin, Piney Grove, and Herring High Schools. (Courtesy of North Carolina Division of Archives and History.)

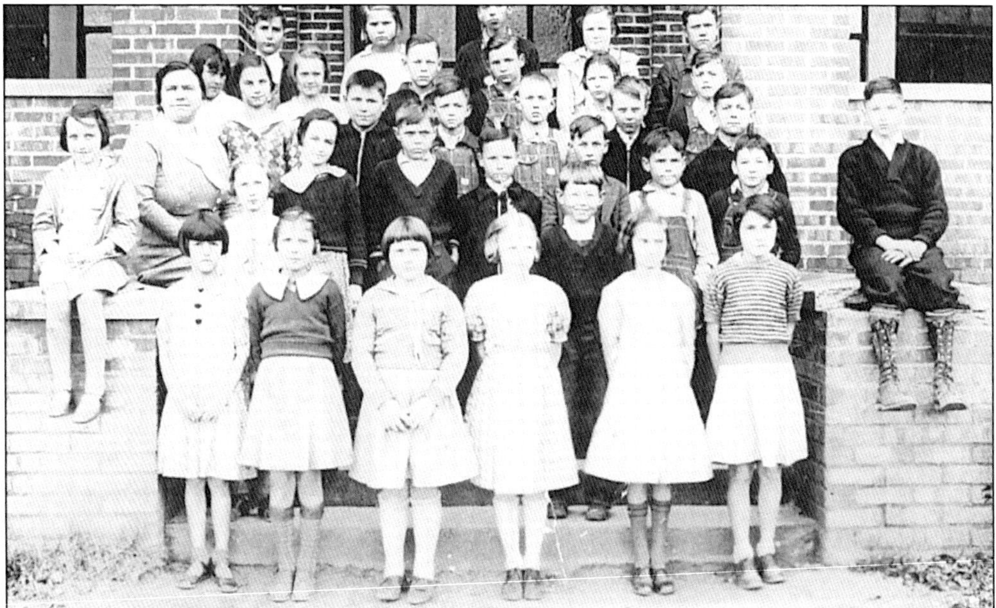

STUDENTS AT ROSEBORO'S SCHOOL, C. 1930. Billy Herring, the present-day chief of the Roseboro fire department, is seated on the banister at right. (Courtesy of Billy Herring.)

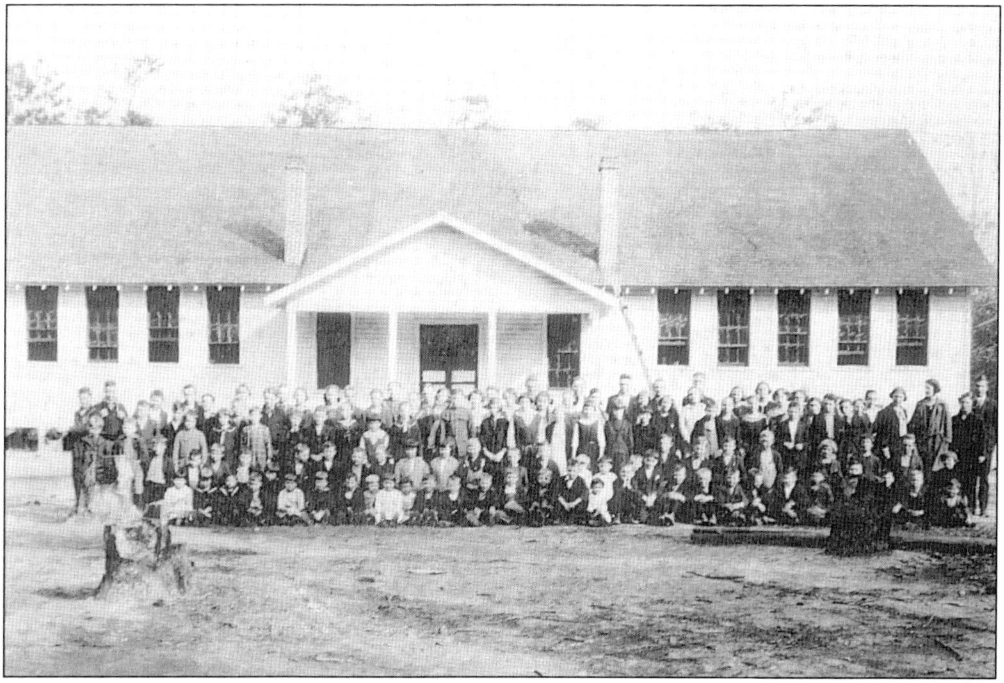

PINE FOREST SCHOOL, C. EARLY 1900S. This school was located in the vicinity of Pine Forest Road in the Mt. Elam community of Mingo Township. (Courtesy of Tom Jackson.)

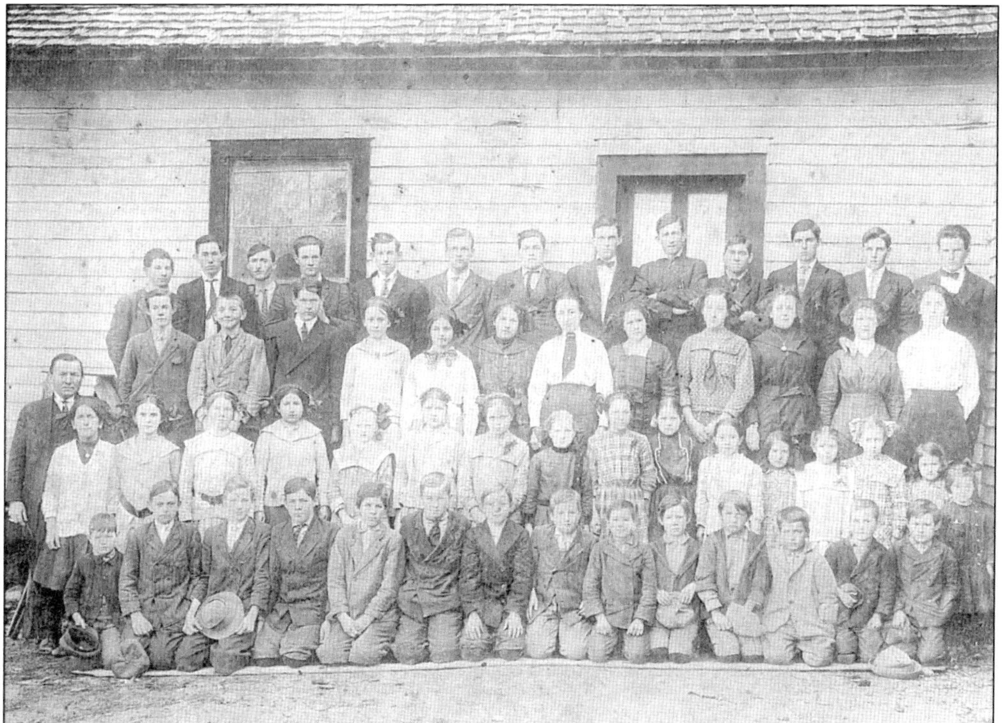

STRAW POND SCHOOL, C. LATE 1800S. This picture is thought to be of the Straw Pond School in the Midway vicinity, off Straw Pond Road. (Courtesy of Tom Jackson.)

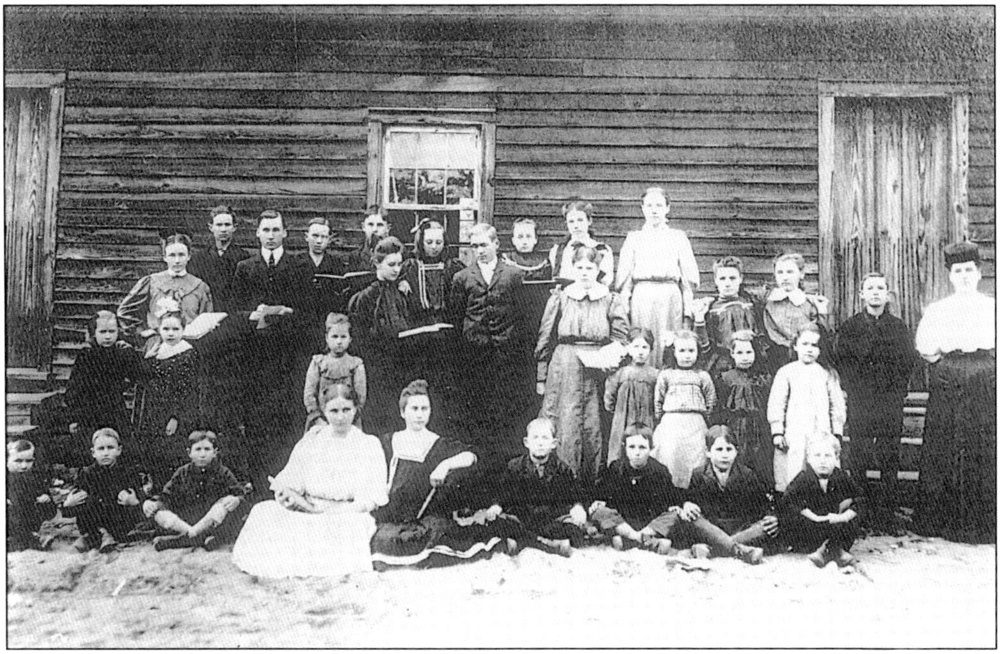

THE NAYLOR SCHOOL, NEAR THE OLD HARNETT CHURCH IN HERRING TOWNSHIP, C. 1909. In rural districts "a weather-boarded box" served as the school building. A few wooden benches and a wood-burning heater furnished the school room. (Courtesy of Clarence E. McLamb Jr.)

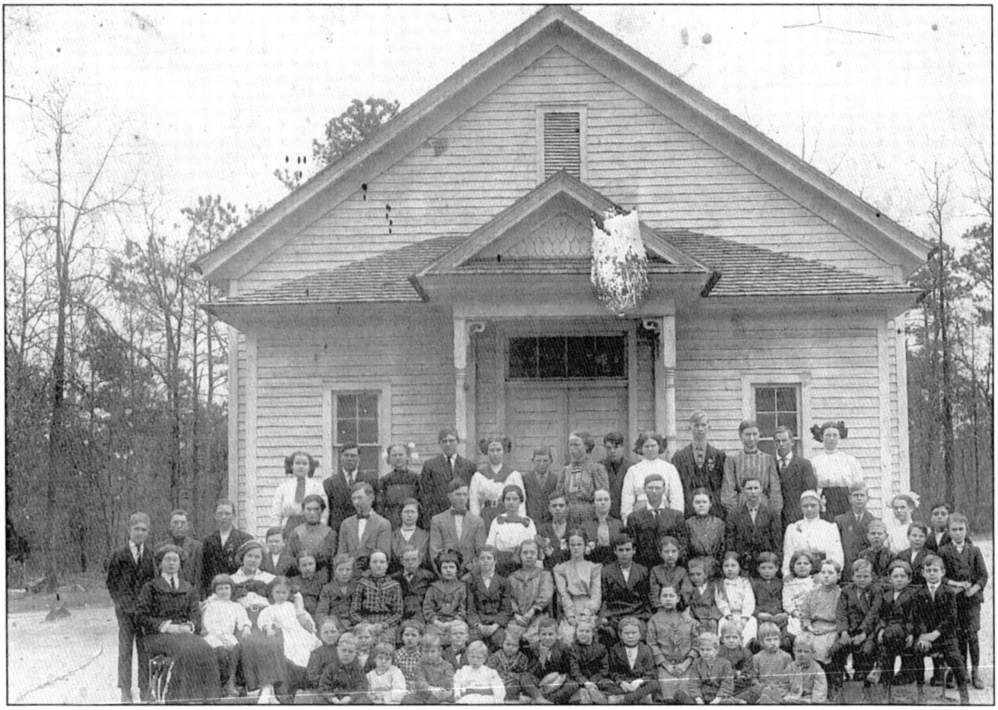

COOPER SCHOOL, C. 1910. Once located on U.S. Highway 13 near the Cumberland County line, this school was destroyed when a pan full of grease on the stove was accidentally knocked off and began a devastating fire. (Courtesy of Edna Page.)

ORANGE SCHOOL IN DISMAL TOWNSHIP, C. EARLY TWENTIETH CENTURY. The schoolteacher here was T. Jackson. The Hayes child in the wagon was pulled to school by his brother; unfortunately, he did not live to adulthood. (Courtesy of Clarence E. McLamb Jr.)

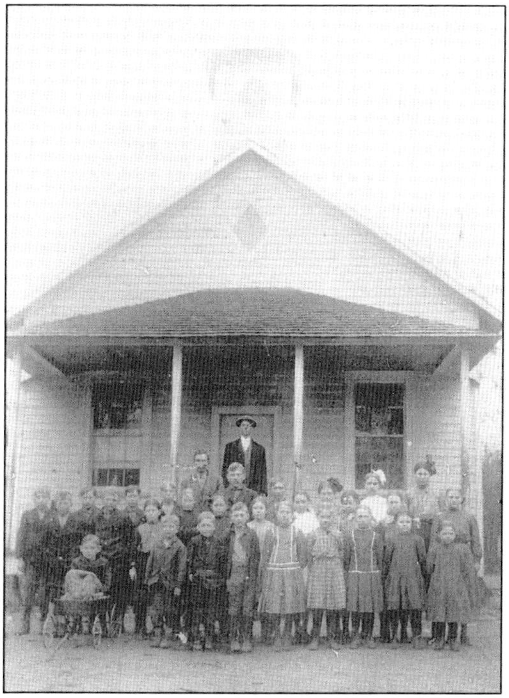

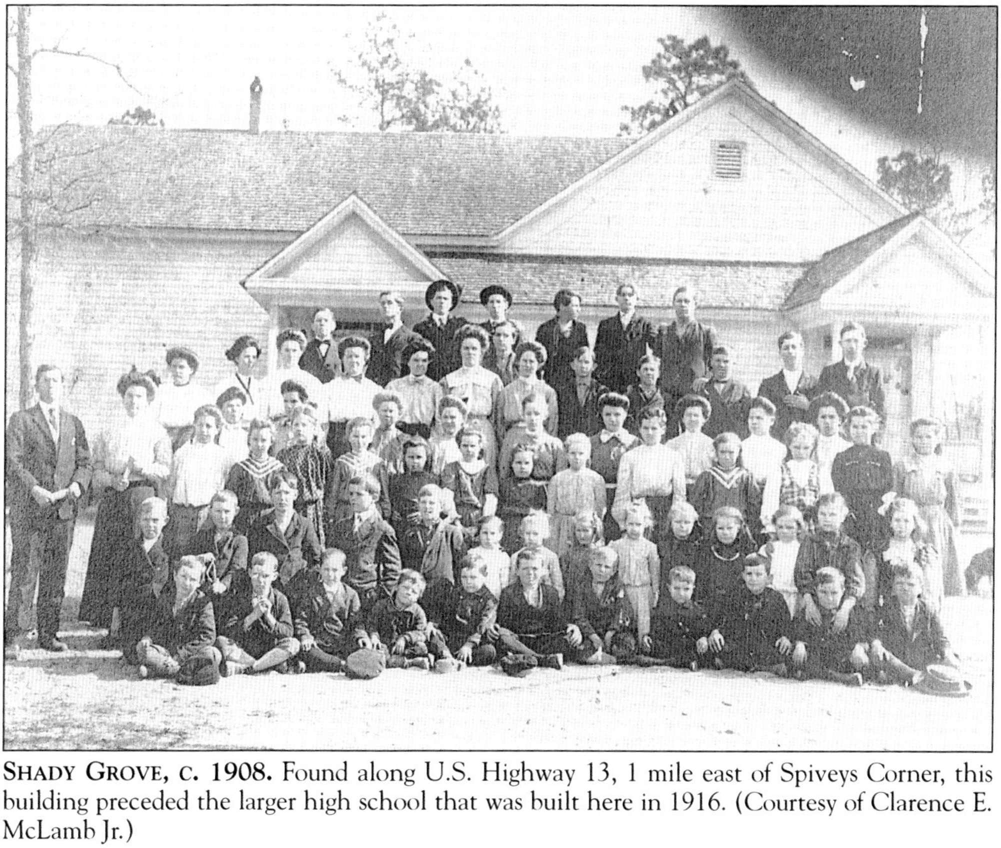

SHADY GROVE, C. 1908. Found along U.S. Highway 13, 1 mile east of Spiveys Corner, this building preceded the larger high school that was built here in 1916. (Courtesy of Clarence E. McLamb Jr.)

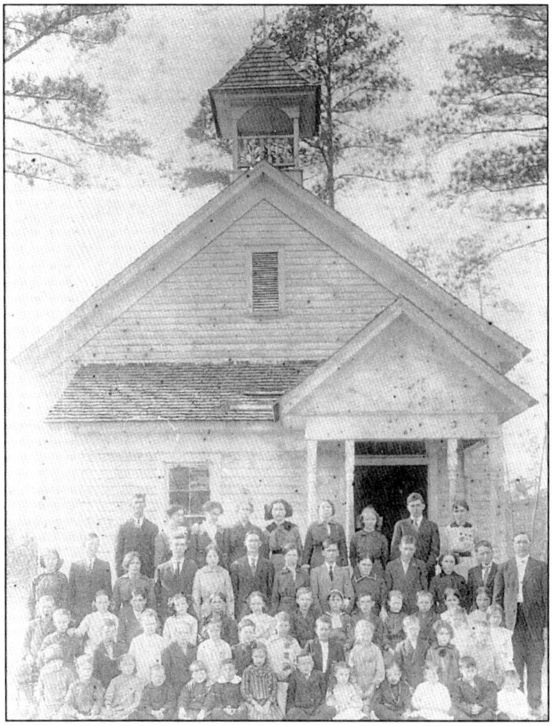

MAPLE GROVE SCHOOL, C. 1915. Paschal Willford taught the students Maple Grove, which was located near Timothy in Westbrook Township. Nature provided toilets for many rural schools, with a "his" and "her" path leading into the bushes. (Courtesy of Clarence E. McLamb Jr.)

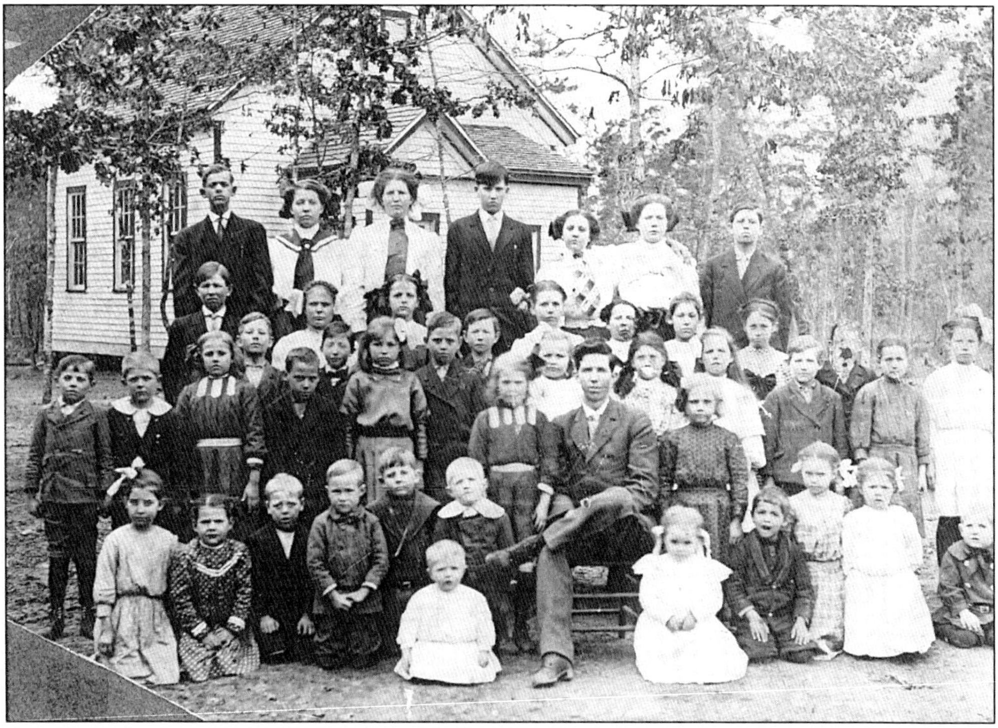

THE KING SCHOOL, 1912. Located in what became the Piney Grove community, near modern-day Skeeter Point, this school served students with surnames that included King, Sutton, Oates, Lee, Jordan, and others in this four-month school term. (Courtesy of David King.)

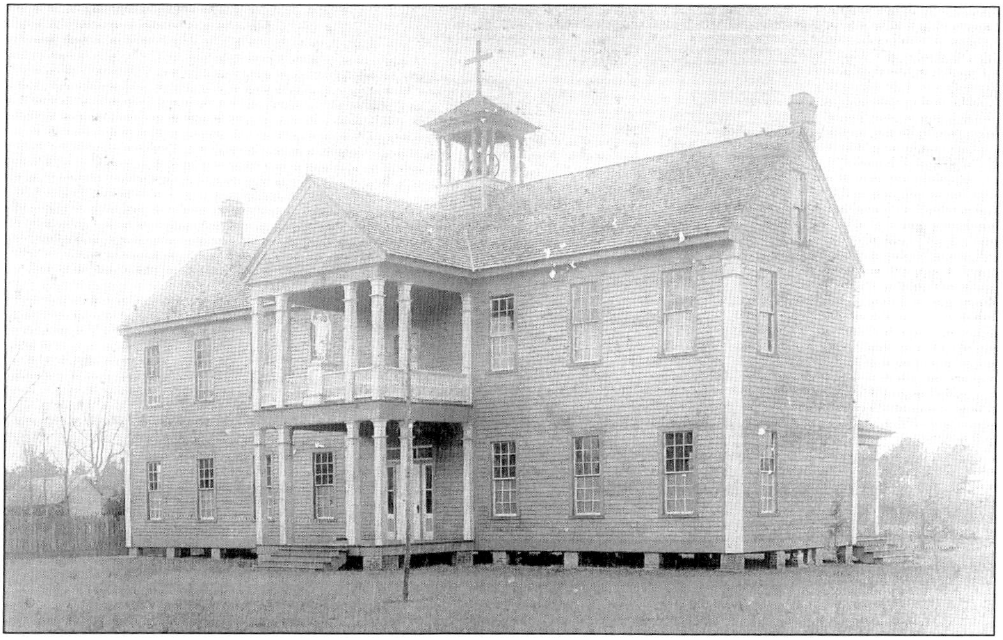

The Catholic School in Newton Grove. Built *c.* 1900 and operated as a school until *c.* 1940, this building had an upstairs that was used for symposiums on Sunday afternoons. In its later days, the building served as a movie house. (Courtesy of Albert and Ann Herring.)

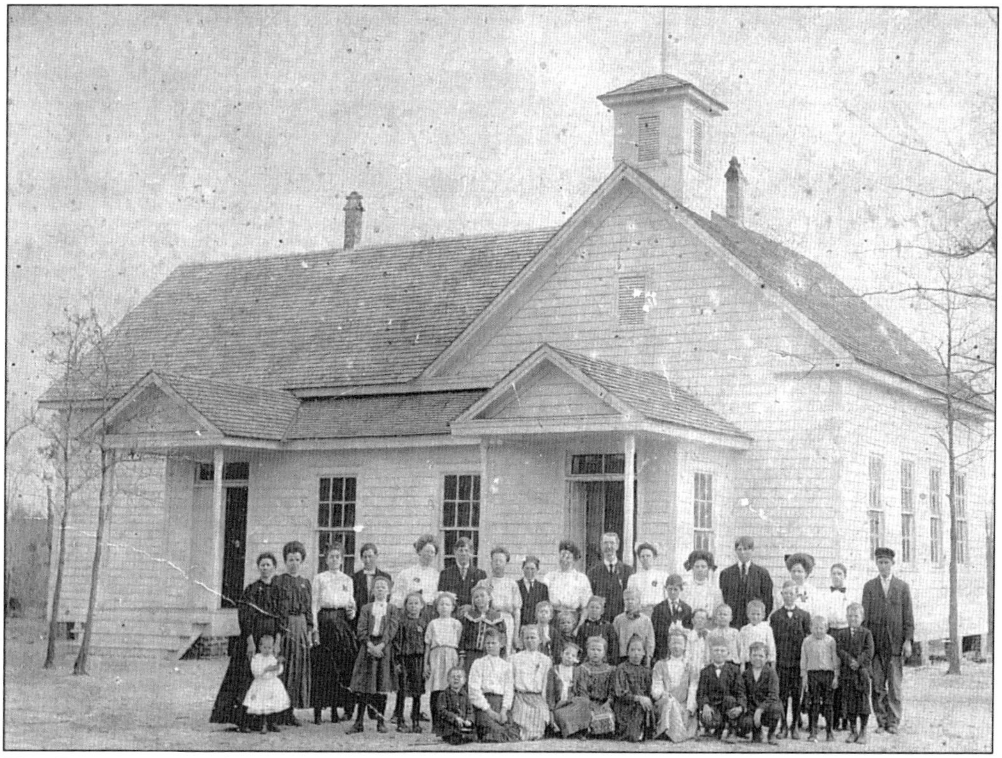

The Parkersburg School, c. 1900. Miss Lizzie C. Smith was the teacher at this school in 1897. (Courtesy of Hazel P. Smith.)

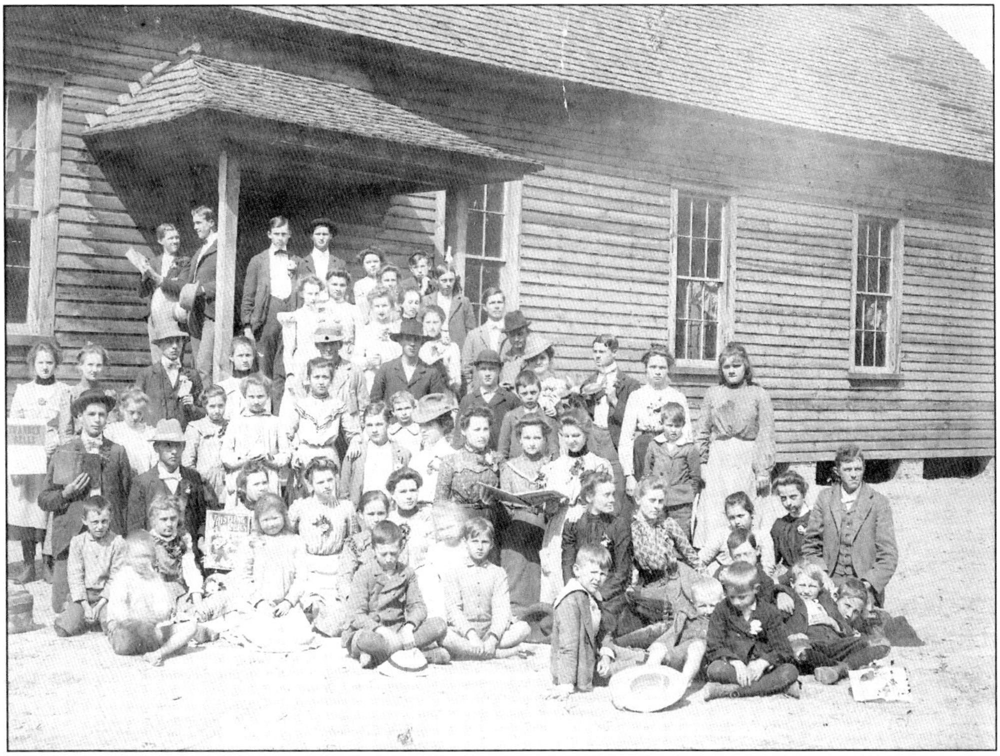

NEWTON GROVE'S EARLY SCHOOL DAYS. In 1896 and 1897, D.P. Dameron and N.B. Lee were teachers in Newton Grove. The list of books used by students here might have included *Webster's Speller*, *Reed & Kellogg's Grammar*, *Sanford's Arithmetic*, *Holme's Reader*, *Maury's Geography*, and *Holme's History*. (Courtesy of Sampson County History Museum, Inc.)

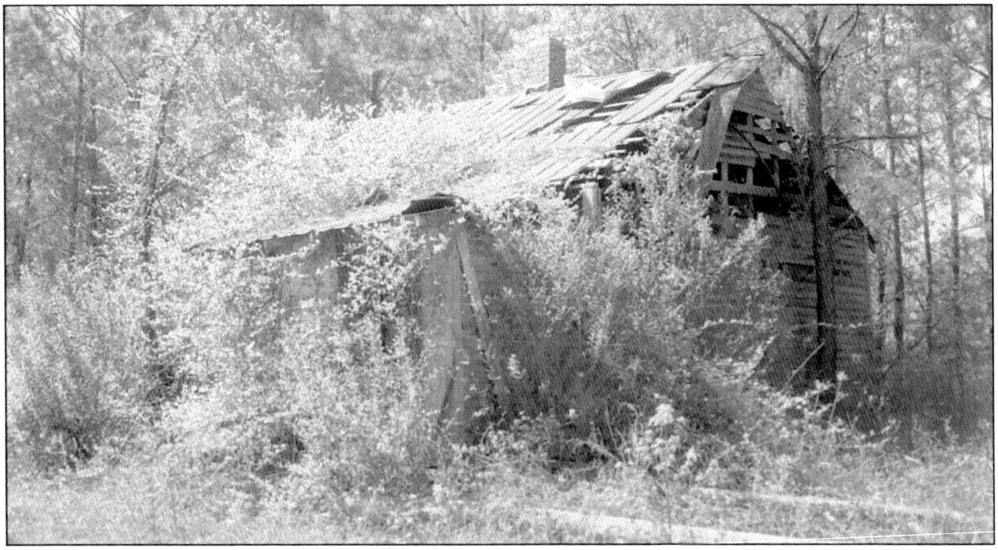

POINT LEVEL GRADE SCHOOL FOR AFRICAN-AMERICAN STUDENTS. Pictured here in the present day, Point Level Grade School was located on the Wyre Branch Road in Herring Township. In 1884, there were 31 African-American schools in the county; by 1897, the number had grown to 51.

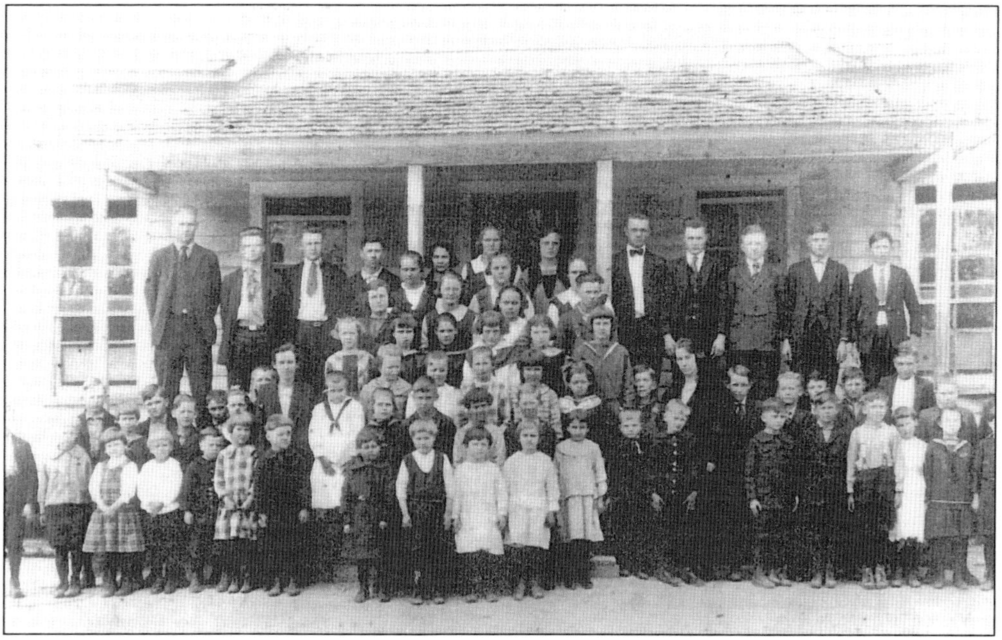

THE TWO-ROOM WELCOME SCHOOL BUILDING, 1920. This school was located along Welcome School Road in Dismal Township. Mittie Autry Williams taught in the "big room" and Ila Autry Williams taught in the "little room." (Courtesy of Preston and Lib Page.)

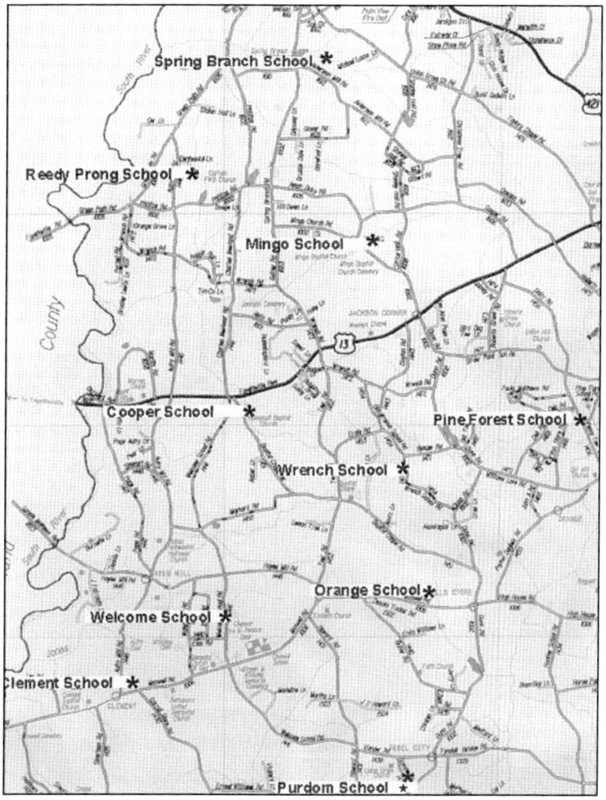

A RURAL SCHOOL MAP. The plotting of schools on this map demonstrates the placement of the one- and two-room schools around 1900. School buildings were spaced apart in a manner that made it possible for students to walk to school. The area shown includes most of Dismal and part of Mingo Townships.

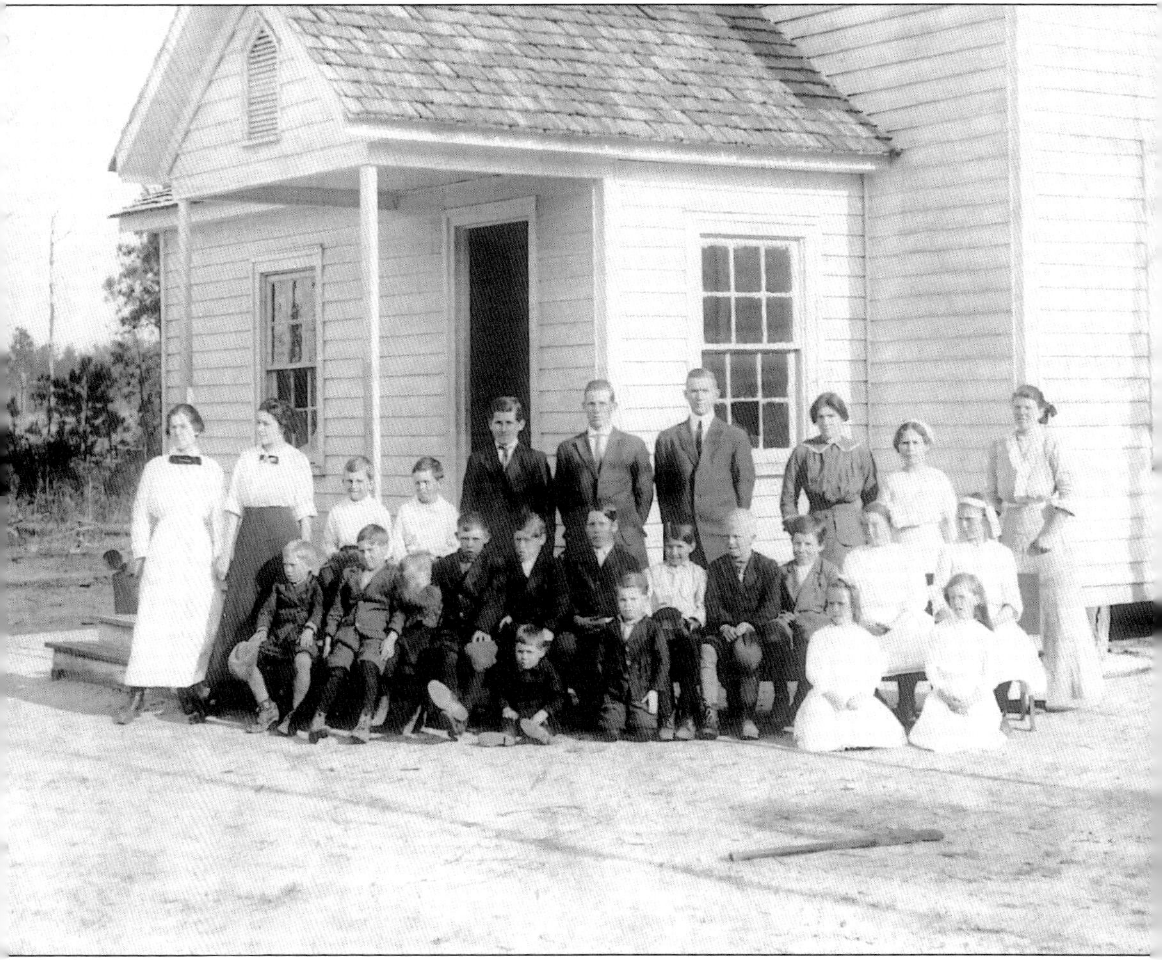

EUREKA SCHOOL, C. 1913. Eureka School was located about 4 miles north of Ingold and was adjacent to the current Union Grove Baptist Church. Students came from families with the surnames Ezzell, Alman, Cannady, Vann, Johnson, Carters, Fryars, and others. (Courtesy of Don Carter.)

Four

The Home Place

The home place of earlier days was the pivotal location for family gatherings, Sunday dinners, family reunions, wakes for the deceased, and a place where returning children were always welcome. The rural home site usually had a smoke house, water well, corn crib, potato hill, mule stables, shade trees, and in summer time, a garden. Most often, the family graveyard was located in a prominent spot near the house.

Home for earlier generations inspired visions of fields planted with corn, hay patches, orchards of peaches and apples, vineyards, rail fences that bordered the tall pine forest, and hens and their broods wandering along the many cart paths. For others, home gives life to memories of fishing in the creek, checking rabbit boxes, swimming in the lake, or maybe riding on a buggy with a favorite uncle.

Uncles, aunts, cousins, and friends often congregated at the home places, especially for Sunday dinner. If you were a young child, you knew that you would have to wait until the old folks ate, before you were called to the second table.

Often the old folks were cared for by a younger member of the family who inherited the home place, and the cycle was repeated by the next generation. Some of Sampson's old homes still occupy the ground that they were built on, while many others have fallen into everlasting ruin and decay.

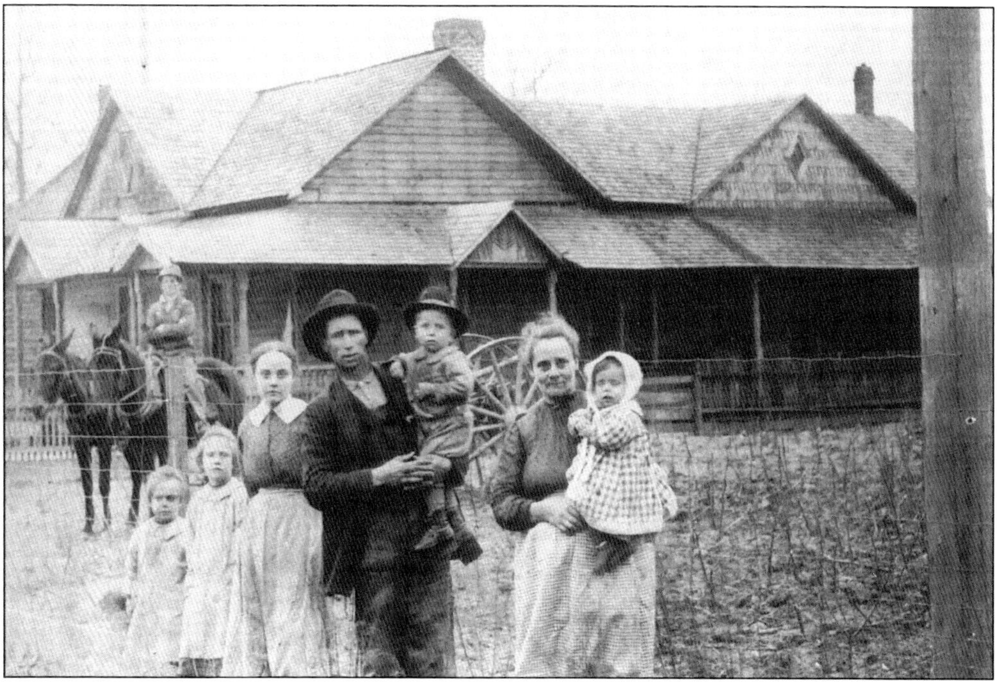

The Robbie Barefoot Family of Dismal Township, c. 1915. The cypress telephone pole (right) was cut from the banks of the South River. The poles and lines were installed and maintained by neighborhood work crews. The ring of the party line invited all the neighbors to pick up and listen to the latest gossip. (Courtesy of Floy Barefoot Carroll.)

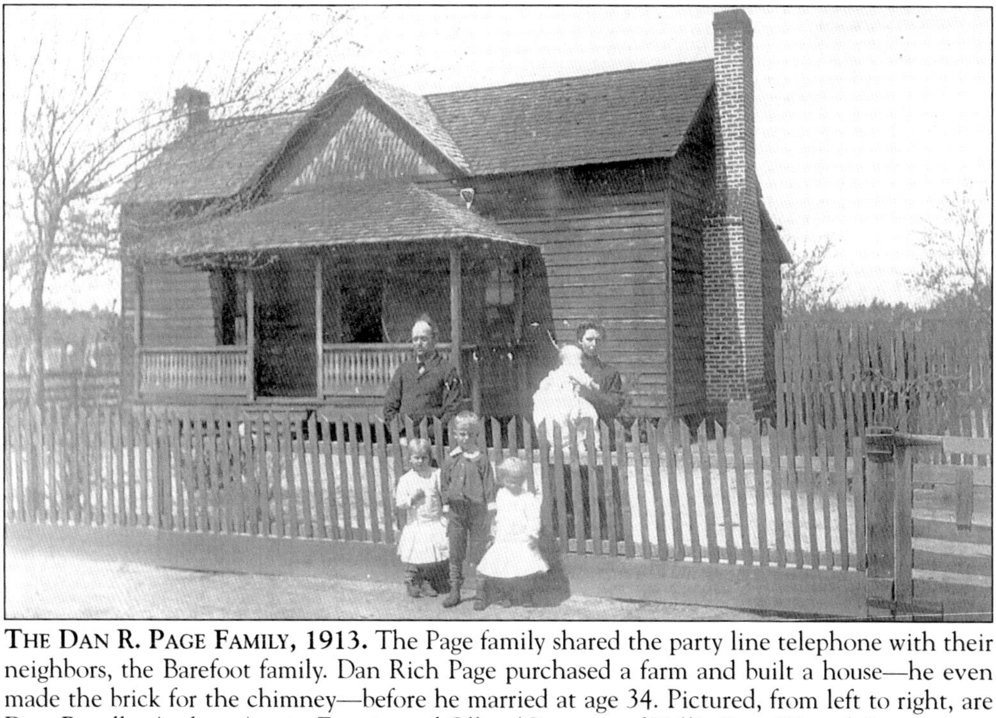

The Dan R. Page Family, 1913. The Page family shared the party line telephone with their neighbors, the Barefoot family. Dan Rich Page purchased a farm and built a house—he even made the brick for the chimney—before he married at age 34. Pictured, from left to right, are Dan, Rosella, Author, Annie, Fannie, and Ollie. (Courtesy of Vallie Page Wrench.)

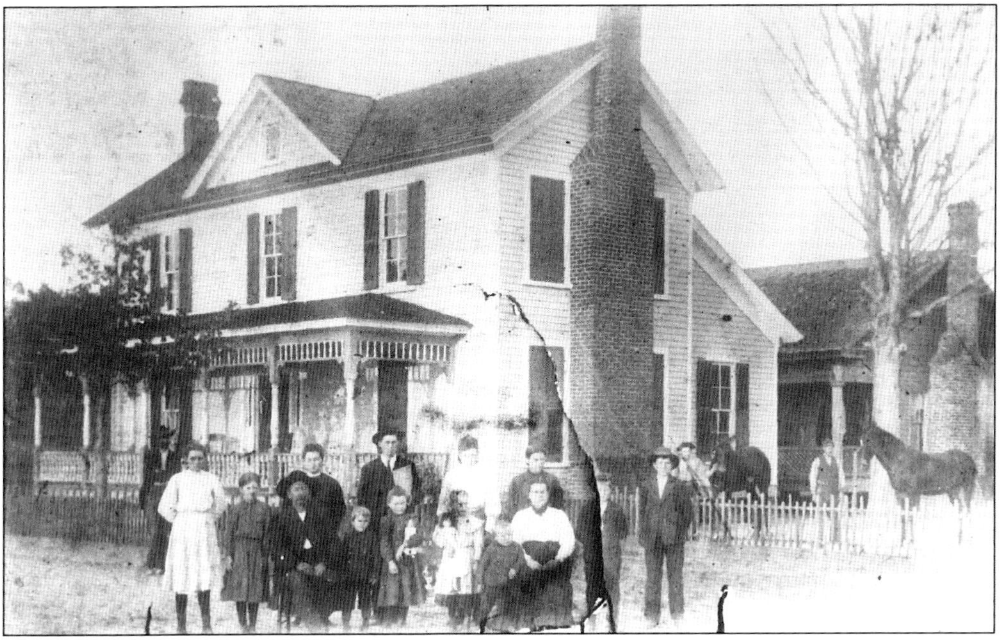

THIRTEEN OAKS IN THE NEWTON GROVE VICINITY. Lovett Warren planted an oak tree upon the birth of each of his 13 children, hence the home's name, Thirteen Oaks. The house was built in 1902. (Courtesy of Clarence Lee Warren.)

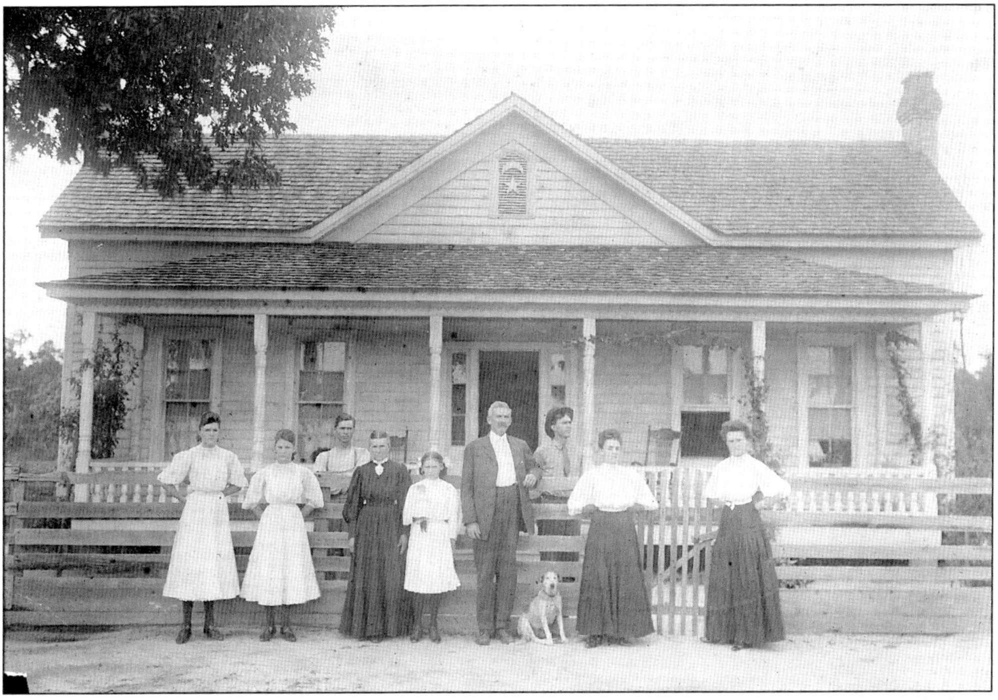

THE J.R. WESTBROOK HOME, BUILT C. 1880S, IN WESTBROOK TOWNSHIP. Pictured, from left to right, are twins Burtie and Murtie ("Big Sis" and "Little Sis"), Milton, Callie, Nannie, J.R., Claude, and Cary Westbrook. The dog's name is lost in history. (Courtesy of Callie Jones Hinson.)

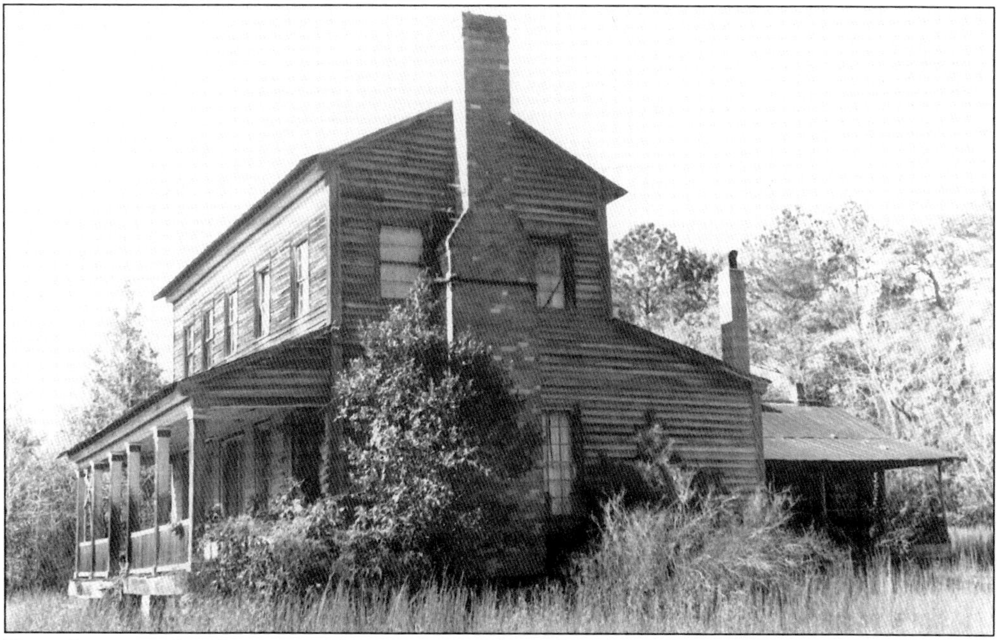

THE CHARLES B. CORBETT HOUSE. Located in the Ivanhoe vicinity, the Corbett house was built in 1832, according to the date on the chimney. This house is considered to be the oldest remaining structure in the Ivanhoe area. (Courtesy of North Carolina Division of Archives and History.)

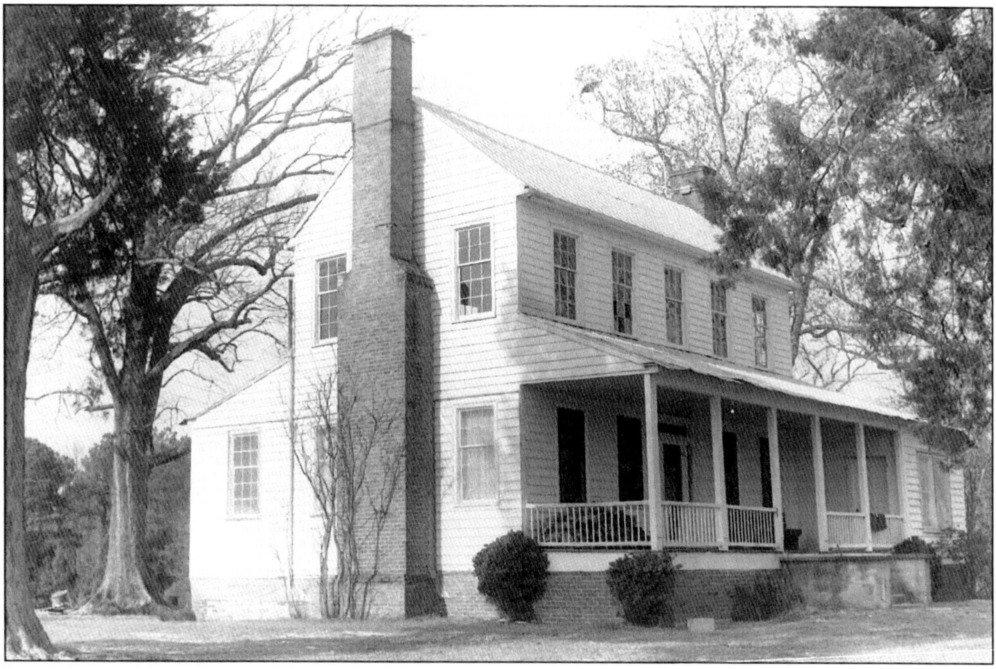

THE ARCHIBALD MURPHY HOUSE, BUILT C. 1835, IN THE GARLAND VICINITY. Near the house is a small Murphy family cemetery. The house was given to Allen Lamb and became known as the Murphy-Lamb house. (Courtesy of North Carolina Division of Archives and History.)

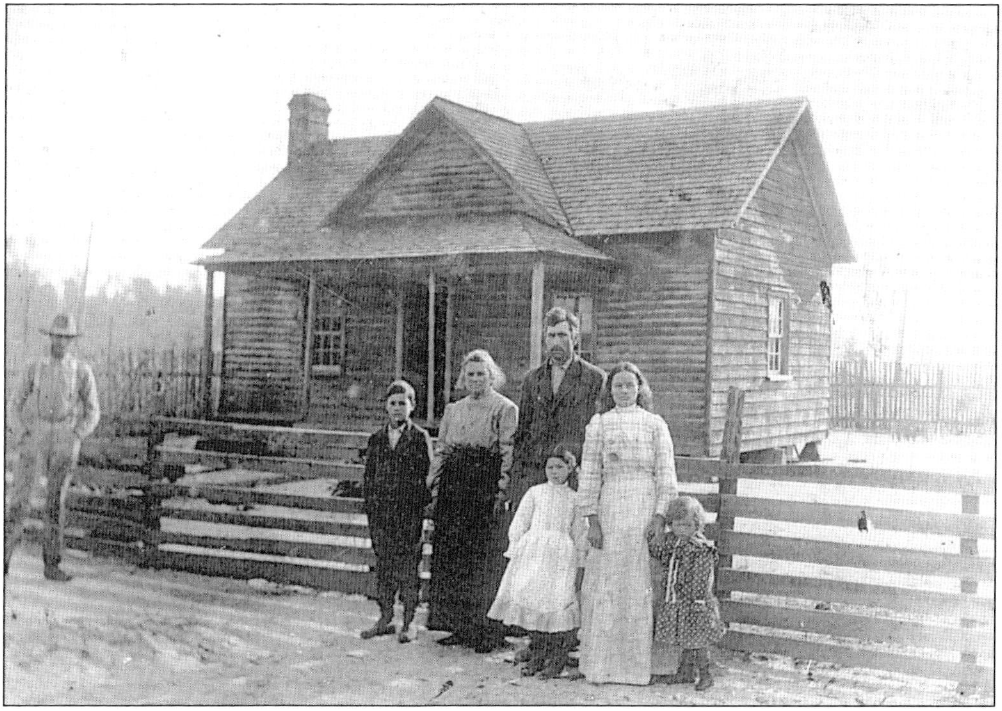

The Native American Family of W.L. Bedsole. The Bedsoles lived along the Autry Mill Road. They are believed to be, from left to right, Henry, Author, Amanda, W.L., and Hannah Bedsole. The young girls are Rosa and Pauline. (Courtesy of Joe Williams Studio.)

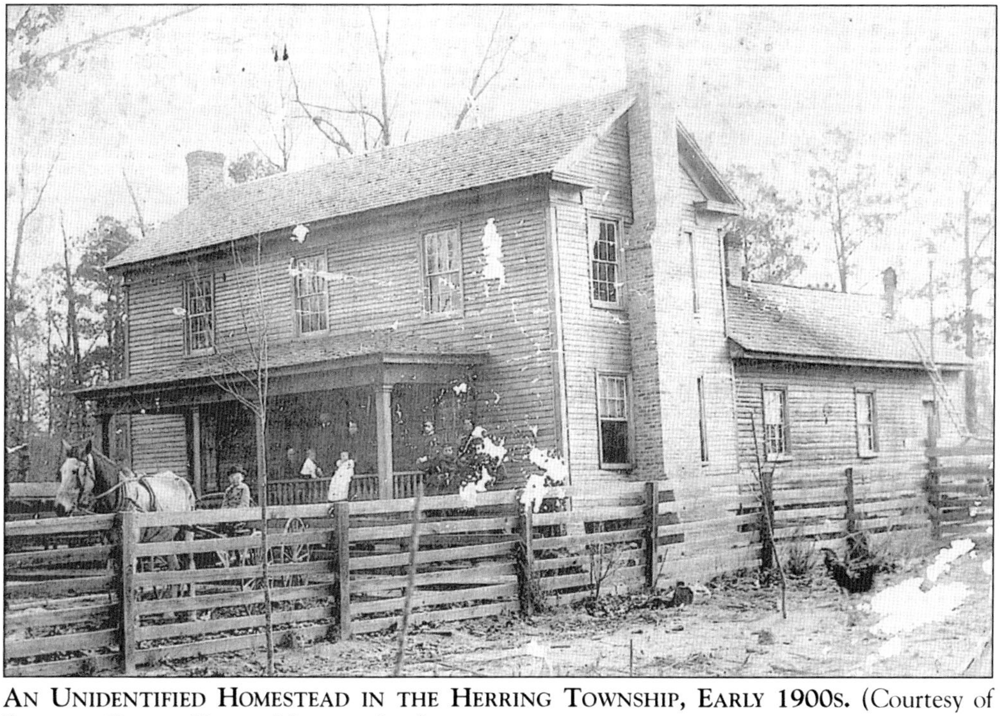

An Unidentified Homestead in the Herring Township, Early 1900s. (Courtesy of Sampson County History Museum, Inc.)

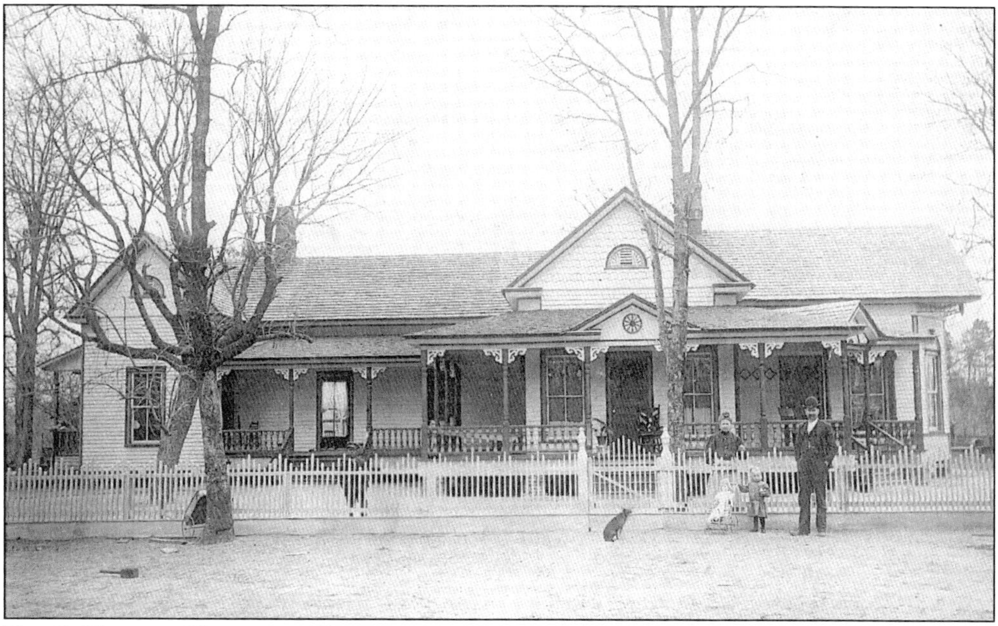

THE J. THOMAS WILLIAMS'S HOME PLACE IN MINGO TOWNSHIP, C. 1915. From left to right are J.T. Williams, Daisy Williams, and Willa Williams Jackson. The child is unidentified. This house burned earlier in the twentieth century. (Courtesy of Tom Jackson.)

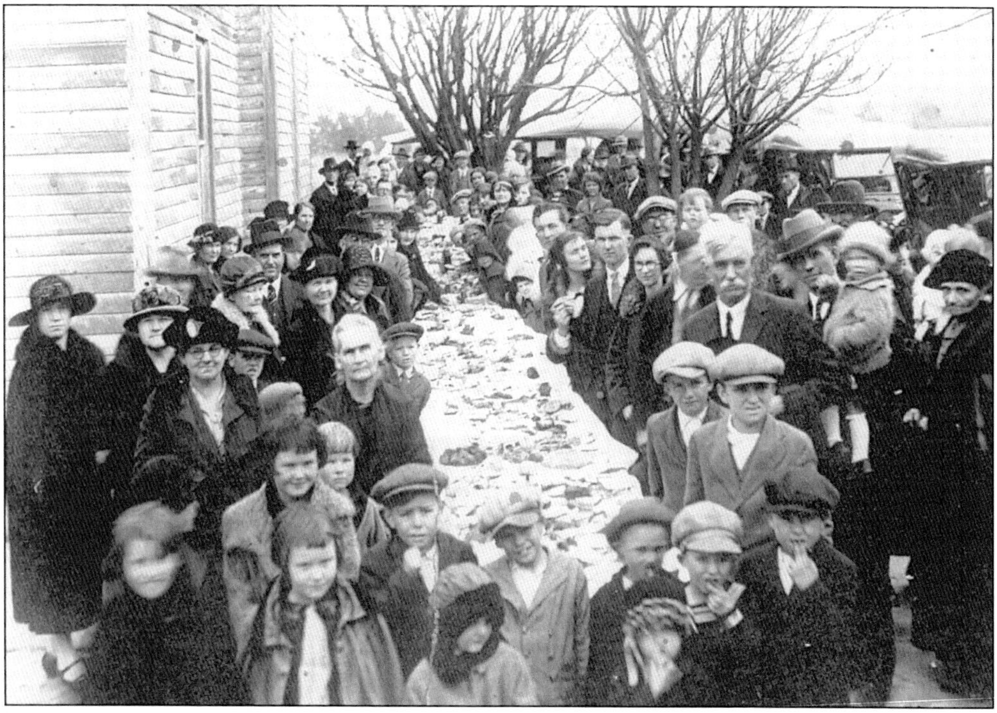

ROBERT ALLEN CARTER'S FAMILY GATHERING AT THE HOME PLACE ALONG THE OLD RALEIGH ROAD IN CLINTON, C. 1918. Robert Carter is the bareheaded figure with a mustache in the right side of the picture. His second wife, Kissy Warwick Carter, is pictured across the table from him. (Courtesy of Joyce Bass Binkley.)

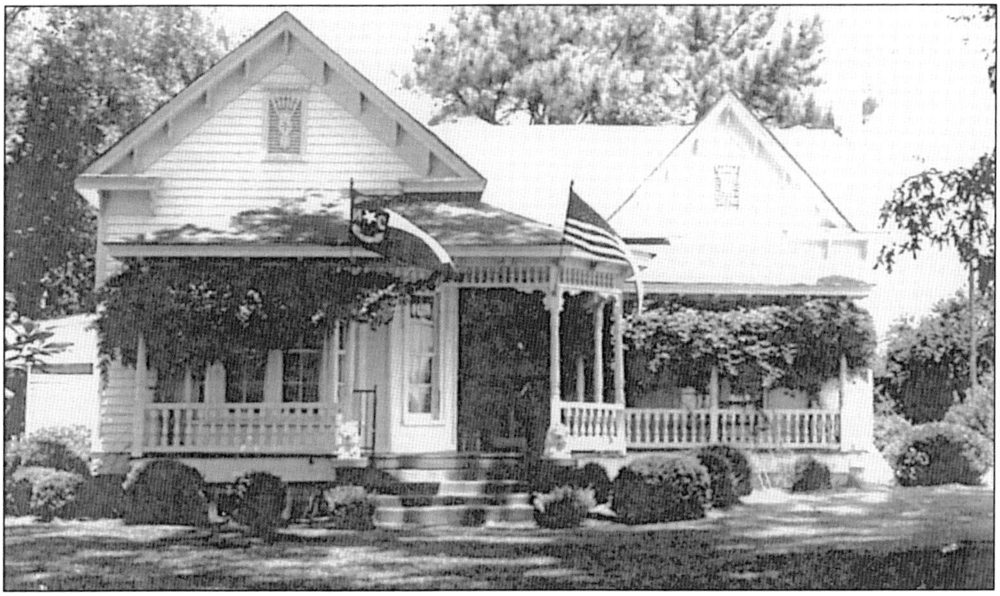

THE MARION ALASKA BASS HOME PLACE IN THE NEWTON GROVE VICINITY. The first part of this house was built in 1886 by Marion Alaska's father, who insisted that he build a house before he married. Clayton Warwick lived in the house in recent history. (Courtesy of Joyce Bass Binkley.)

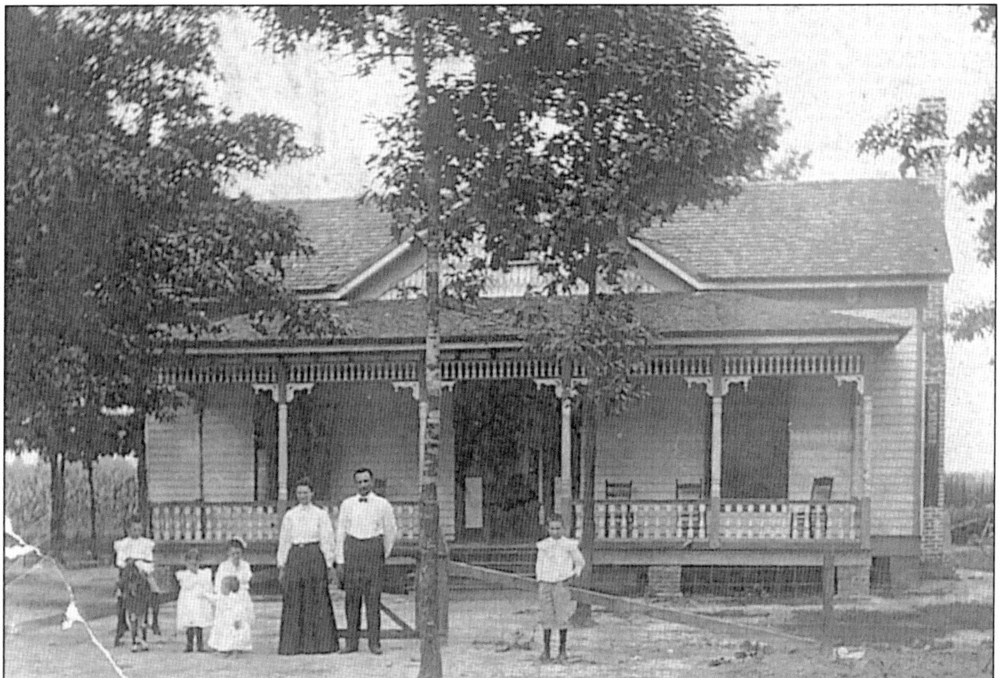

THE HOME PLACE OF BENJAMIN FRANKLIN "BUD" THORNTON IN THE PLEASANT UNION COMMUNITY OF UPPER SAMPSON, LATE 1800S. From left to right are Ezra ("Sonny"), riding a goat; Irene; Griffin; Harold; Julianne Weaver; Benjamin; and Isaac Thornton. (Courtesy of Shirley T. Warren.)

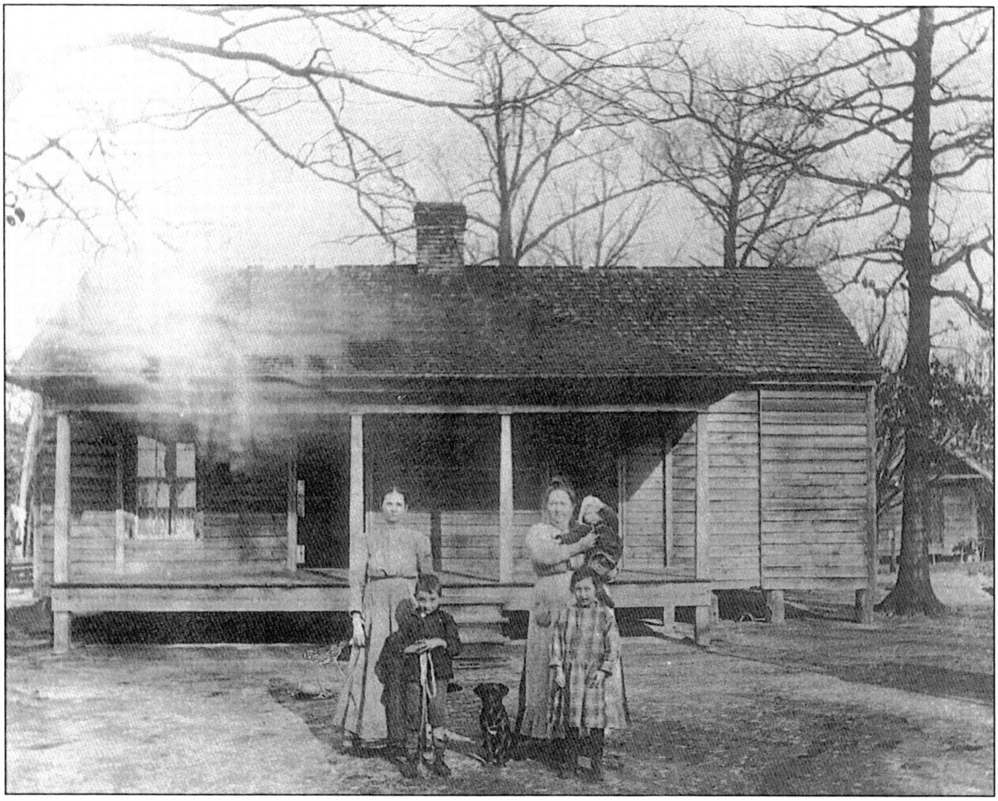

The Martian Dixon Jackson Home Place along Dunn Road, near Hall's Store, c. 1907. From left to right are Caldonia Naylor Jackson; Fuller Jackson; Mrs. Horne, holding Bynum Jackson; and a neighbor's daughter. (Courtesy of Graham Jackson.)

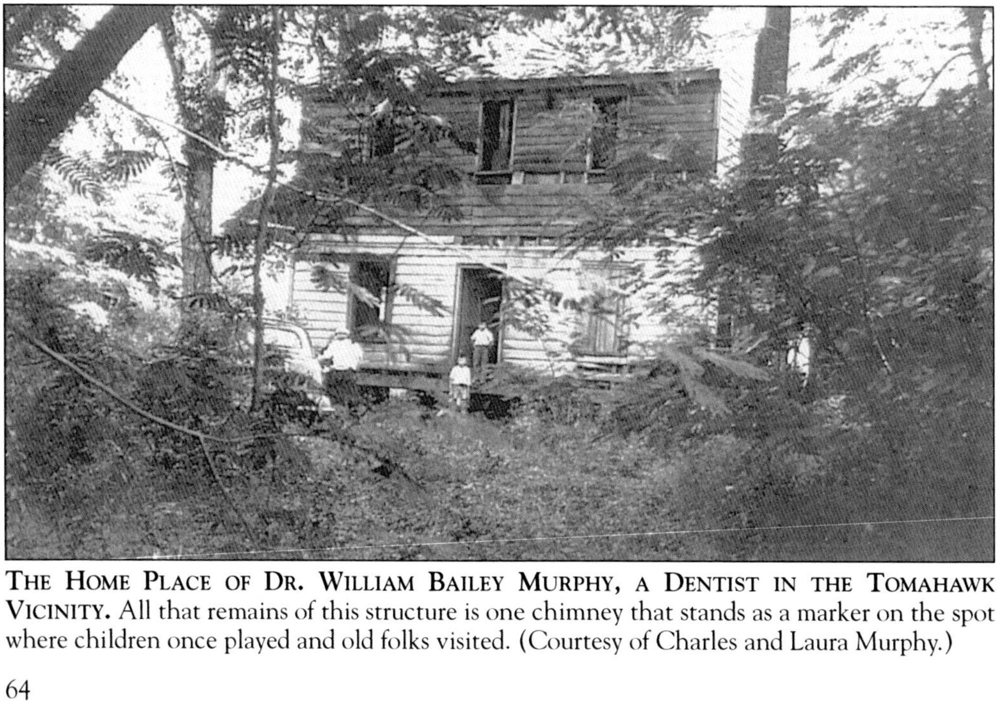

The Home Place of Dr. William Bailey Murphy, a Dentist in the Tomahawk Vicinity. All that remains of this structure is one chimney that stands as a marker on the spot where children once played and old folks visited. (Courtesy of Charles and Laura Murphy.)

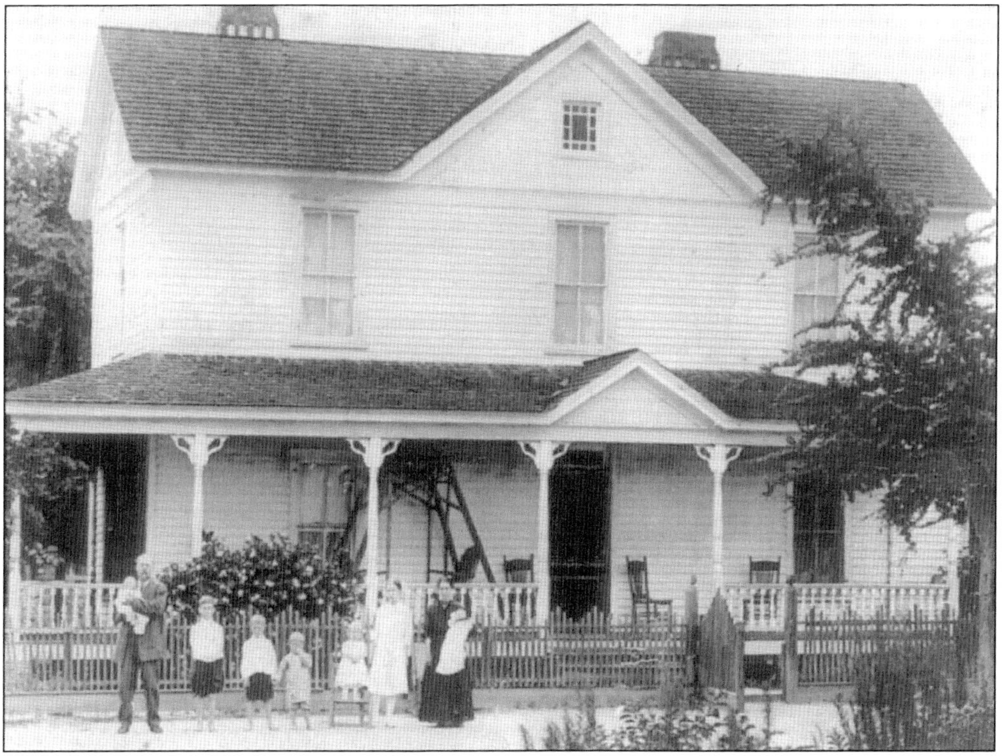

THE O.B. TEW FAMILY HOME ALONG U.S. HIGHWAY 13, NEAR THE CUMBERLAND COUNTY LINE, C. 1915. Mrs. O.B. Tew taught school at Purdom before becoming a mother. Mr. Tew taught school at Cooper and, for a time, was also the horse-and-buggy mail carrier. (Courtesy of Mrs. Earl Draughon.)

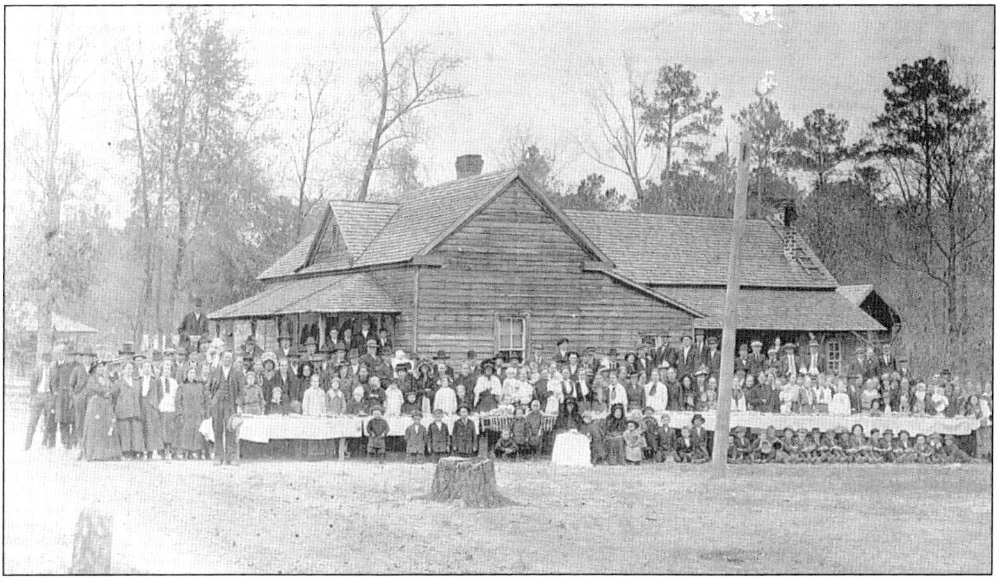

THE GEORGE A. DANIELS HOME AT ROUTE 1, BOX 46 IN COOPER, C. 1910. Note the telephone pole in the foreground. The community built and maintained what were known as the farmer's telephone lines. (Courtesy of Lee Ronald Daniels.)

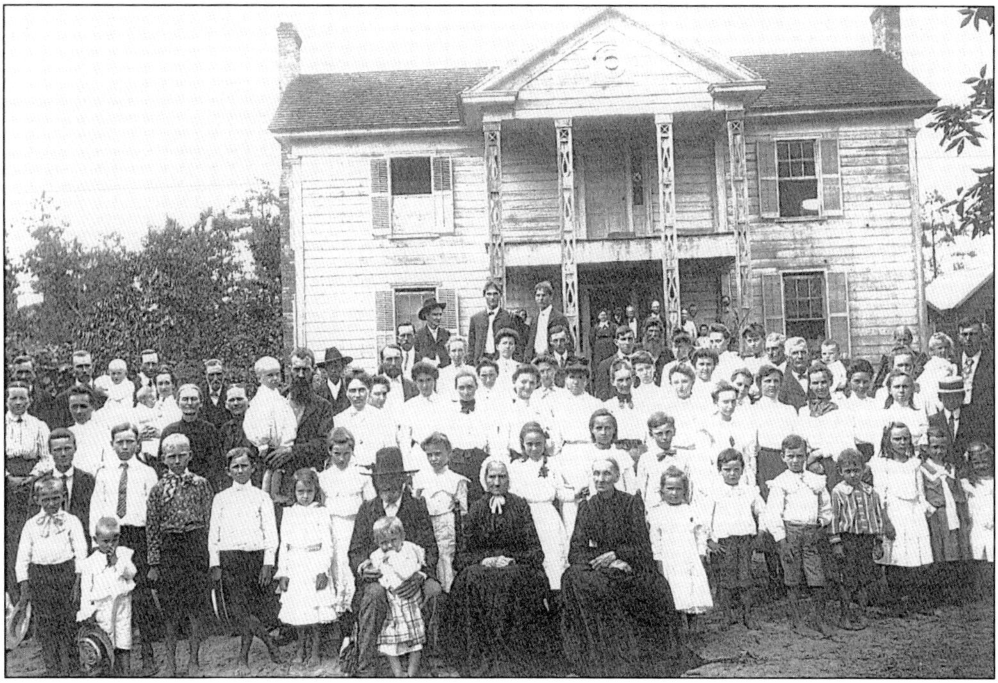

THE JACOB COOPER HOWARD FAMILY REUNION, 1904. This gathering was held in the present-day vicinity of Laurel Lake, near Salemburg. Jacob Howard, the patriarch of the clan, is seated on the front row wearing a hat and a beard. His wife, Betsy Williams Howard, is at his side. The boy in front of him is Dr. Charles Howard. (Courtesy of Lee Ronald Daniels.)

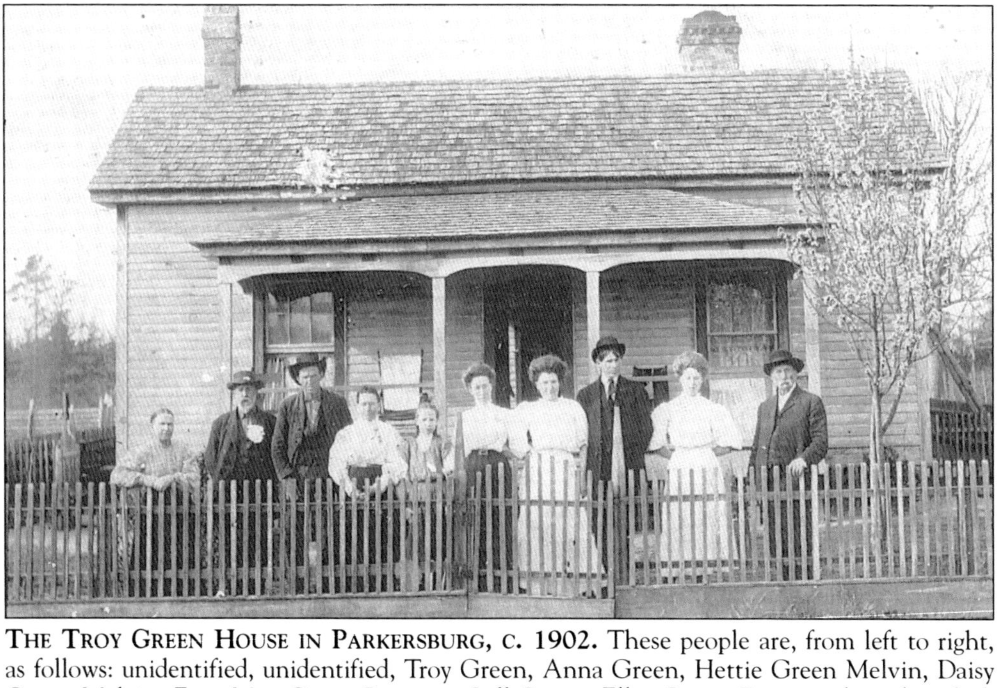

THE TROY GREEN HOUSE IN PARKERSBURG, C. 1902. These people are, from left to right, as follows: unidentified, unidentified, Troy Green, Anna Green, Hettie Green Melvin, Daisy Green Melvin, Eura Mae Green Peterson, Jeff Green, Ellie Green Price, and unidentified. (Courtesy of Hazel P. Smith.)

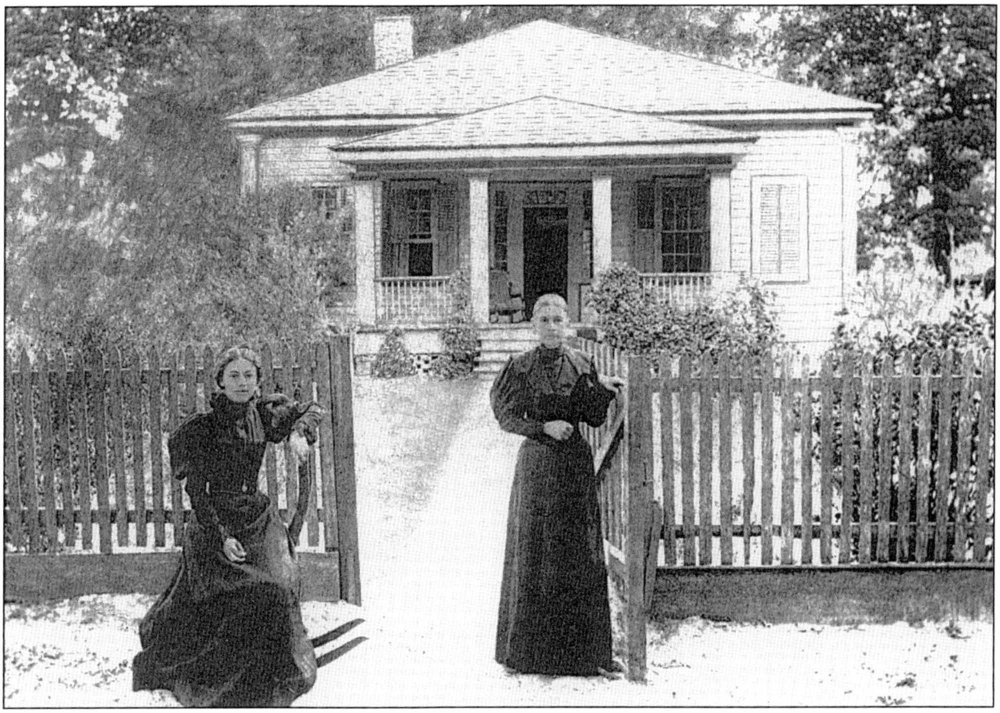

THE 1894 HOME OF DR. JOHN CARR MONK, A NEWTON GROVE PHYSICIAN. This house was built in 1855 and was located on Erwin Drive. John Catherine Monk and Euphemia Eason Monk, the daughter and wife of John Monk, are pictured here. (Courtesy of Albert and Ann Herring.)

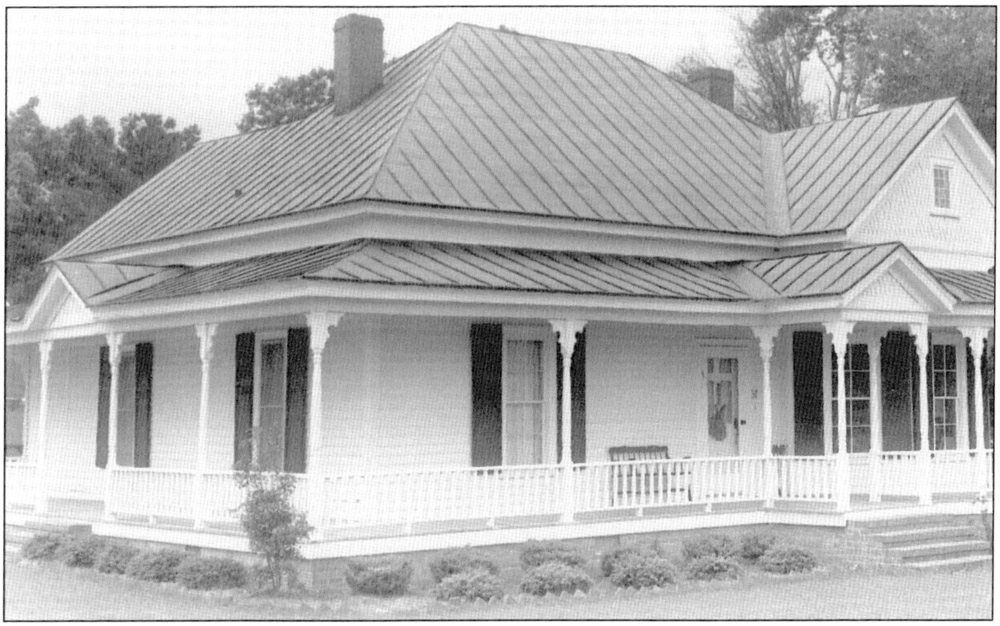

THE JESSIE MARTIAN JACKSON HOME. Built *c.* 1905 and originally located near the present-day Wesley Chapel Church, the house has been relocated and is, today, the home of Amelia and Pete Wrench. (Courtesy of North Carolina Division of Archives and History.)

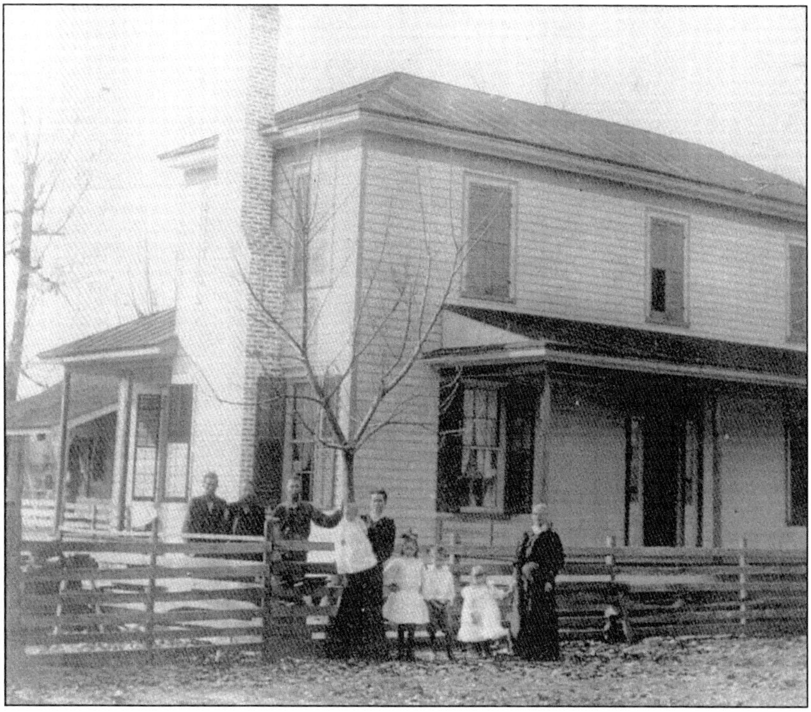

THE MOORE HOME PLACE IN THE SOUTH CLINTON VICINITY. (Courtesy of David King.)

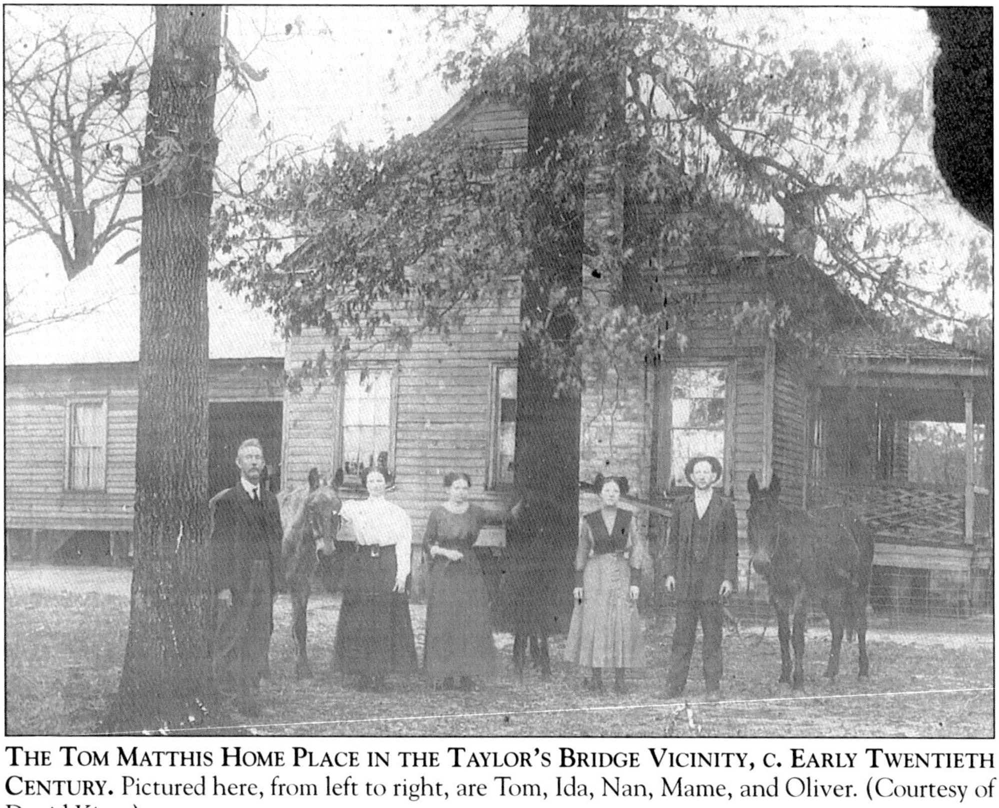

THE TOM MATTHIS HOME PLACE IN THE TAYLOR'S BRIDGE VICINITY, C. EARLY TWENTIETH CENTURY. Pictured here, from left to right, are Tom, Ida, Nan, Mame, and Oliver. (Courtesy of David King.)

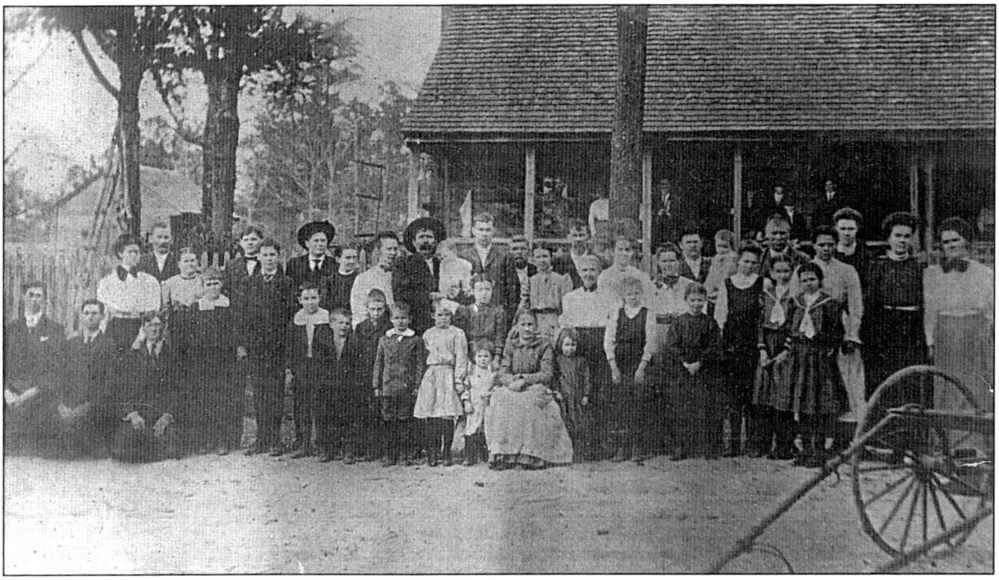

GRANNY BETSY'S BIRTHDAY PARTY, FEBRUARY 2, 1907. Betsy Ann Robinson Matthis is seated in the center. She could eat red meat with her natural teeth and read a newspaper without the aid of glasses at the age of 90. (Courtesy of Roland E. Matthis.)

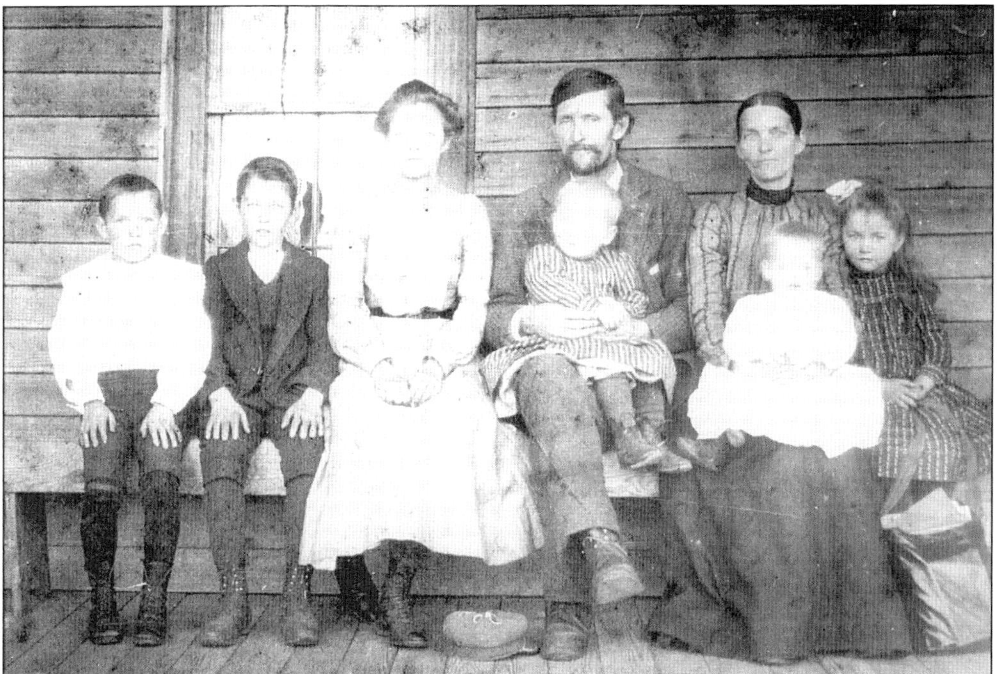

THE DANIEL LOVE McLAMB FAMILY IN WESTBROOK TOWNSHIP, C. 1902. From left to right are Minson, Norman, Eva, Daniel, child Martian, Florence, child Clarence, and Lenna. (Courtesy of Clarence E. McLamb Jr.)

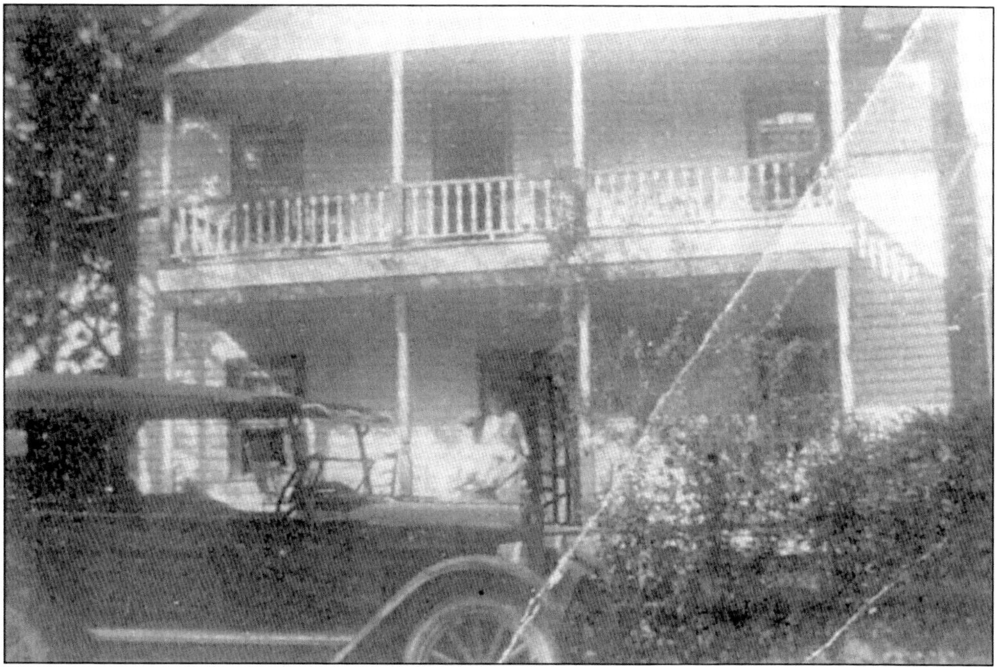

The Bass-King Place. Located in the Keener vicinity, this house was built by Everette Bass in the early part of the nineteenth century. The house was inherited by Rebecca Eliza Bass, who married Henry King. The building next became the home of William King. (Courtesy of Joyce Bass Binkley.)

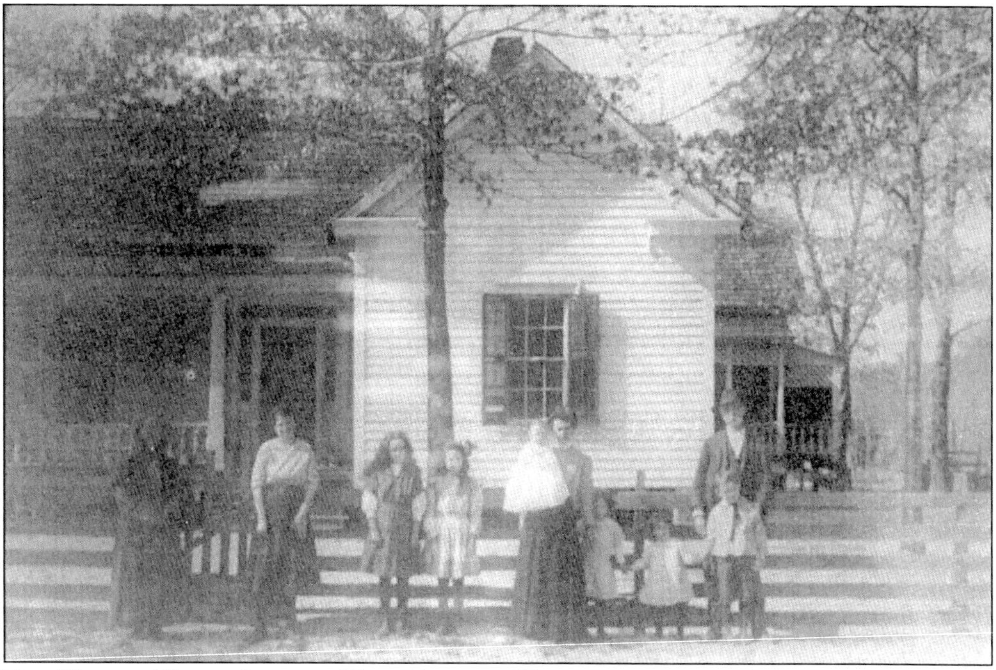

The William Henry Colwell Home Place in Turkey, 1912. From left to right are pictured Maid, Kate, Thelma, Mildred, Eugenia (in arms), Martha, Caroline, Betty, James, and William Henry. (Courtesy of Martha Coffield.)

Five

SAMPSON'S MANY FACES

The people who settled and carved out farms and villages in Sampson County were a tough and durable lot. Our early citizens lived almost entirely off the land, and if they had any need, a way was found to fill it. They lived through good times and hard times and made life more comfortable for their children.

The hardy people who make up the strong fabric of our county's history are portrayed here—grannies who have numerous descendants that cleave to loving memories of them; the soldiers from history's wars, whose stories are retold; widows who managed family and farm after the untimely death of a mate; and men who became patriarchs of large families with deep roots in this county. Claude Crumpler, one of our oldest citizens ever, is portrayed here. Native Americans have been with us from our earliest beginnings. Most of these faces have already slipped into history.

The faces presented in these pages represent the almost uncountable numbers that have woven their life's experience into Sampson County's historical tapestry.

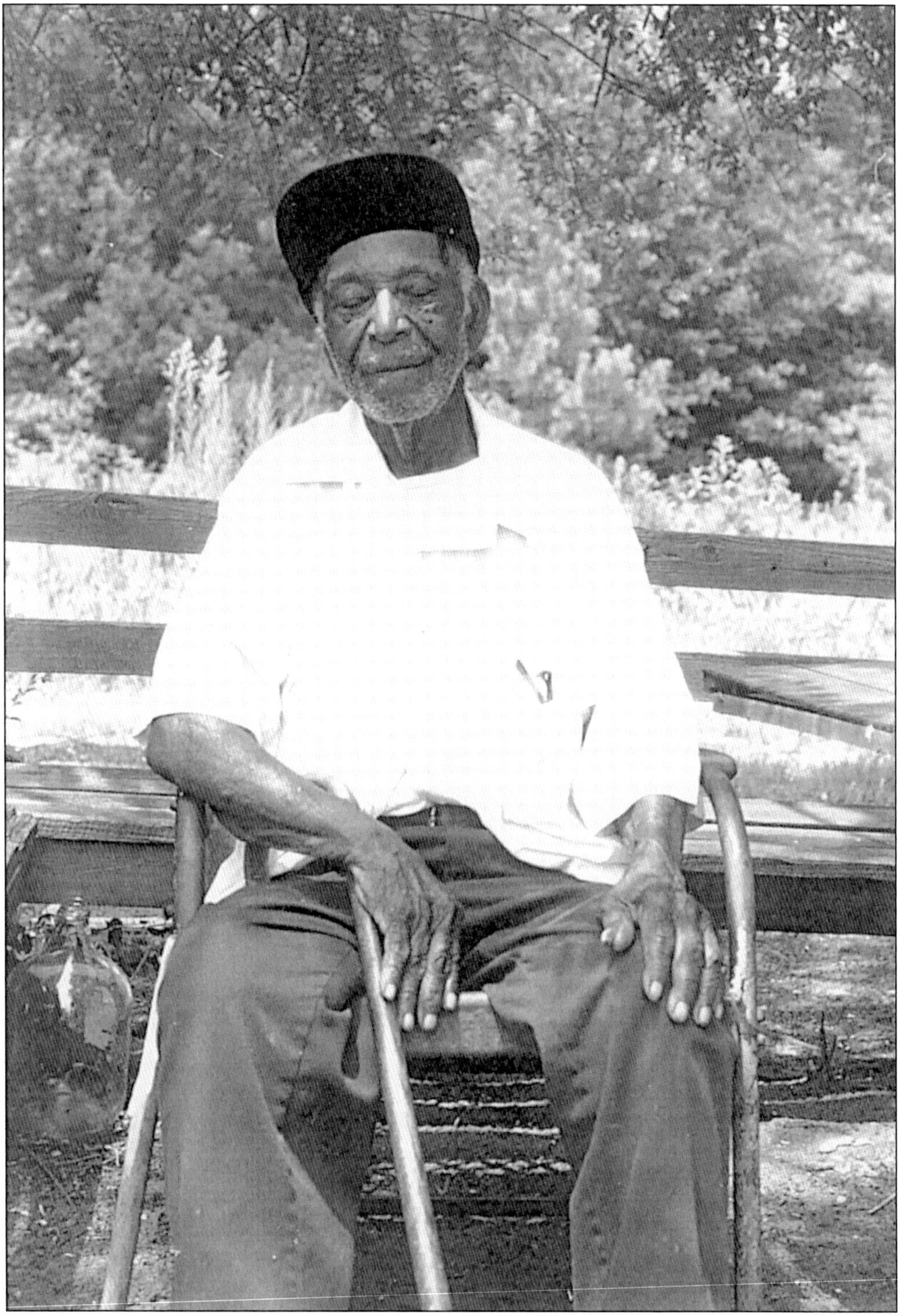

Claude Crumpler of the Salemburg Vicinity. Crumpler lived to be 107 years of age; he was born in 1880 and died in 1987. In an interview late in his life, he expressed concern for his 85-year-old daughter's health. (Courtesy of Clarence E. McLamb Jr.)

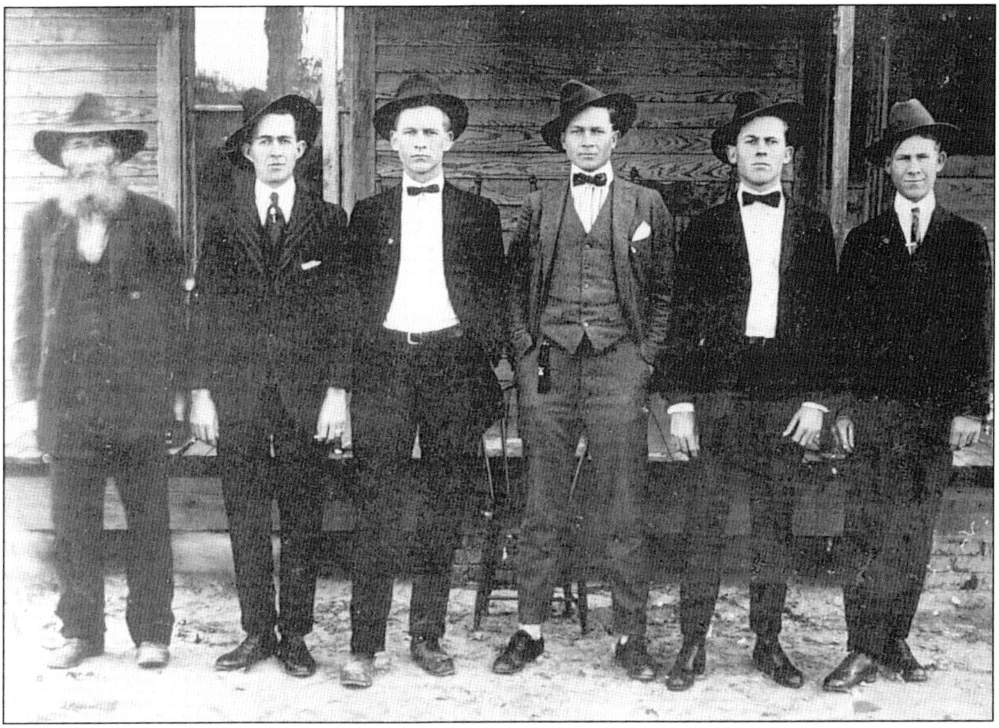

The "Roaring Twenties Gang" from Newton Grove. From left to right are father David Howell, sons Richard E. Howell, David Howell, Silas E. Howell, Paul Howell, and Bennett Howell. (Courtesy of John Howell.)

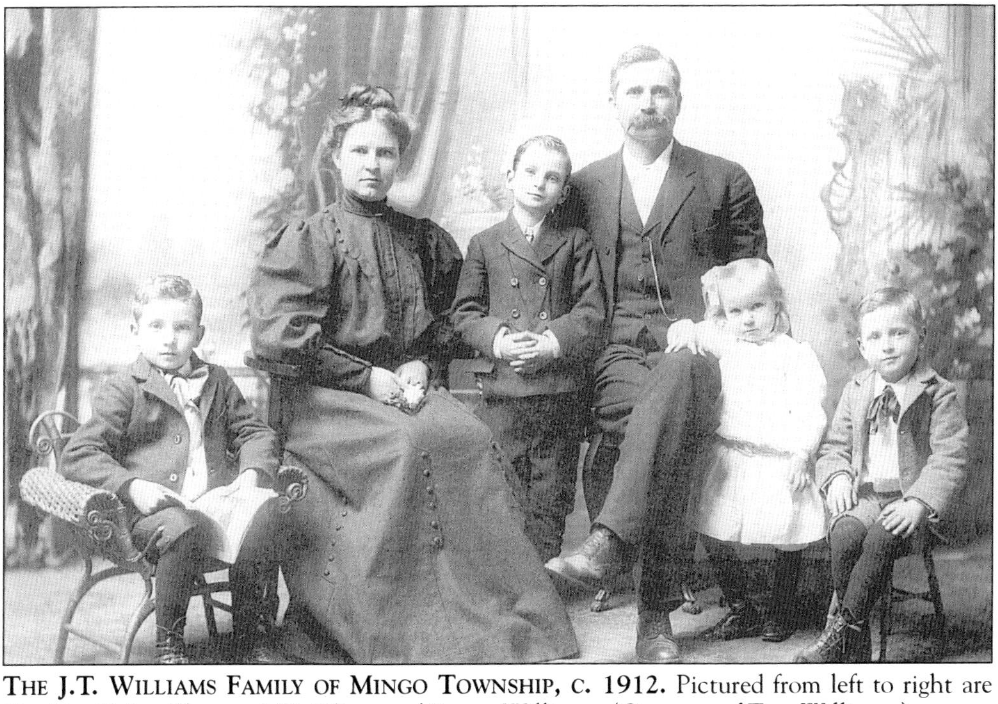

The J.T. Williams Family of Mingo Township, c. 1912. Pictured from left to right are Garthie, Daisy, Clayton, J.T., Olive, and Stuart Williams. (Courtesy of Tom Williams.)

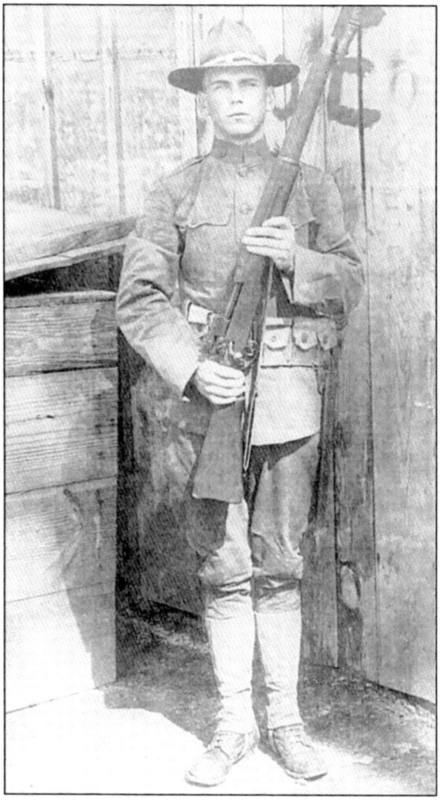

Henry A. Bizzell, 1917. Bizzell served in World War I in the "Wildcat" Division. (Courtesy of Sampson County History Museum, Inc.)

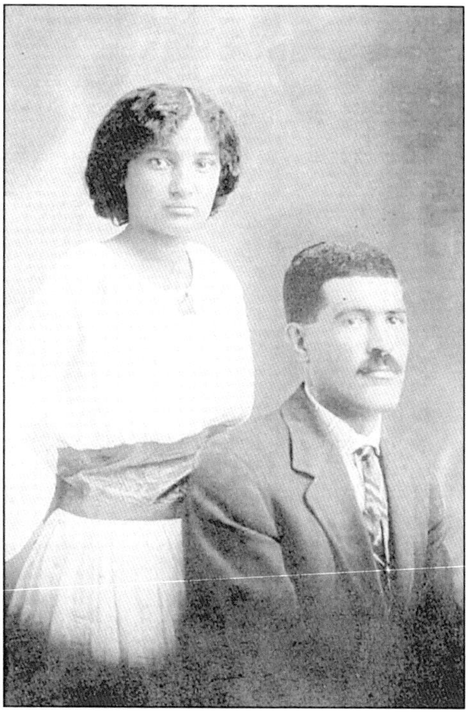

Wilkie Maynor and His Wife, c. 1918. This Native American couple were from Dismal Township. Wilkie served in France during World War I. (Courtesy of Golden Maynor.)

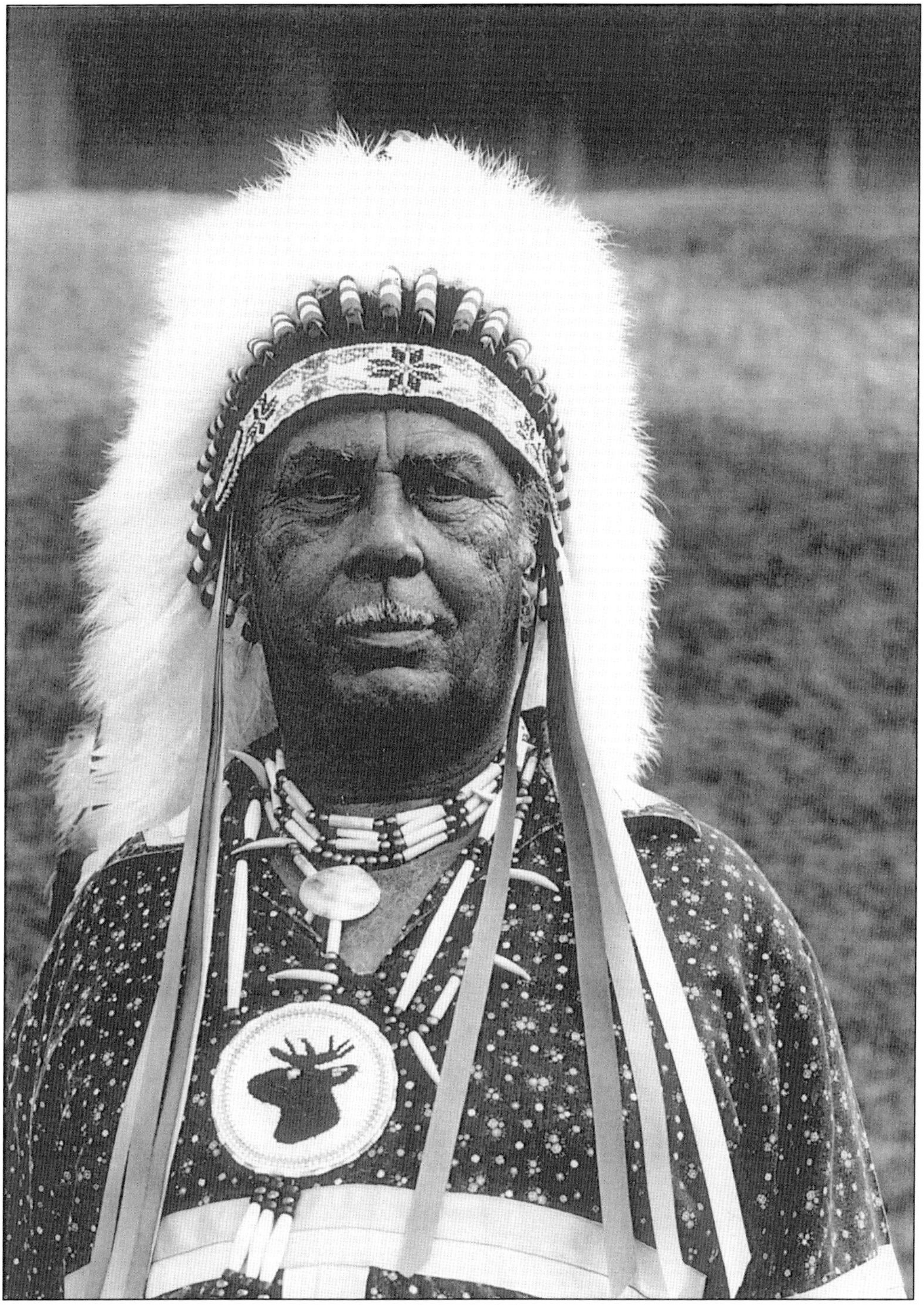

TOM CARTER. Carter occupied the office of chief of the Crotan Indians for several years, and he is pictured here in ceremonial dress. (Courtesy of Coharie Intra-Tribal Council, Inc.)

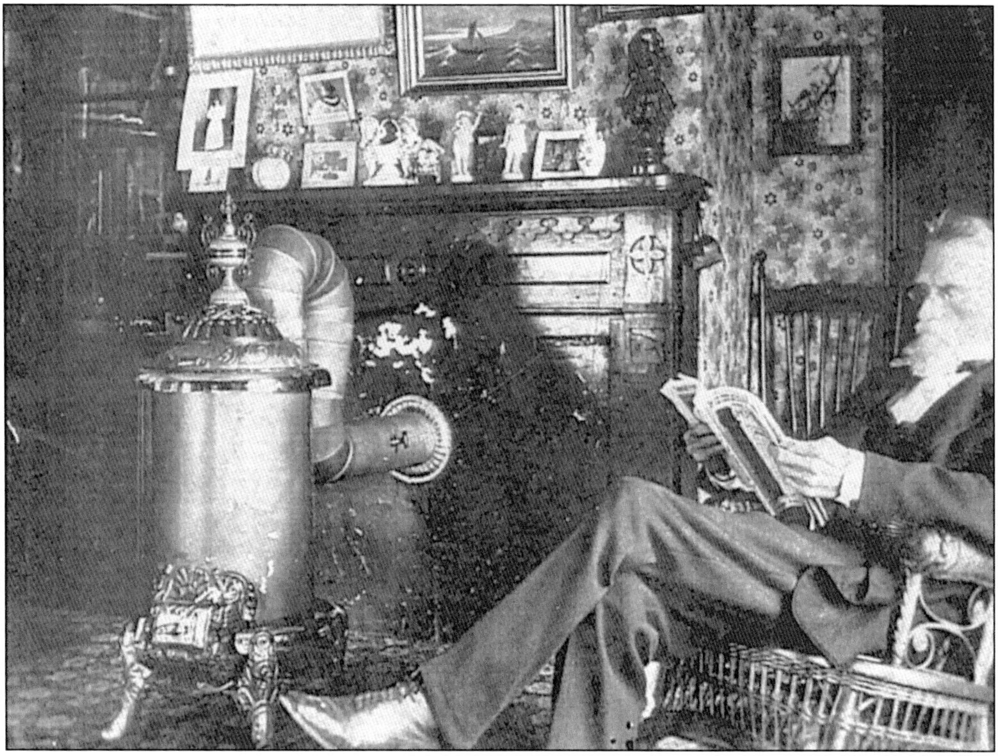

ISAAC ALDERMAN FROM TOMAHAWK, C. LATE 1800S. Isaac is the great-grandfather of Charles Murphy, who lives in this home today. (Courtesy of Charles and Laura Murphy.)

JOHN HENRY ALDERMEN'S FAMILY OF THE TOMAHAWK VICINITY. John was born in 1828 and died in 1900. (Courtesy of Charles and Laura Murphy.)

JAMES M. PARKER. From the McGee Methodist Church neighborhood, Parker was born 1835 and died in 1904. He served in Company A, Regiment 30, Infantry of the Confederate Army. He was present at the April 9, 1865 Confederacy surrender at Appomattox Court House in Virginia. (Courtesy of Fannie Widener.)

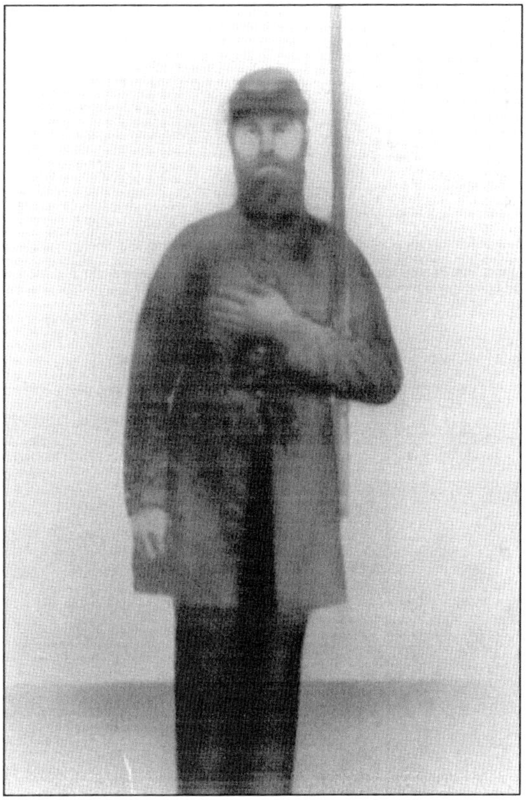

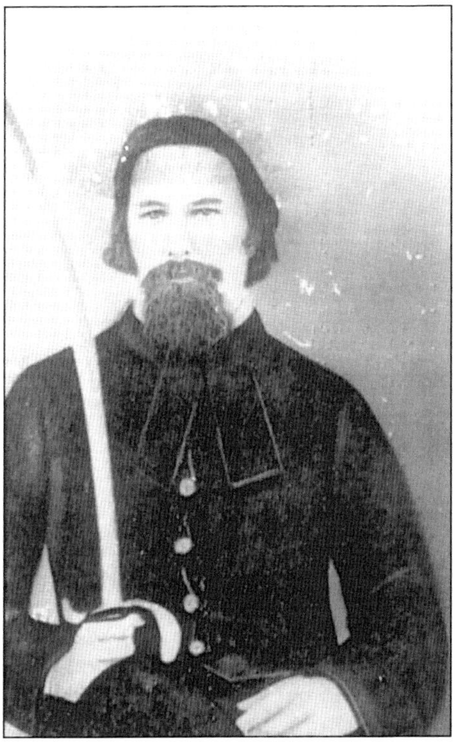

WILLIAM WARWICK. A Civil War cavalry veteran, Warwick rode with Jeb Stuart in the War Between the States. (Courtesy of Joyce Bass Binkley.)

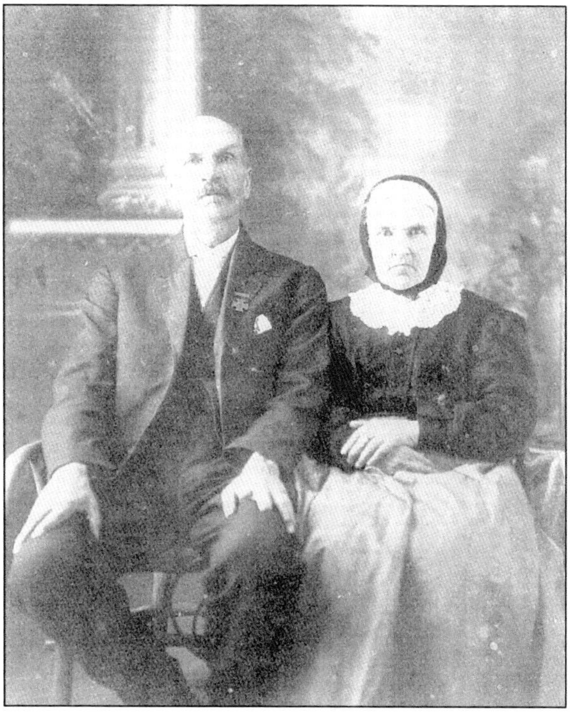

WILLIAM HENRY MCLAMB AND HIS WIFE, ZILPHA WARREN MCLAMB, FROM THE MT. ELAM COMMUNITY, C. 1902. William was a veteran of the Civil War and lost his fingers in battle. (Courtesy of Clarence E. McLamb Jr.)

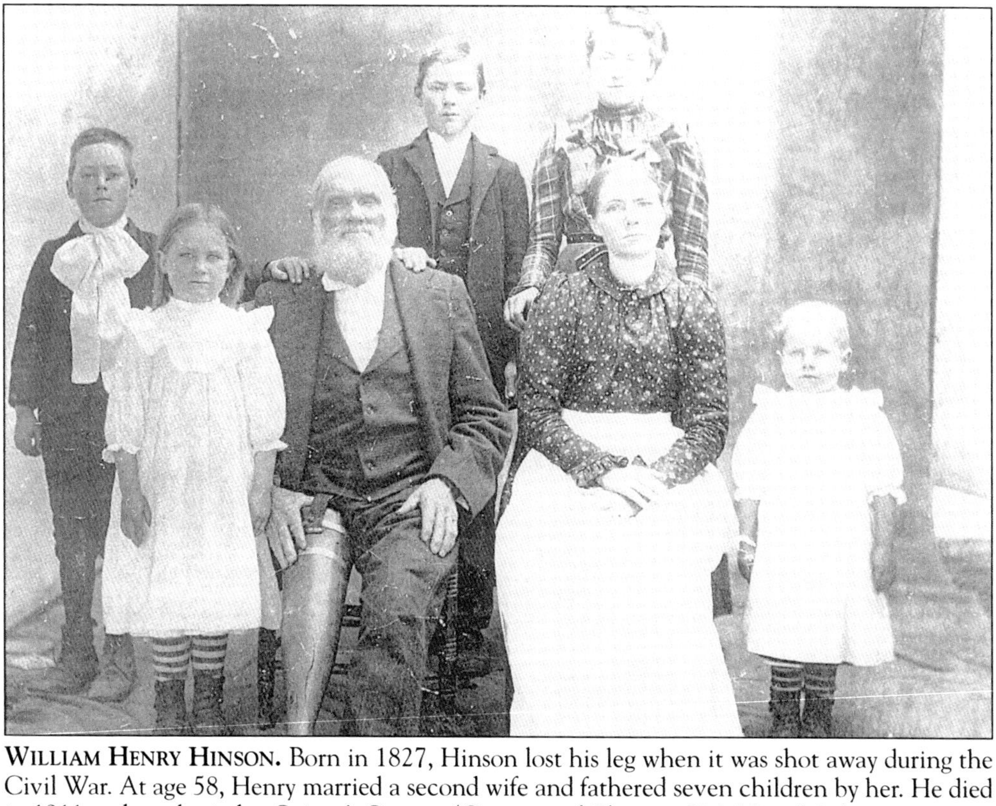

WILLIAM HENRY HINSON. Born in 1827, Hinson lost his leg when it was shot away during the Civil War. At age 58, Henry married a second wife and fathered seven children by her. He died in 1911 and was buried at Spivey's Corner. (Courtesy of Clarence E. McLamb Jr.)

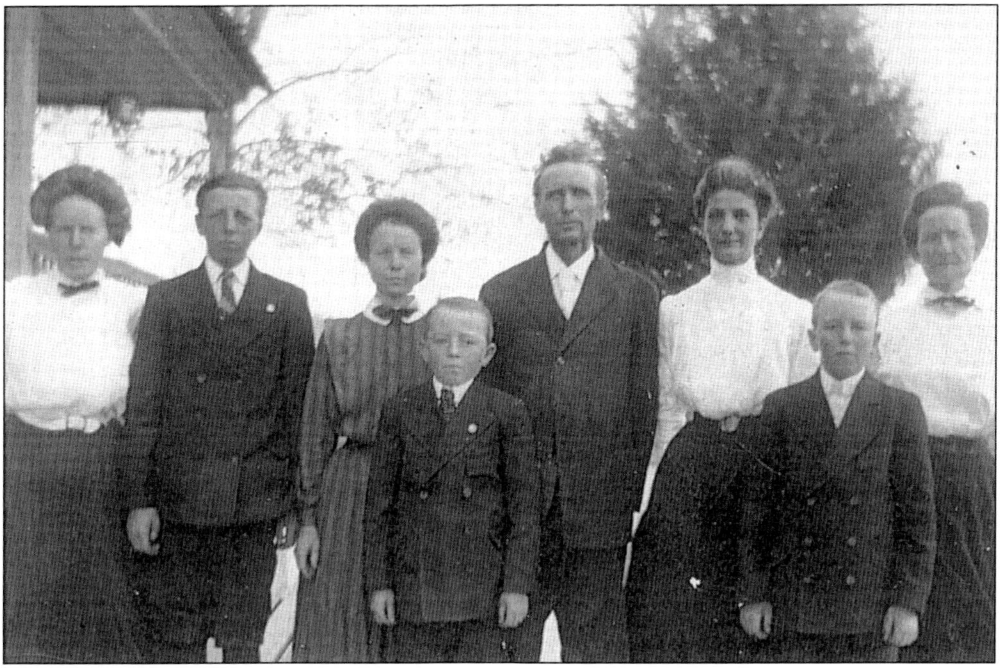

THE MELVIN FAMILY OF THE HARRELLS STORE VICINITY, C. 1909. From left to right are Carrie, Raymond, Lizzie, Herbert, John C., Betty G., Edwin, and Sara Melvin. The three boys established R.H. Melvin's business in Harrells Store. (Courtesy of Lela Harrell.)

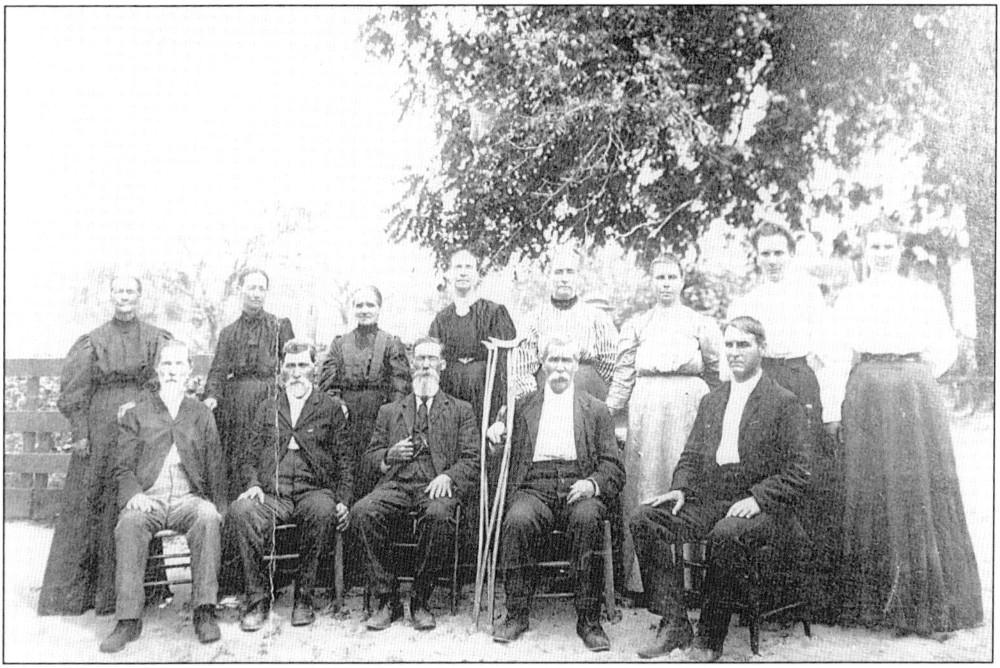

THE BAREFOOT FAMILY. This group of Barefoots added greatly to Sampson's population. They include, from left to right, the following: (front row) Nathan, Noah B., William Bright, Handy Minson, and Archie Barefoot; (back row) Amelia, Nancy, Meady Eliza, Neggelina, Serena, Silvania, Betthany, and Louphemia Barefoot. (Courtesy of Clarence E. McLamb Jr.)

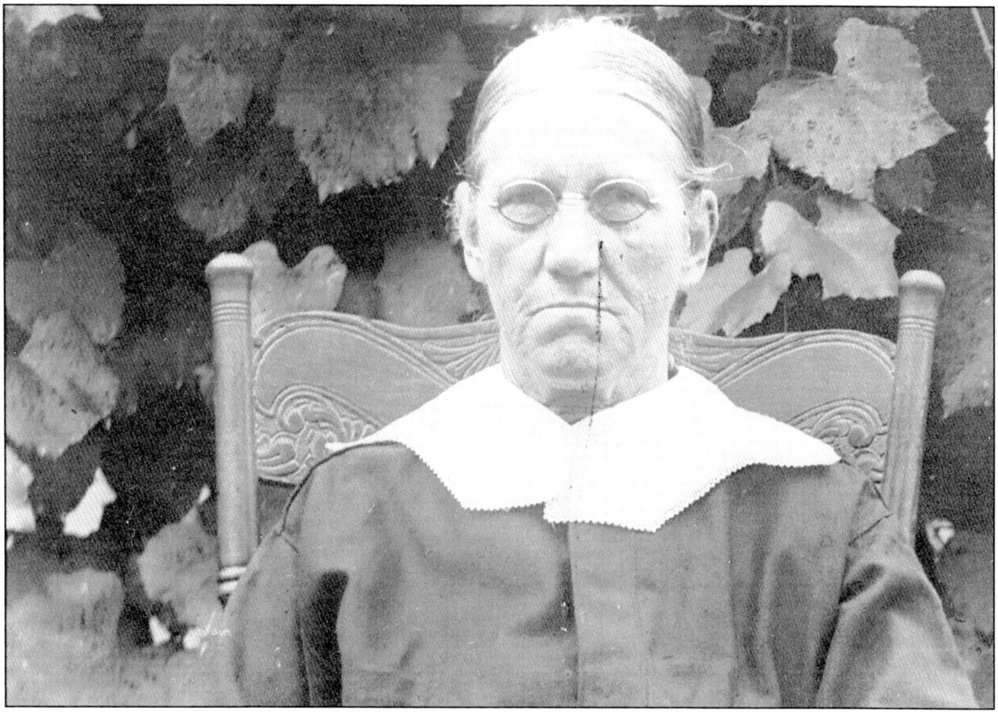

Sylvania Williams Page. Born on February 2, 1847, Page represents the many faithful and steadfast mothers that have loved and disciplined Sampson County's children. She died on January 10, 1923, in Dismal Township. (Courtesy of Ollie Page.)

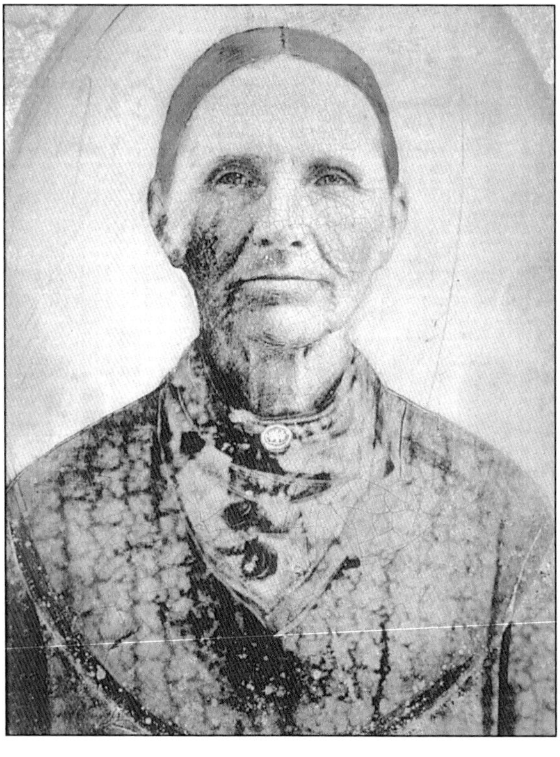

Mary Baggett Warren. After losing her husband during the Civil War, Warren was left, as were many women, to manage the farm and family in one of the most difficult periods of Sampson's history. Born in 1826, Warren died in 1898 and her grave is in a field near Bethesda Church in Plainview Township. (Courtesy of Clarence E. McLamb Jr.)

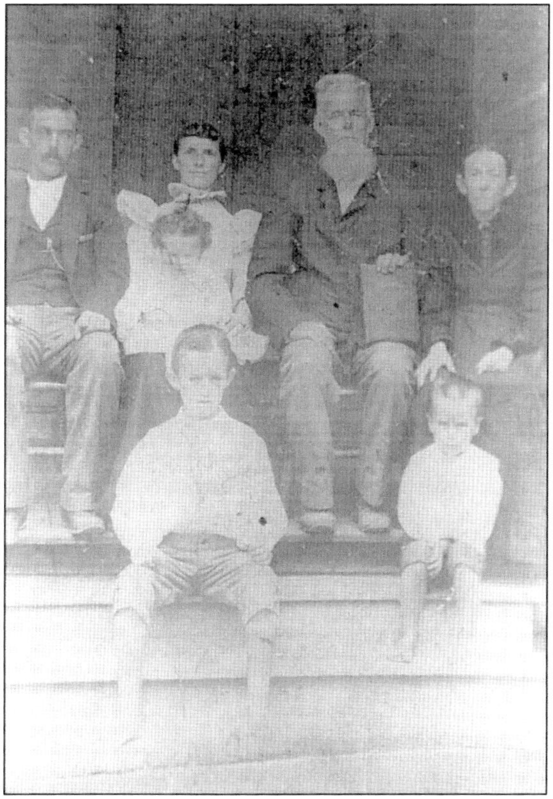

A FAMILY PORTRAIT. From left to right are Marion Alaska, Mollie Bass, James Warwick, and his wife, Elizabeth Wilson Warwick. The children pictured are Hosea, Howard, and Allen Bass. The Bible, also seen here, was one of the few books that many Sampson County families owned. (Courtesy of Joyce Bass Binkley.)

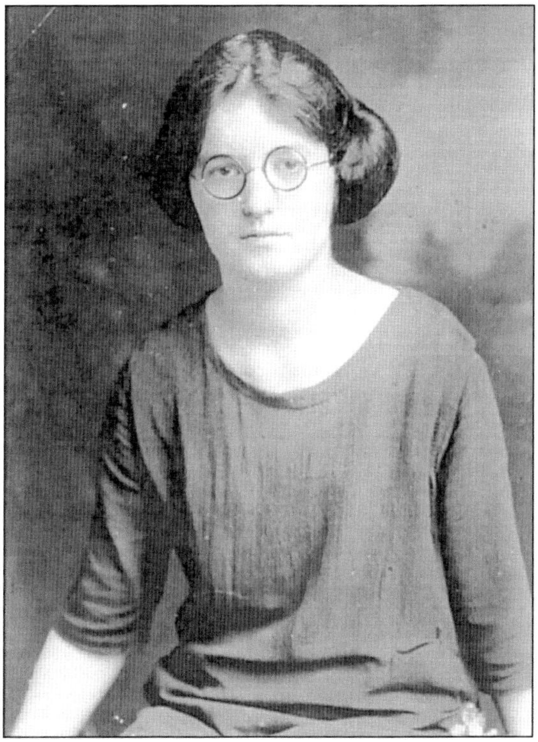

ELEMN WARWICK, AGE 15. Elemn was the daughter of Hosea and Mary Carter Warwick. (Courtesy of Joyce Bass Binkley.)

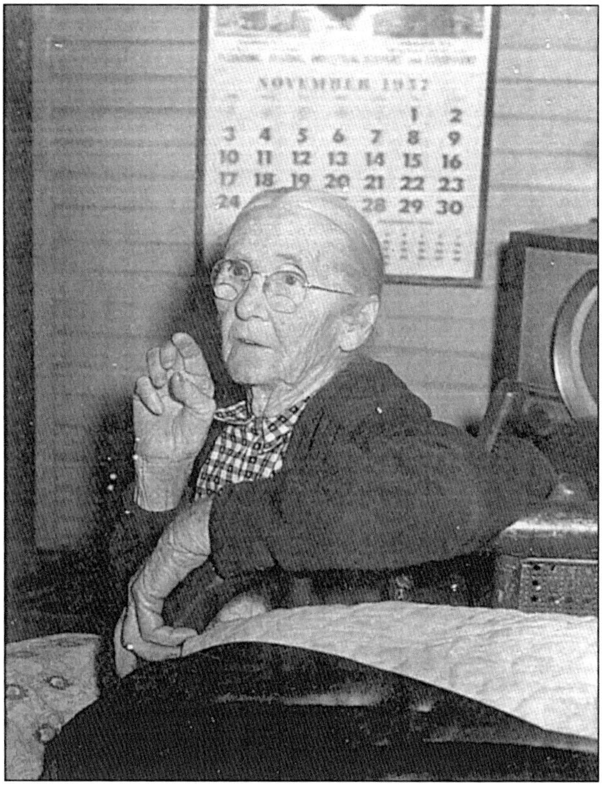

“MAMIE” LIZZIE MATTHIS KNOWLES. Knowles lived her entire life in the Taylor’s Bridge section of Sampson. She inspires special memories of Sampson County grannies from our past. (Courtesy of George C. Burton.)

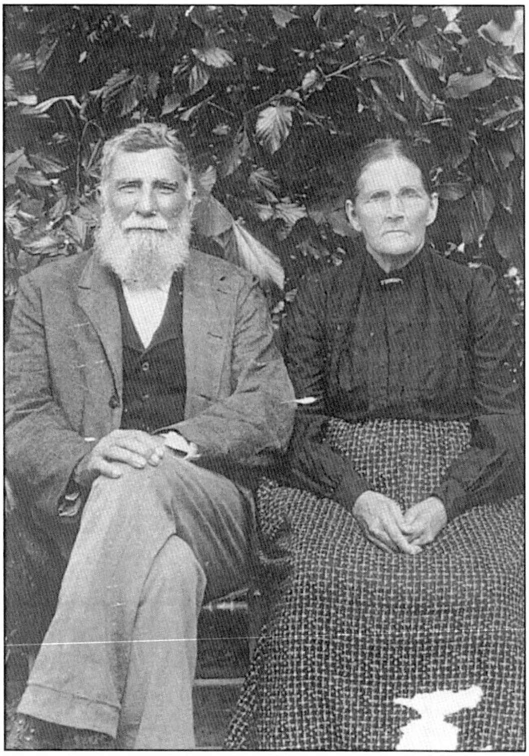

DAVID J. KNOWLES AND MARGARET ROBINSON KNOWLES. This couple was married in 1856, and they lived in the Taylors Bridge vicinity. It is said that Margaret made the clothes that they both are wearing. Universalists in faith, they believed in music and dancing and held parties to celebrate almost anything. (Courtesy of Roland E. Matthis.)

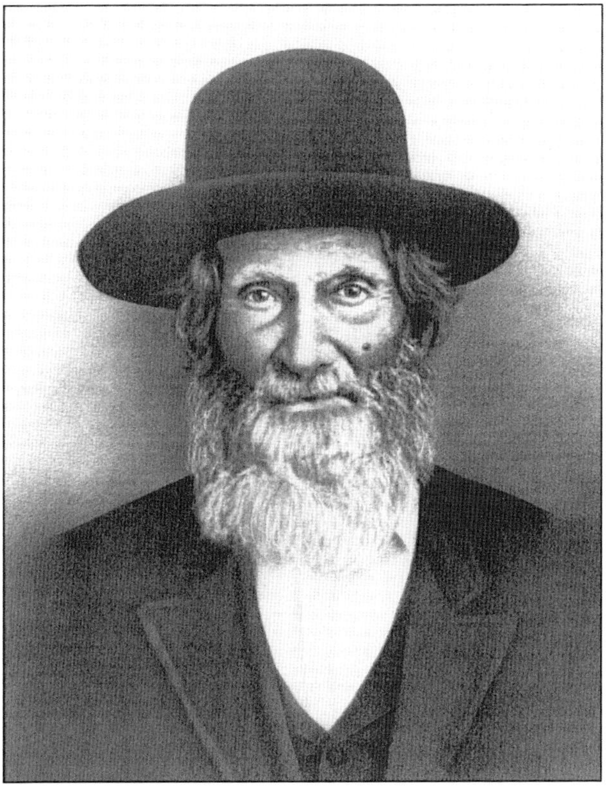

JACOB COOPER HOWARD. One of Sampson's patriarchs, Howard was born in 1819. He operated a gristmill, powered by the waters of what is now Laurel Lake, near Salemburg, and his home was noted for the big family gatherings that were held there. Howard died in 1914. (Courtesy of Lee Ronald Daniels.)

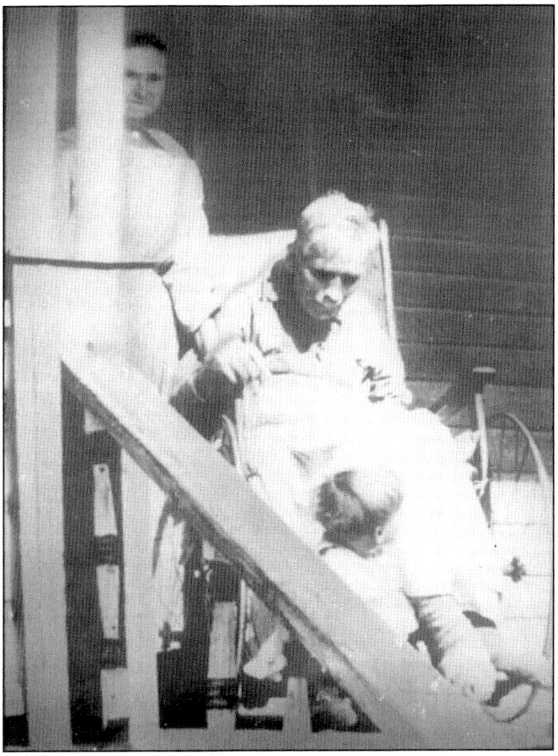

A NORRIS PORTRAIT. Pictured, from left to right, are Sarah Amanda Page Norris, Sampson Norris, and Fletcher Keith Norris, their grandson. Sampson and Amanda are buried in a grove of scrub oaks near their home in the Parkersburg vicinity. (Courtesy of Edna Merritt.)

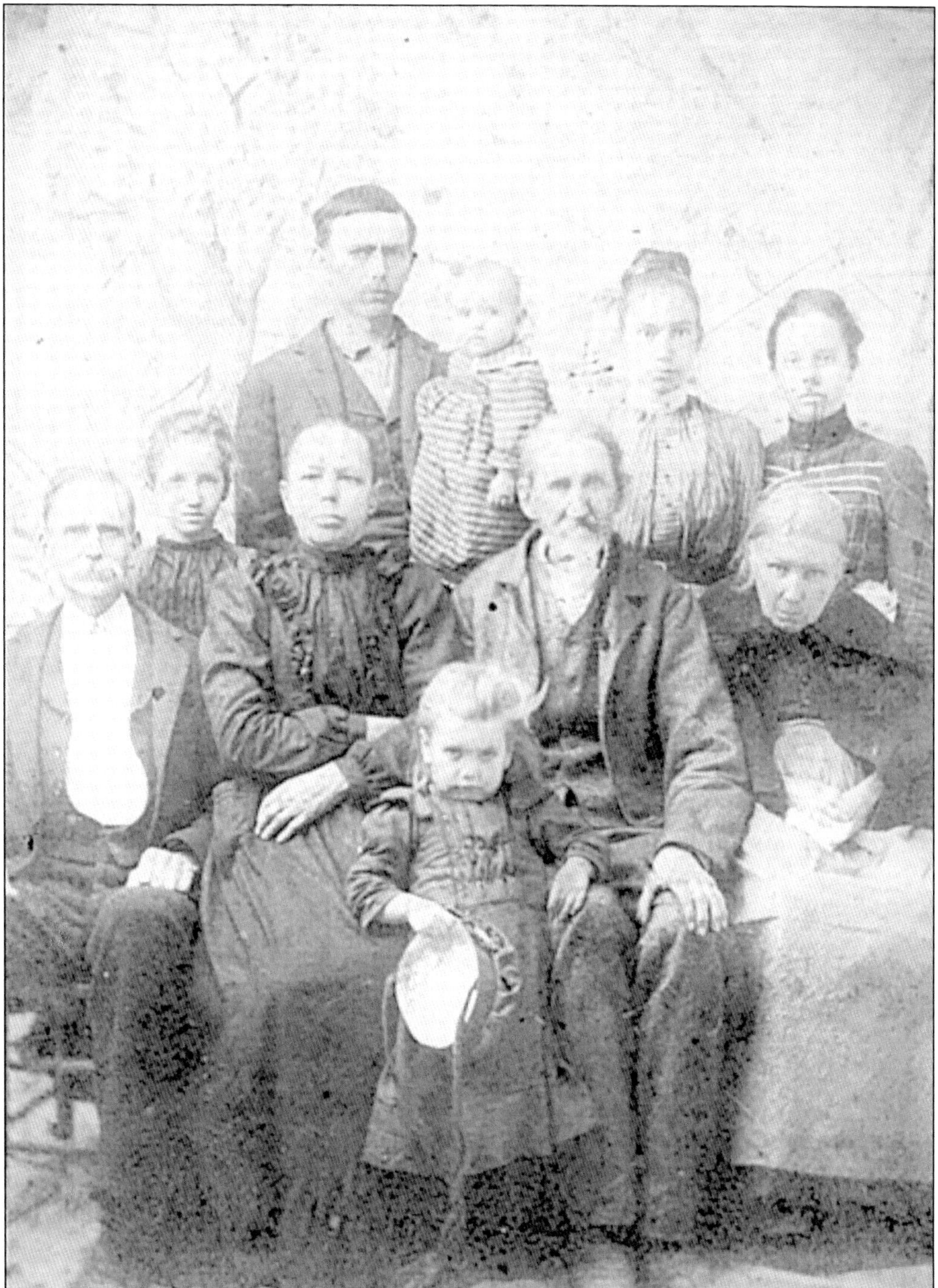

A 1902 Portrait. All the adults in this 1902 picture are resting in graves scattered over Sampson County. The older folks, from left to right, are as follows: (seated) Joel William Wrench, Edia Lee Wrench, John Love Daniel, and Luiza Carroll Daniel; (standing) Frank Wrench and Anner Daniel Wrench. Joel and John were veterans of the Civil War. (Courtesy of Vallie Page Wrench.)

JOHN WRENCH. While serving in Company E, 2nd North Carolina Infantry for the pay of $16.50 per month, Wrench was wounded in the left leg by a round ball on September 19, 1864, in Winchester, Virginia. He was treated for his wounds in a field hospital and was later imprisoned in Point Lookout, Maryland. After the war, John returned to Sampson County, where his wife had died in childbirth during the war years. (Courtesy of Gary Jackson.)

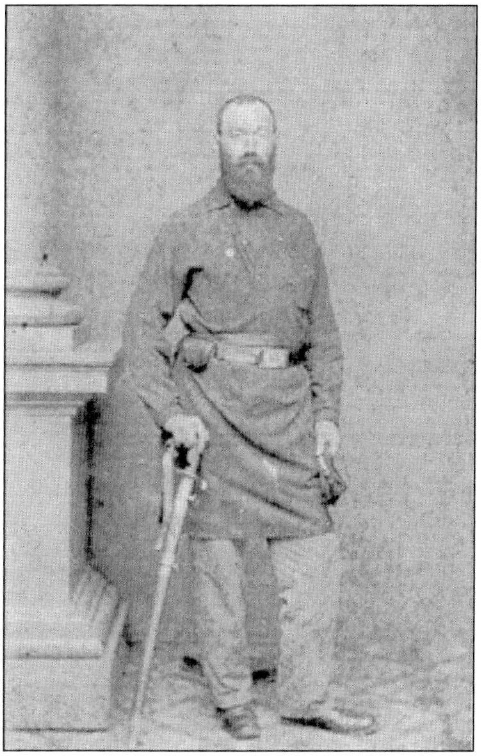

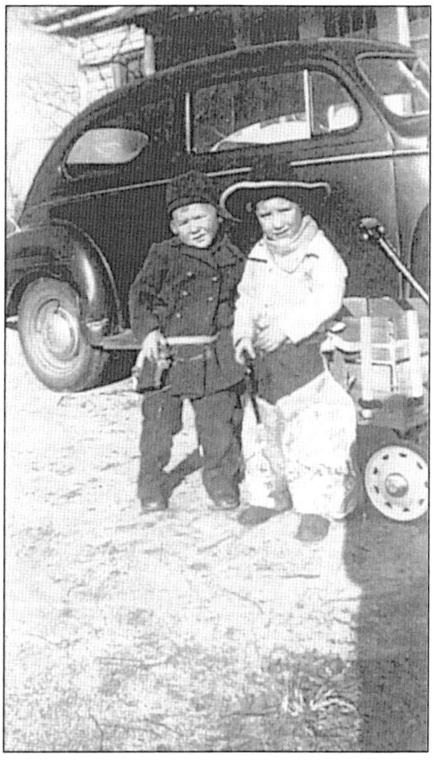

JULIAN BLACKMAN AND DAVID F. KING OF THE INGOLD COMMUNITY, 1948. David, a North Carolina highway patrolman, has retired back to the Ingold vicinity. (Courtesy of Lascar King.)

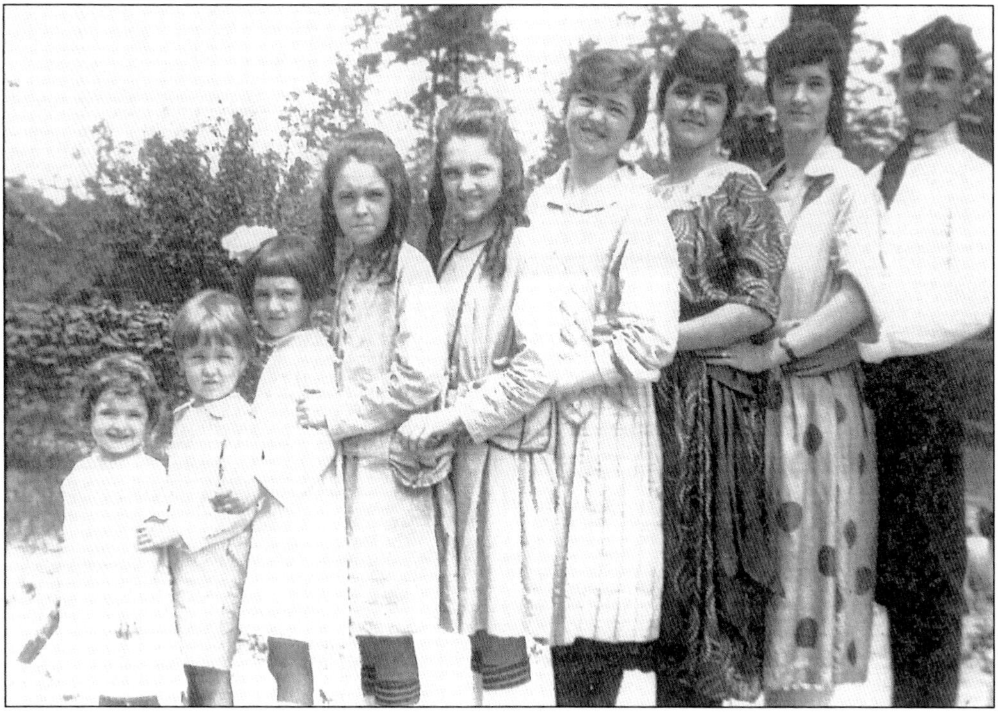

The William Henry Colwell Family of Turkey, 1920. From left to right are Dorothy, William, Lucile, Eugenia, Betty, Caroline, Mildred, Thelma, and James. (Courtesy of Martha Coffield.)

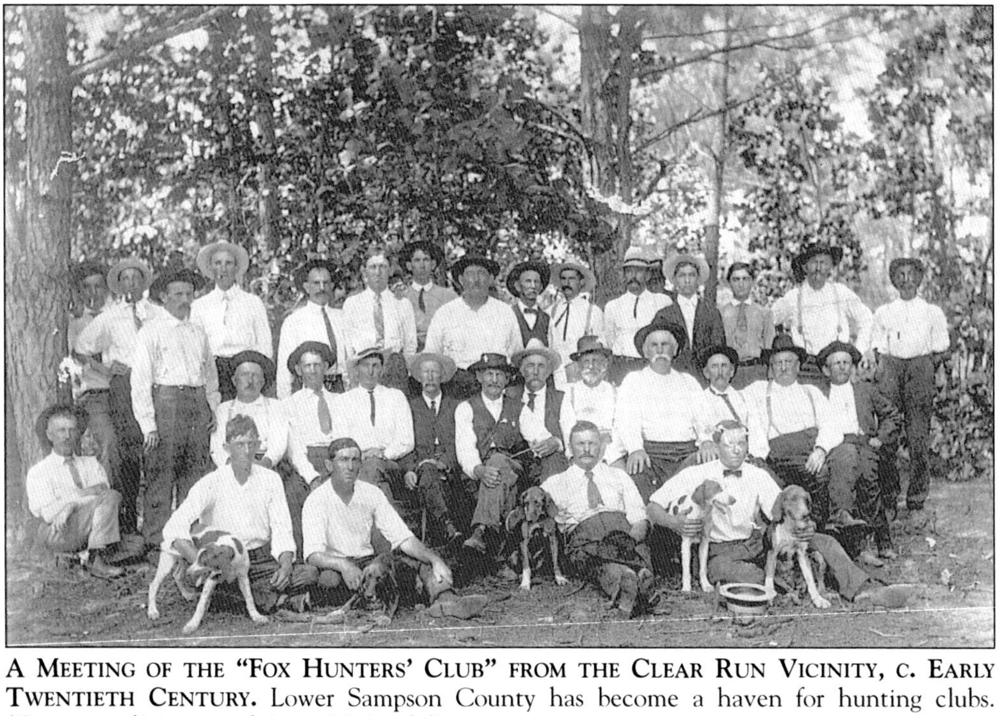

A Meeting of the "Fox Hunters' Club" from the Clear Run Vicinity, c. Early Twentieth Century. Lower Sampson County has become a haven for hunting clubs. (Courtesy of Merrie and Amos McLamb.)

Six

Towns and Villages

Autryville, Garland, Harrells, Newton Grove, Roseboro, Salemburg, and Turkey are Sampson's incorporated towns and villages. Other would-be villages include Ivanhoe, Lisborn, Mintz, Owensville, Parkersburg, Tomahawk, Ingold, Clear Run, and many other noted crossroads.

Lisborn was the only trading center in Sampson County in 1784. The town was located on the Coharie River at the site of the present-day Lisborn bridge. Flatboats poled upstream above tidewater, and in times of high-water even steamboats plied between Lisborn and Wilmington. However, the town suffered a slow death starting in the mid-1880s. Today there is no visual sign that this town ever existed.

Owenville was a small county community about 1 mile north of present-day Roseboro. Owenville flourished before the Civil War and had a post office as well as being a major stopping point on the old stage road from Fayetteville to Wilmington, but the village was killed by the coming of the railroad through the new town of Roseboro.

The images presented in this chapter give a glimpse, however brief, into the past history of Sampson's towns and villages.

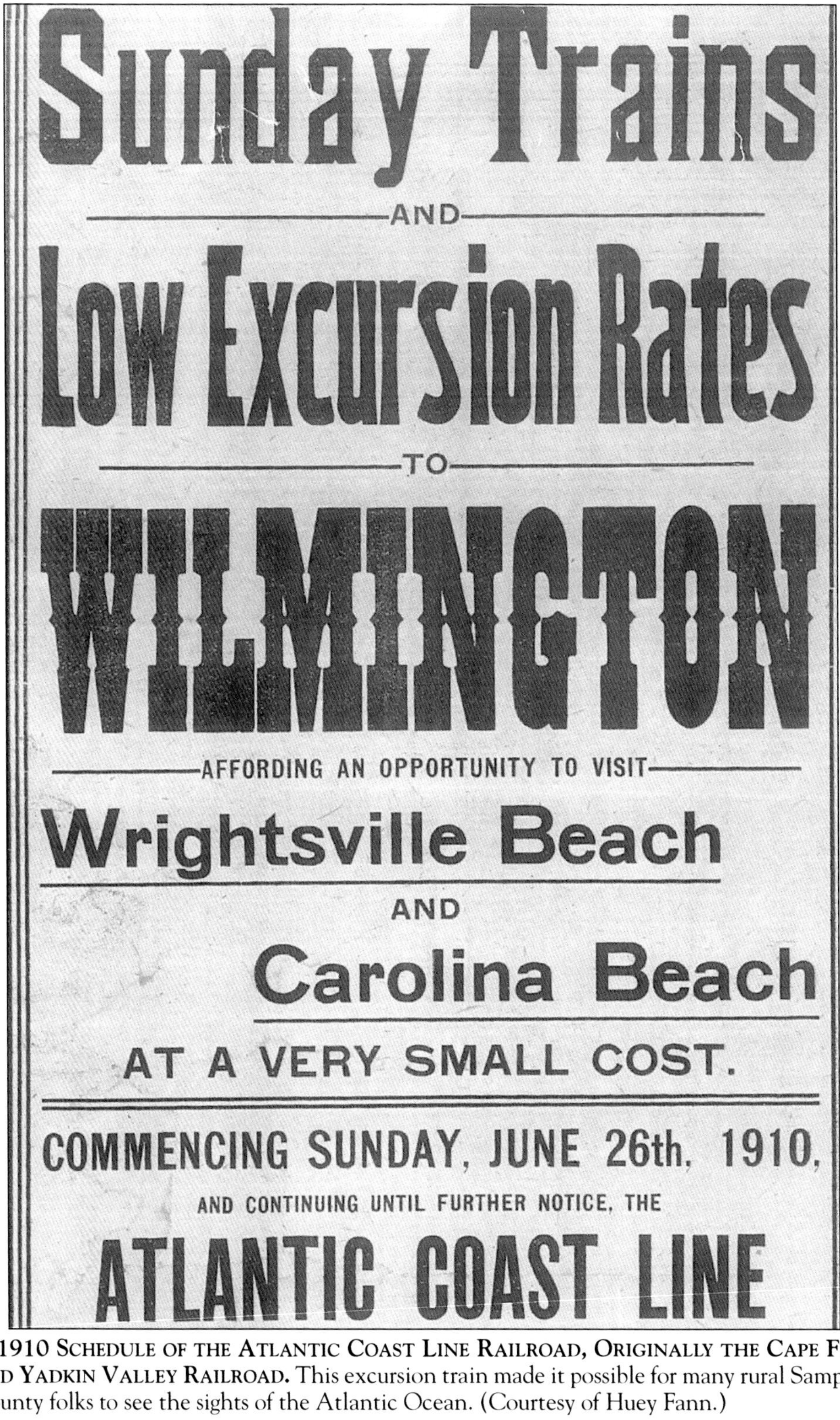
Sunday Trains

AND

Low Excursion Rates

TO

WILMINGTON

AFFORDING AN OPPORTUNITY TO VISIT

Wrightsville Beach

AND

Carolina Beach

AT A VERY SMALL COST.

COMMENCING SUNDAY, JUNE 26th, 1910,

AND CONTINUING UNTIL FURTHER NOTICE, THE

ATLANTIC COAST LINE

A 1910 SCHEDULE OF THE ATLANTIC COAST LINE RAILROAD, ORIGINALLY THE CAPE FEAR AND YADKIN VALLEY RAILROAD. This excursion train made it possible for many rural Sampson County folks to see the sights of the Atlantic Ocean. (Courtesy of Huey Fann.)

WILL OPERATE

Sunday Excursion Trains

From SANFORD and Intermediate Points to WILMINGTON on the Following Convenient Schedule and

VERY LOW ROUND-TRIP RATES.

TICKETS LIMITED TO DATE OF SALE.

FROM	Schedule.	FARE.
Lv. Sanford	6:00 a. m.	$2.00
" Jonesboro	6:05 a. m.	2.00
" Swann	6:18 a. m.	1.95
" Rock Branch	6:22 a. m.	1.90
" Spout Springs	6:38 a. m.	1.75
" Manchester	6:55 a. m.	1.65
" Fayetteville	7:25 a. m.	1.50
" Vander	7:45 a. m.	1.50
" Steadman	7:55 a. m.	1.50
" Autryville	8:02 a. m.	1.40
" Roseboro	8:20 a. m,	1.30
" Mintz	8:28 a. m.	1.25
" Parkersburg	8:40 a. m.	1.15
" Garland	8:50 a. m.	1.05
" Tomahawk	9:04 a. m.	95
" Kerr	9:15 a. m.	85
" Ivanhoe	9:24 a. m.	75
" Atkinson	9:40 a. m.	60
" Currie	9:53 a. m,	45
" Montague	9:58 a. m.	40
" Richards	10:12 a. m.	25
Ar. Wilmington	10:35 a. m.	....

RETURNING { LEAVE WILMINGTON 5:25 P. M., ARRIVE FAYETTEVILLE 8:35 P. M. and SANFORD 10:00 P. M., Stopping at all stations to let off passengers

WRIGHTSVILLE BEACH

IS

MORE ATTRACTIVE THAN EVER.

W. J. CRAIG, Passenger Traffic Manager.

T. C. WHITE, Gen'l Passenger Agent.

WILMINGTON, N. C.

TRAIN EXCURSIONS. The train stopped at eight depots on its journey through Sampson County. One could travel from Autryville to Wilmington in just 2 hours and 37 minutes. Today, this rail line is only a memory, and some of the rail villages have disappeared. (Courtesy of Huey Fann.)

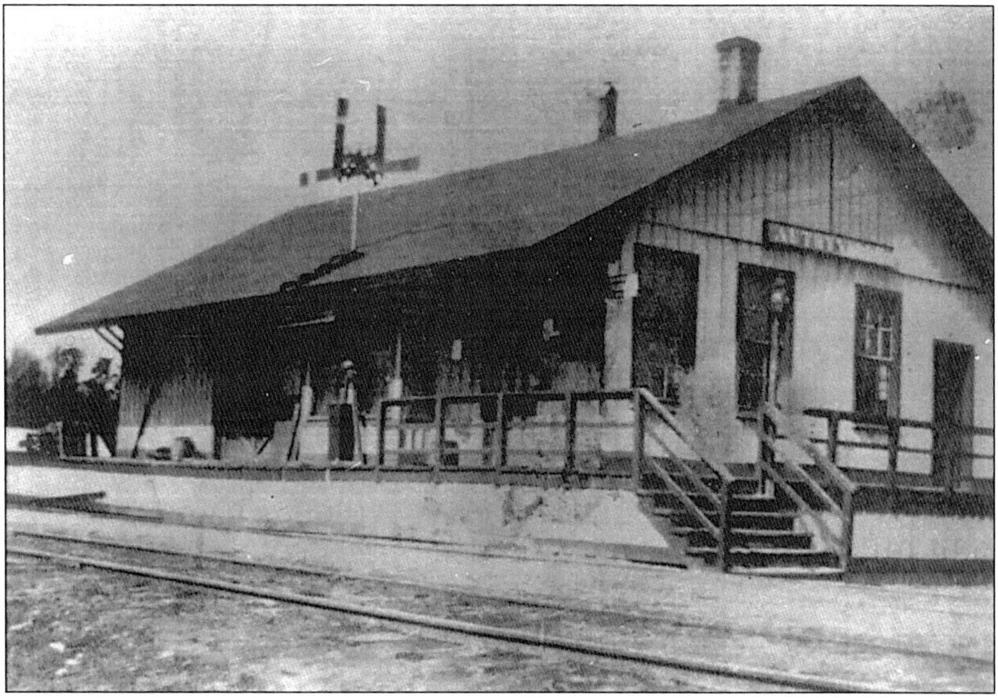

AUTRYS. In 1889, Autrys had only one store. However, during that same year, the Cape Fear and Yadkin Valley Railroad designated Autrys to become a depot for the new railroad, and the town became known as Autryville. In 1908, when I.L. Vinson Sr. came as a depot agent, the railroad had become the property of the Atlantic Coast Line Railroad. (Courtesy of Margaret Vinson Jaynes.)

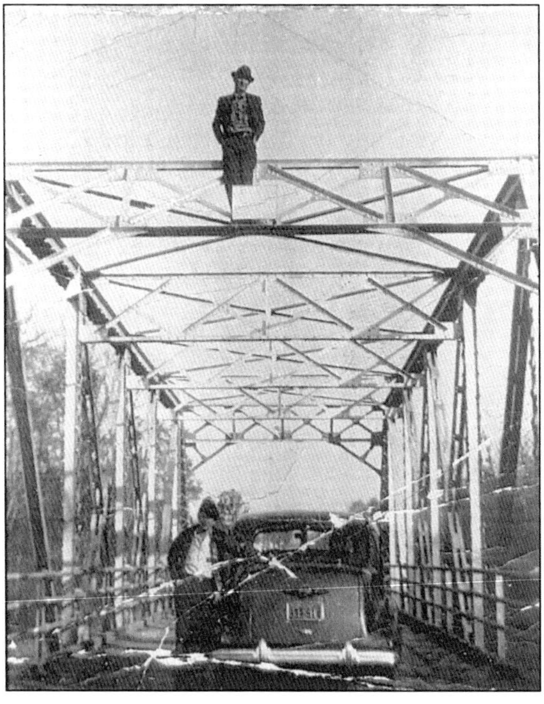

THE SOUTH RIVER BRIDGE. In the 1930s, this bridge brought east-west traffic through downtown Autryville. (Courtesy of Margaret Vinson Jaynes.)

Atlantic Coast Line Railroad Box Cars on the Siding in Autryville, near the Old Water Tank, c. 1920s. Captain James L. Autry was instrumental in bringing the railroad through Autryville. (Courtesy of Margaret Vinson Jaynes.)

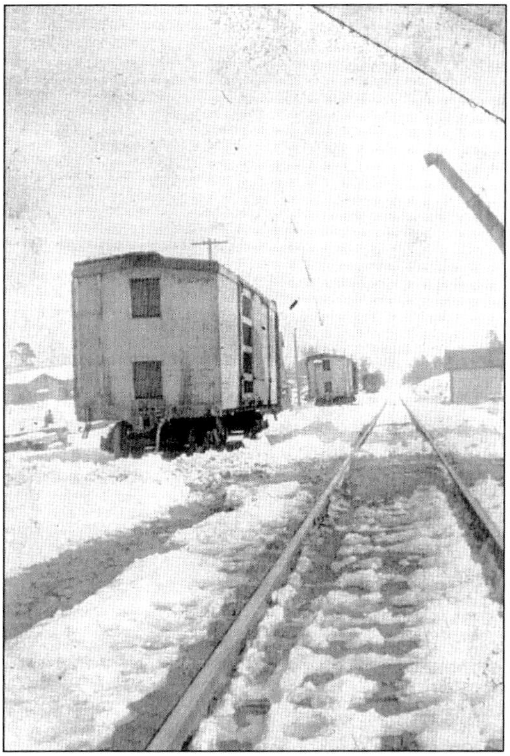

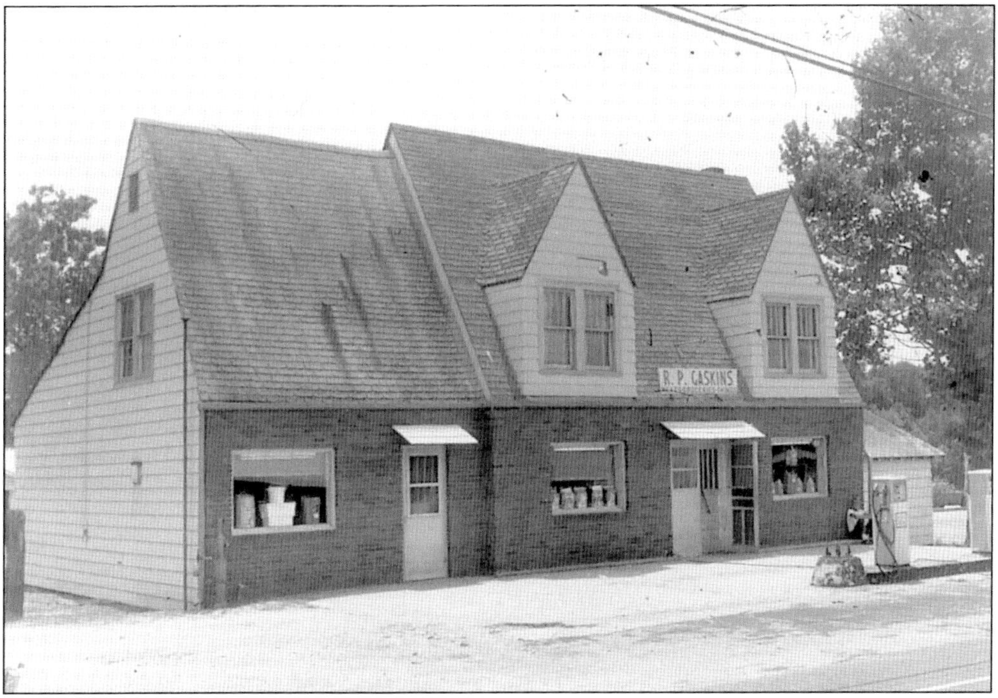

Pure Oil Company Building. The Pure Oil Company built this structure in Autryville, c. 1940. It was remodeled and operated as a general merchandise store for several years. (Courtesy of North Carolina Division of Archives and History.)

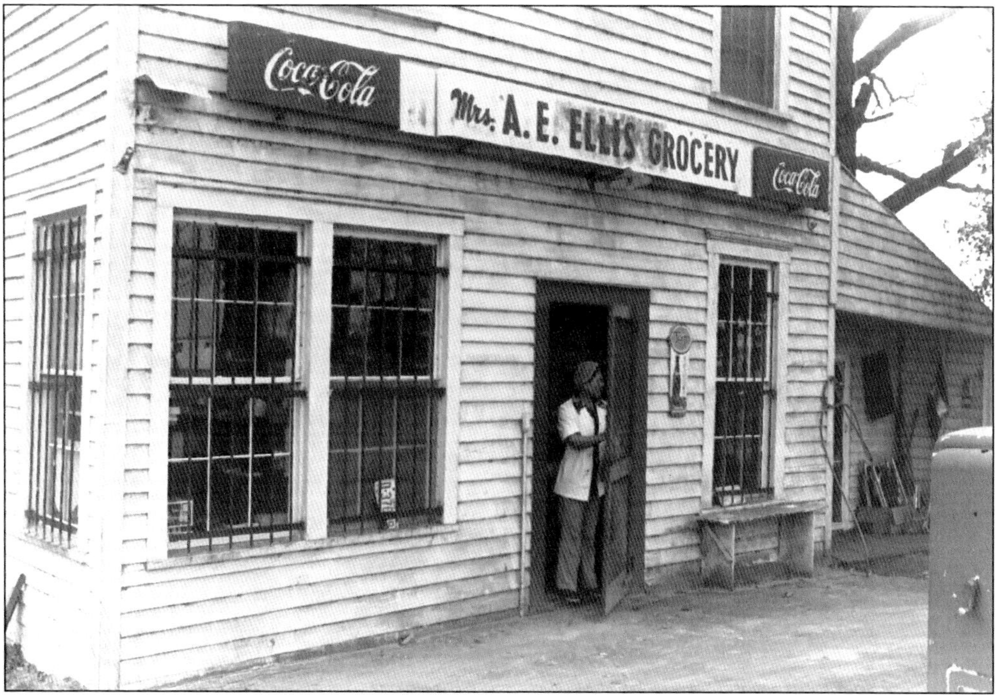

MRS. A.E. ELLIS GROCERY STORE ALONG THE OLD WILMINGTON AND WELDON RAILROAD. (Courtesy of North Carolina Division of Archives and History.)

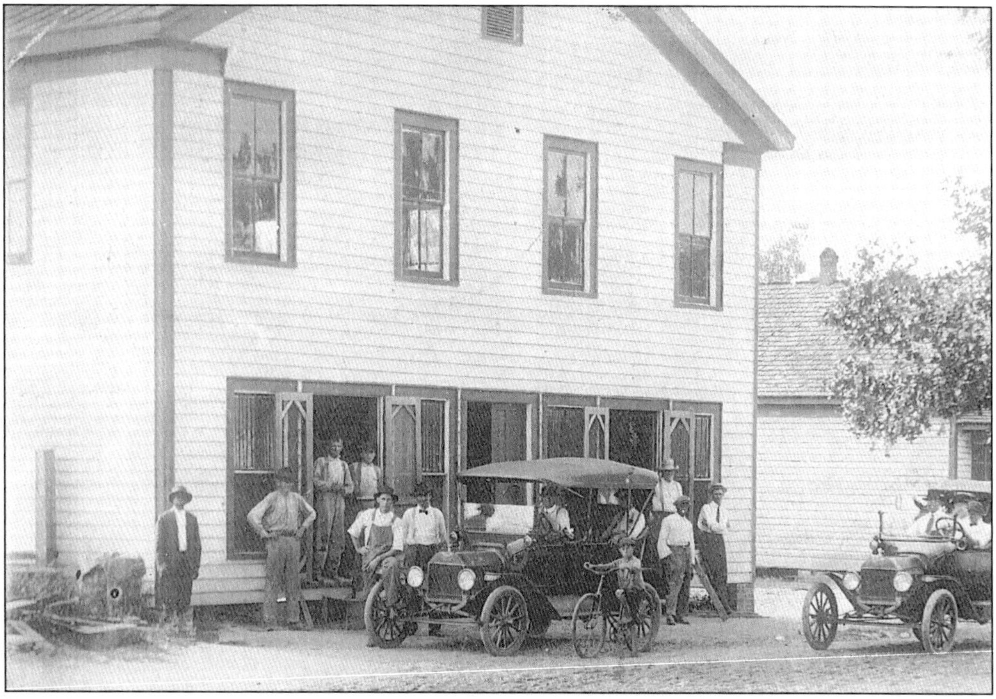

THE O.L. JOHNSON STORE AND INGOLD POST OFFICE BUILDING, C. 1920. The river town of Lisbon disappeared early in the twentieth century, and Ingold replaced Lisbon as the trading center of the nearby communities. (Courtesy of David King.)

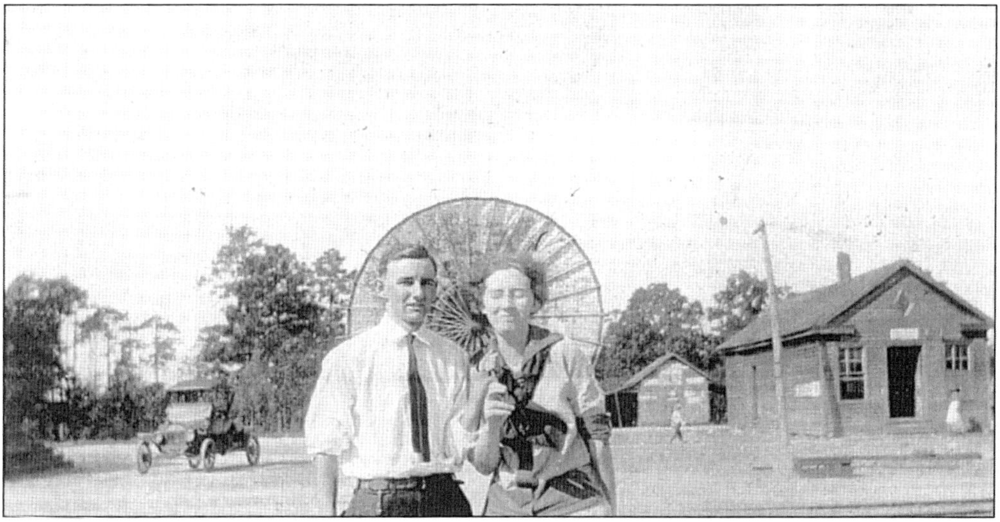

Garland, Once Known as Sloan's Crossing, c. 1910. This building is William Solan's general merchandise store, which also housed the post office. The depot was on the opposite side of Front Street, across from the store. (Courtesy of Catherine Solan.)

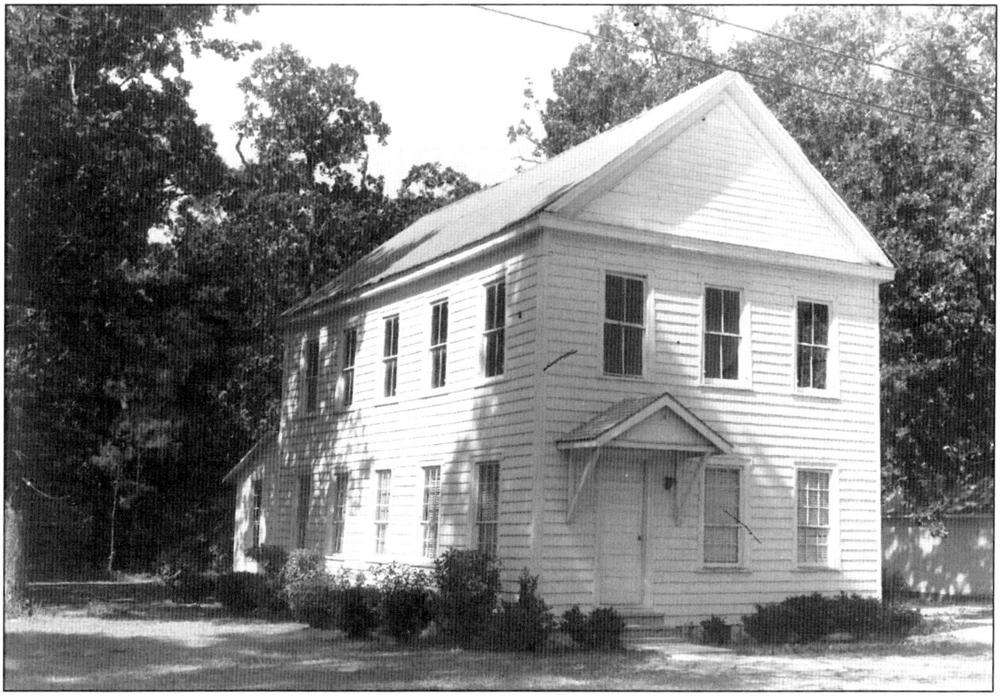

The Old Masonic Building in Harrells Store. Built *c.* 1840, this structure had an upstairs portion that was used by the local Masonic order. The bottom floor served as an academy. (Courtesy of North Carolina Division of Archives and History.)

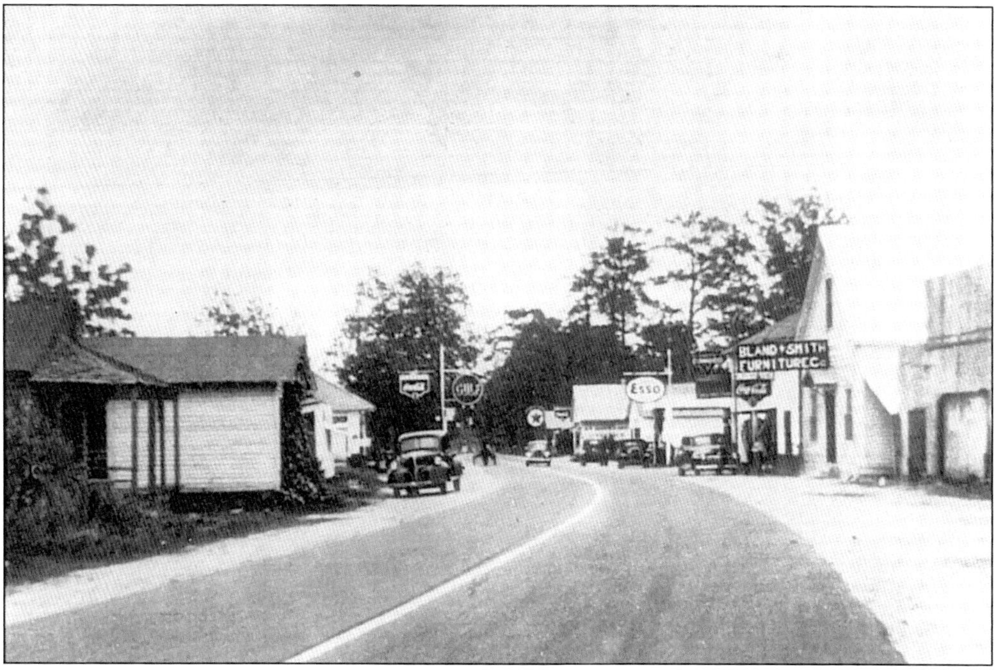

A VIEW OF HARRELLS STORE, C. 1940. A U.S. post office was established in this community in 1874. In the 1940s, the mule and wagon still claimed one half of the highway. (Courtesy of Lela Harrell.)

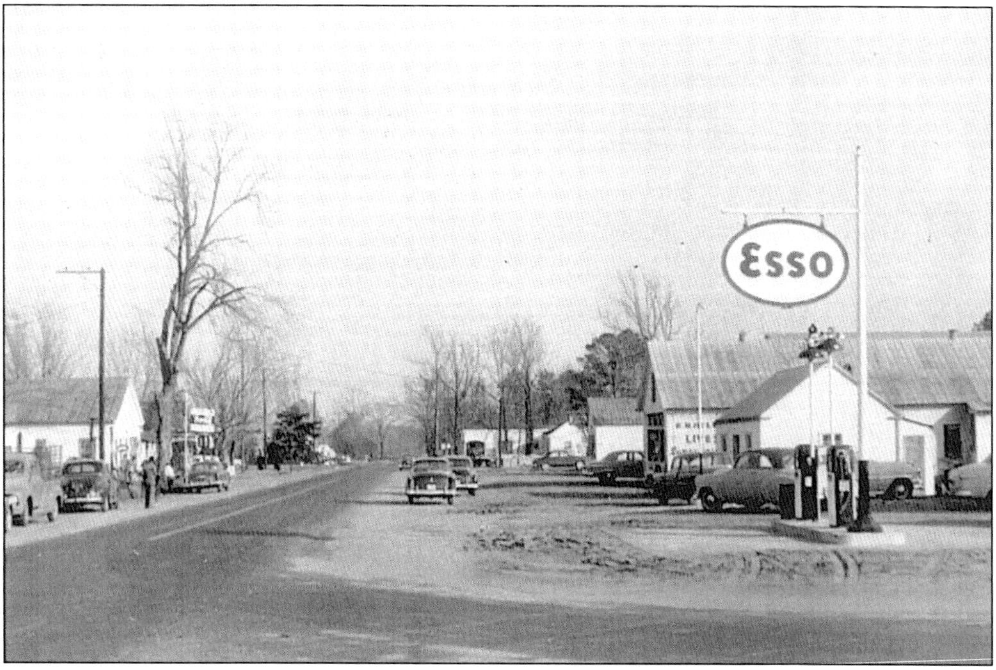

ANOTHER VIEW OF HARRELLS STORE, C. 1950. Harells Store was incorporated in 1943, and the town's name was changed to Harrells in 1952. The R.H. Melvin Brothers store, next to the Esso station, was the first store in Harrells to sell "factory-made cigarettes." (Courtesy of Lela Harrell.)

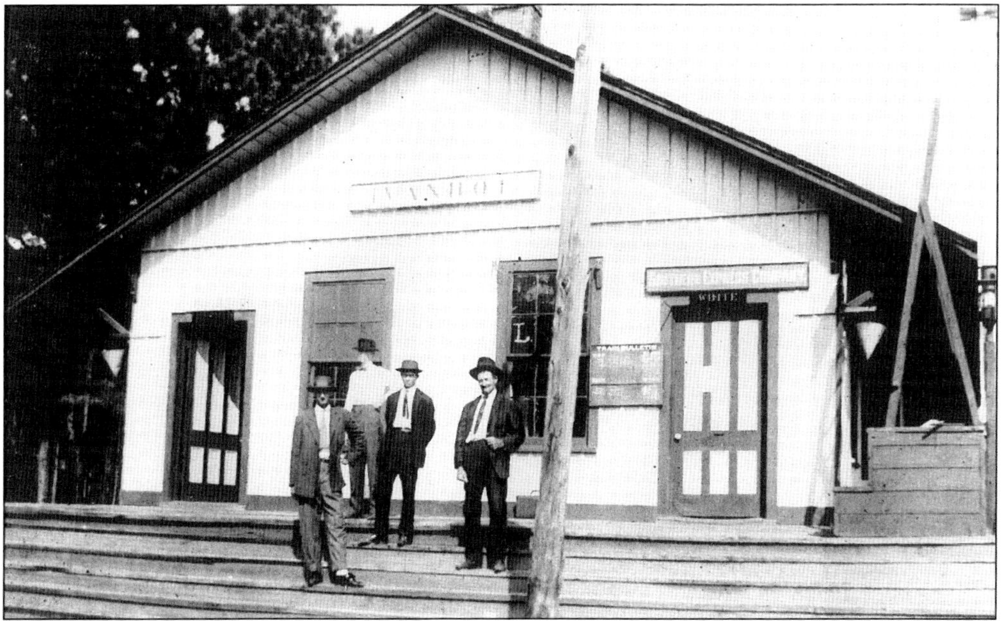

The Ivanhoe Depot. The depot was built when the Cape Fear and Yadkin Valley Railroad came through in1890, but the river village dates back to the 1740s, when Scottish immigrants began to settle here. The name "Ivanhoe" was inspired by the novel of the same name and was suggested by someone to the railroad officials, who adopted it. (Courtesy of Sampson County History Museum, Inc.)

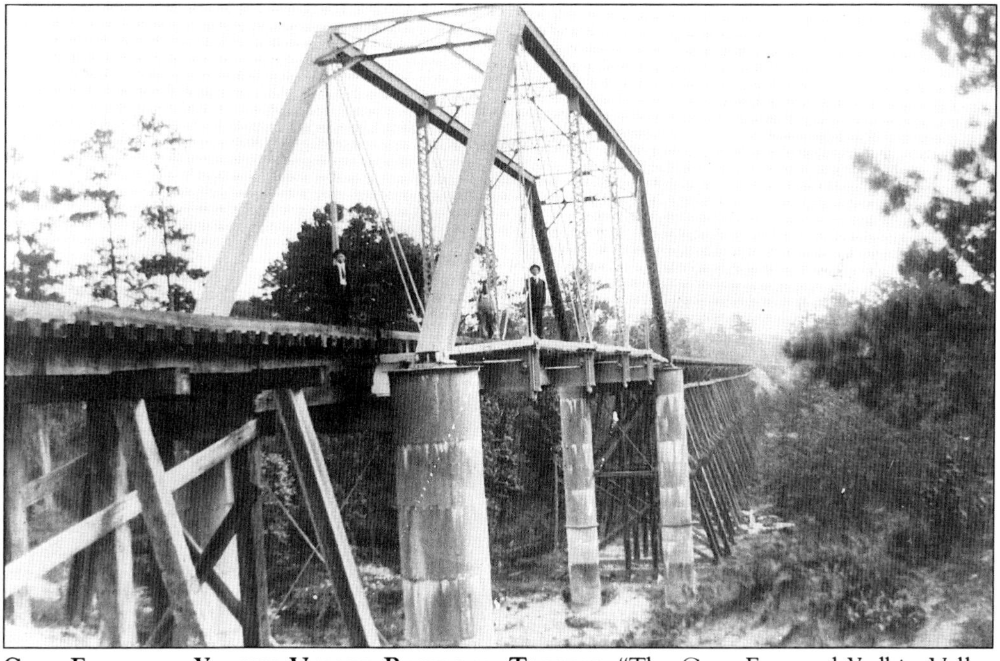

Cape Fear and Yadkin Valley Railroad Trestle. "The Cape Fear and Yadkin Valley Railroad Trestle across the Black River near Ivanhoe is a quarter of a mile long and is one of the prettiest pieces of work in the state," read the *Clinton Caucasian* newspaper on November 7, 1889. (Courtesy of Sampson County History Museum, Inc.)

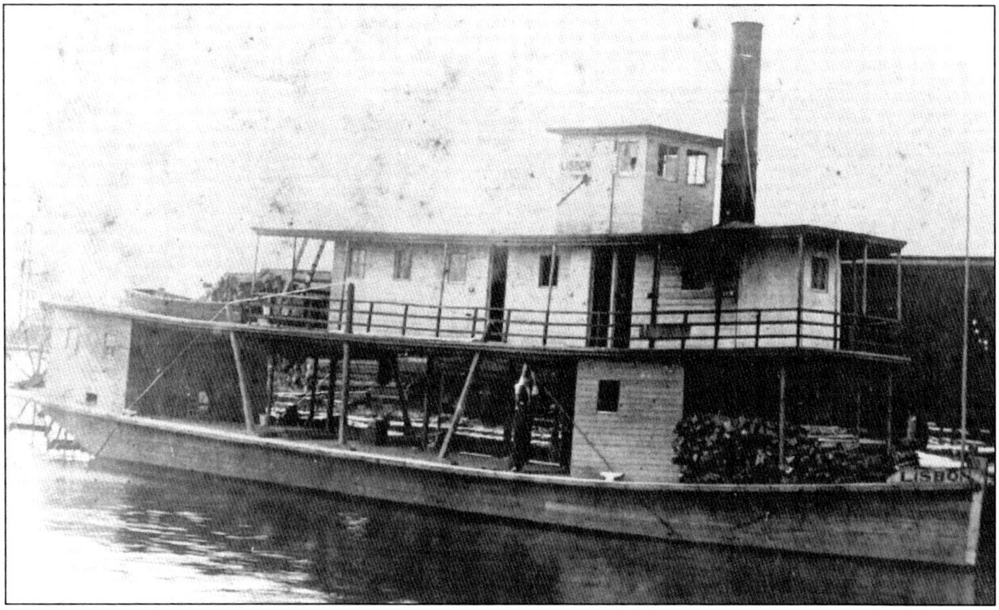

The Lisbon Steamship. This vessel moved goods and passengers up and down North Carolina rivers in the late 1800s. In times of high water, this 77-foot freighter was able to reach the early town of Lisbon along the Black River in lower Sampson County. Both the steamer and the town slipped into history early in the twentieth century. (Courtesy of Philip E. Williams.)

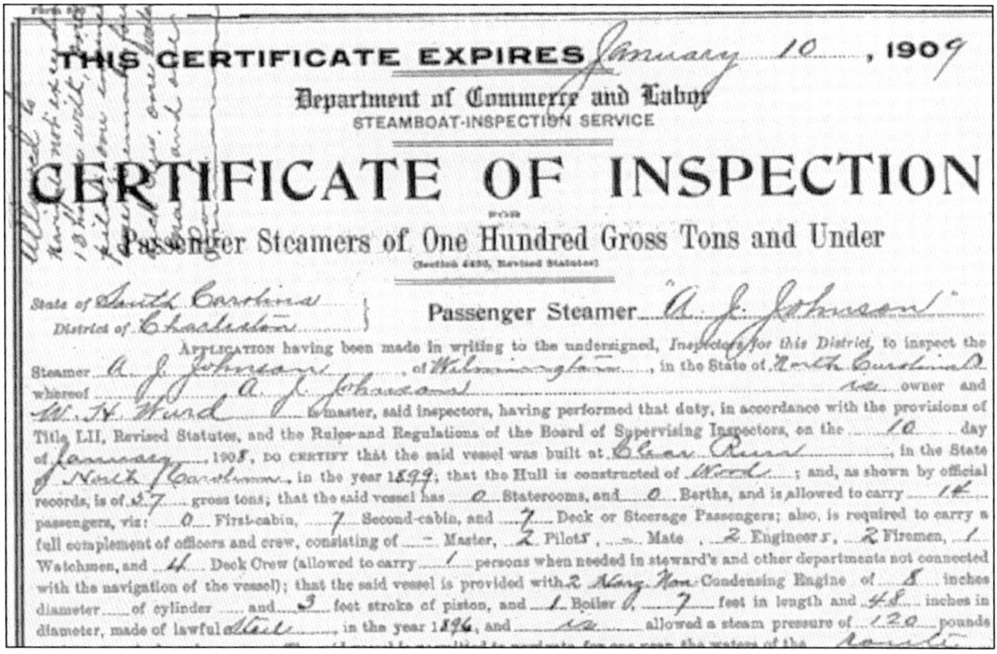

THIS CERTIFICATE EXPIRES January 10, 1909

Department of Commerce and Labor
STEAMBOAT-INSPECTION SERVICE

CERTIFICATE OF INSPECTION
FOR
Passenger Steamers of One Hundred Gross Tons and Under

State of South Carolina
District of Charleston

Passenger Steamer "A. J. Johnson"

Application having been made in writing to the undersigned, *Inspectors for this District*, to inspect the Steamer A. J. Johnson, of Wilmington, in the State of North Carolina whereof A. J. Johnson is owner and W. H. Ward is master, said inspectors, having performed that duty, in accordance with the provisions of Title LII, Revised Statutes, and the Rules and Regulations of the Board of Supervising Inspectors, on the 10 day of January 1908, do certify that the said vessel was built at Clear Run, in the State of North Carolina, in the year 1899; that the Hull is constructed of Wood; and, as shown by official records, is of 57 gross tons; that the said vessel has 0 Staterooms, and 0 Berths, and is allowed to carry 14 passengers, viz: 0 First-cabin, 7 Second-cabin, and 7 Deck or Steerage Passengers; also, is required to carry a full complement of officers and crew, consisting of – Master, 2 Pilots, – Mate, 2 Engineers, 2 Firemen, 1 Watchmen, and 4 Deck Crew (allowed to carry 1 persons when needed in steward's and other departments not connected with the navigation of the vessel); that the said vessel is provided with 2 Horz. Non-Condensing Engine of 8 inches diameter of cylinder and 3 feet stroke of piston, and 1 Boiler 7 feet in length and 48 inches in diameter, made of lawful steel, in the year 1896, and is allowed a steam pressure of 120 pounds

A Steamboat Certificate. This certificate of inspection gives a glimpse into steamboat travel on the tributaries of the Cape Fear River, such as the Black River, following the Civil War. The *A.J. Johnson* steamer left Clear Run early in the morning and arrived in Wilmington in the late afternoon. The ship made two trips every week. (Courtesy of Merrie and Amos McLamb.)

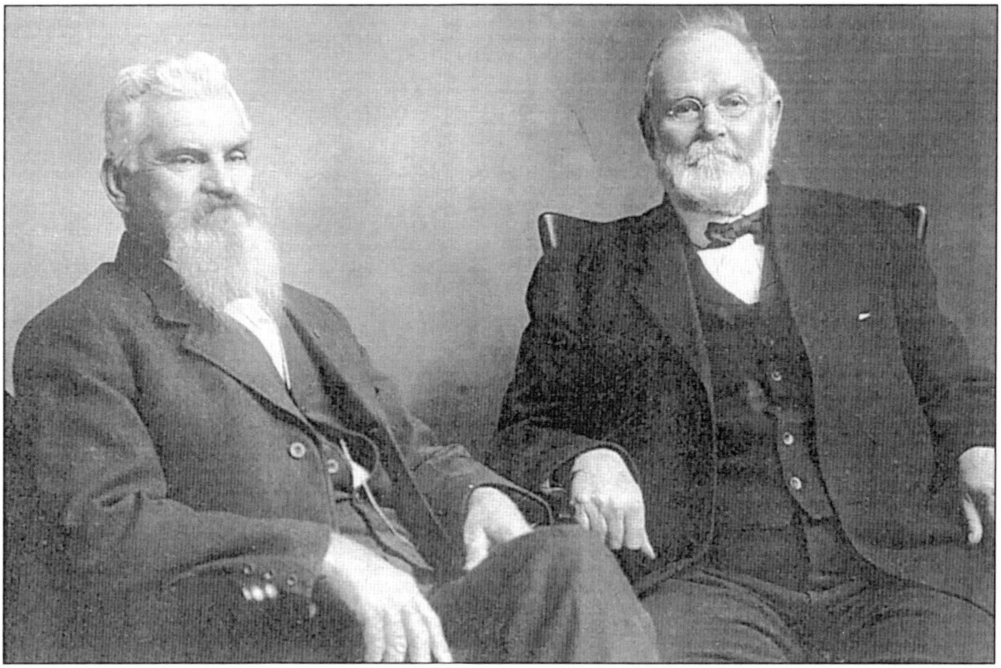

A.J. JOHNSON AND C.I. ROBINSON FROM CLEAR RUN. A.J. Johnson was the owner of the *Lisbon* and *A.J. Johnson* steamboats. The *A.J. Johnson* sank in a storm in 1914, the year of her owner's death. (Courtesy of Merrie and Amos McLamb.)

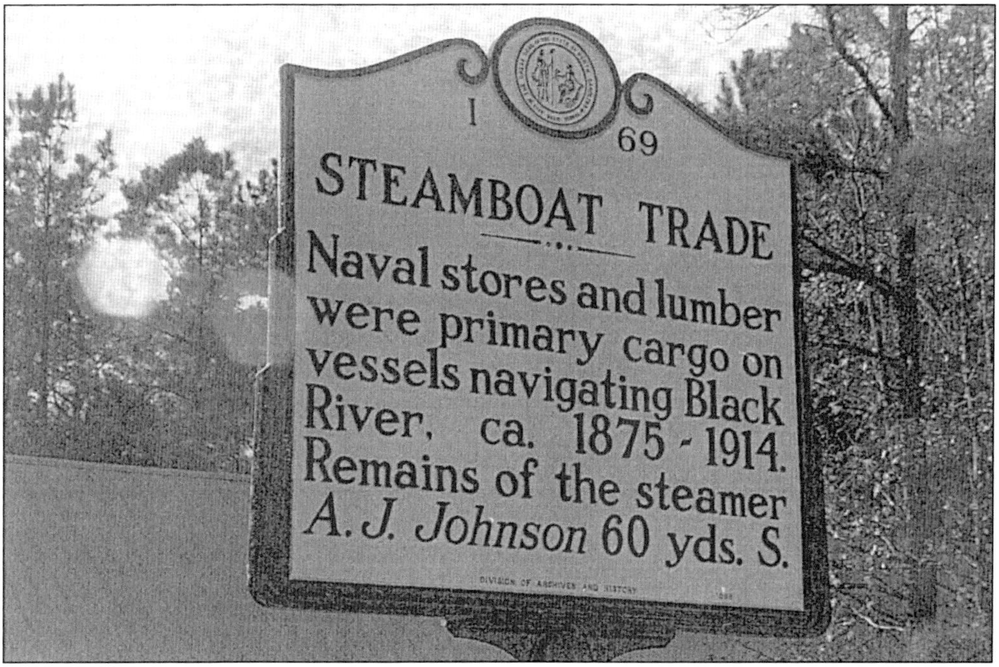

A SIGN MARKING THE LOCATION OF HERRINGSVILLE. A post office was established here in 1873, and riverboats docked here, as well. The name of this Sampson community was changed to Clear Run around 1882. The store in the background was established in 1866 by A.J. Johnson, and it was operated until 1960. (Courtesy of Merrie and Amos Johnson.)

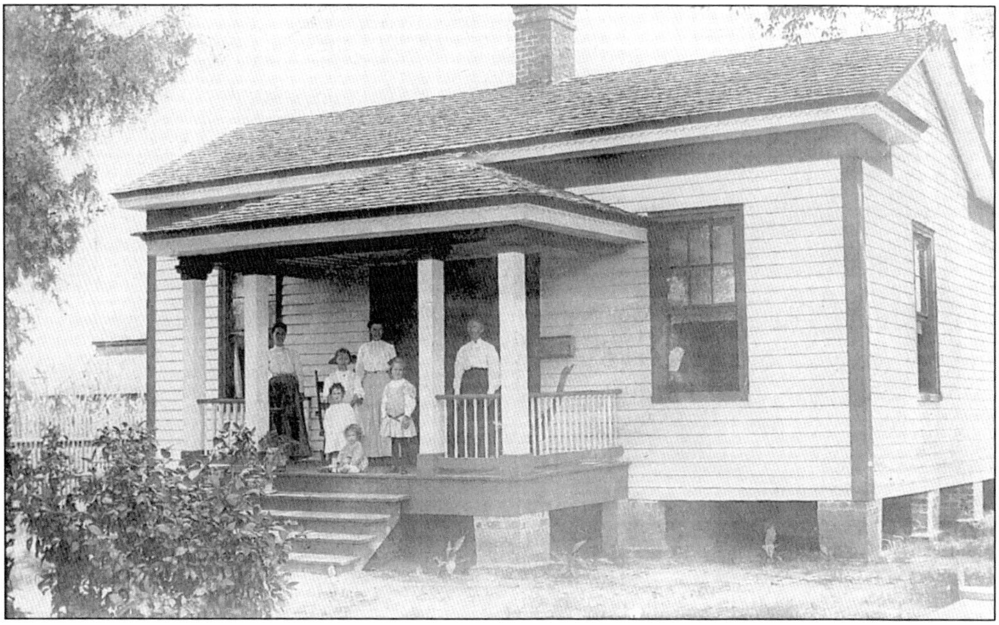

THE NEWTON GROVE POST OFFICE. In earlier days, many post offices were run out of private homes or store buildings. The Newton Grove Post Office was operated out of the Cox home. Mrs. Margaret Cox, seen here, became a postmistress in 1900 and served until 1933. (Courtesy of Albert and Ann Herring.)

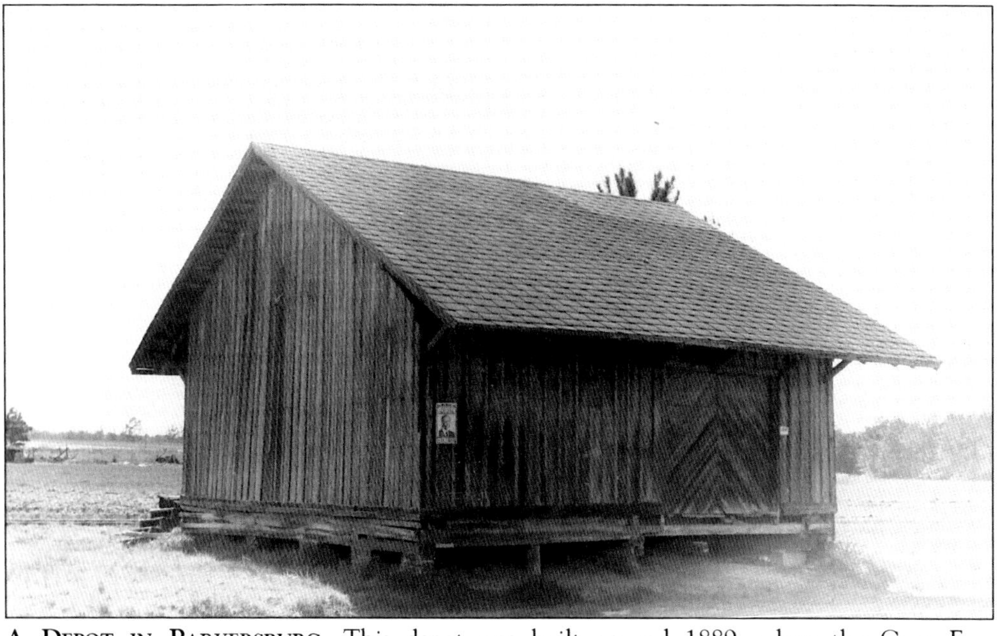

A DEPOT IN PARKERSBURG. This depot was built around 1889, when the Cape Fear and Yadkin Valley Railroad was built through the area. The typical, small railroad town of Parkersburg grew up along the rail. (Courtesy of North Carolina Division of Archives and History.)

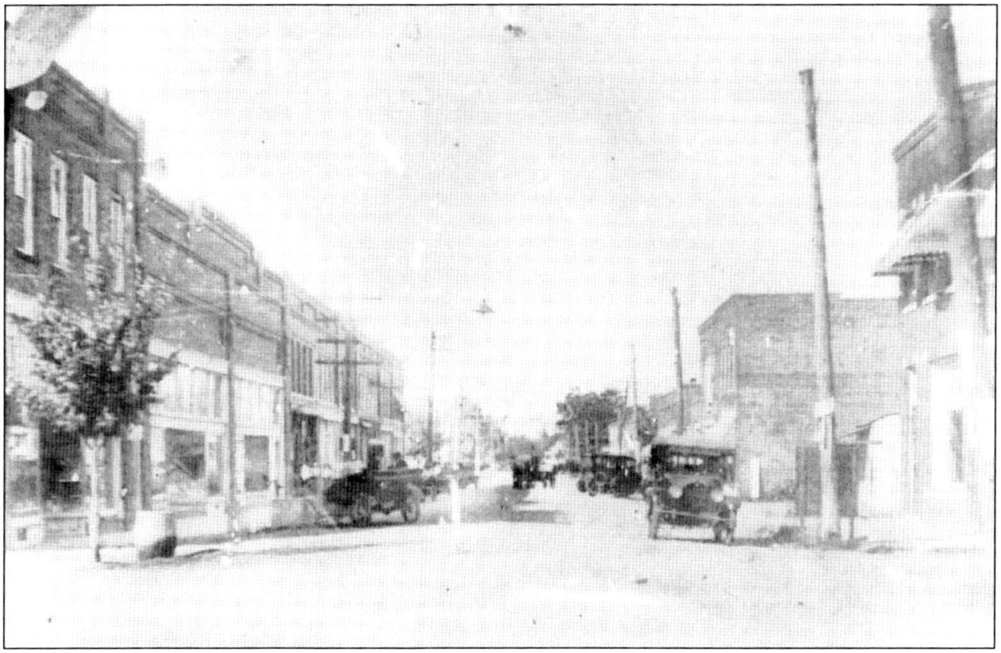

"Autos in Roseboro." This was the headline in the *Clinton News Dispatch* on May 23, 1912. The story goes on to argue that automobiles are becoming so numerous in Roseboro that it is almost dangerous to cross Main Street. (Courtesy of Sampson County History Museum, Inc.)

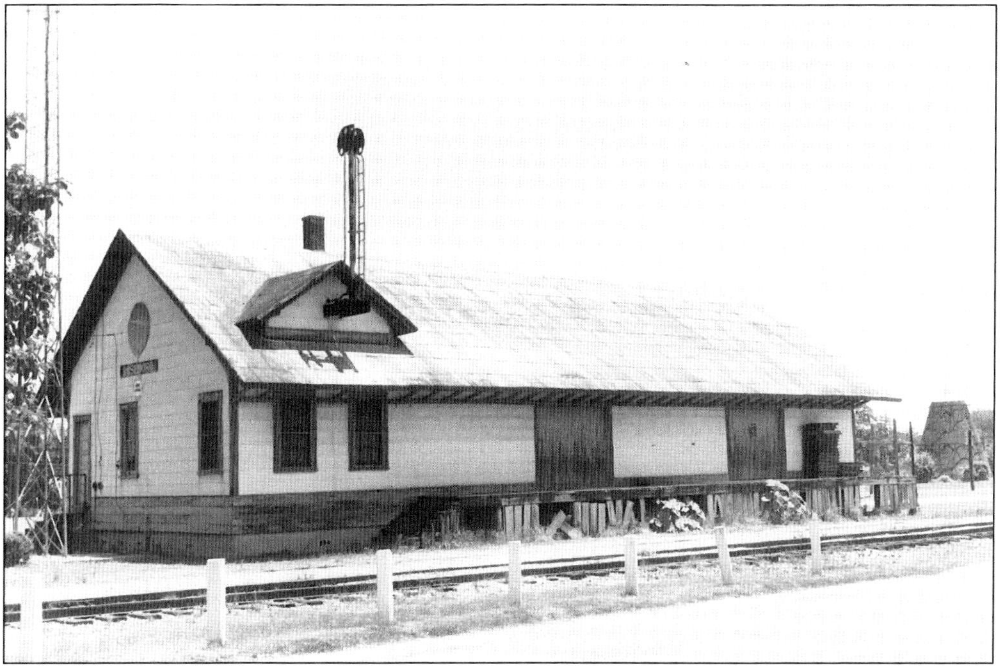

Roseboro Depot. Built by the Cape Fear and Yadkin Valley Railroad in the late 1880s, this depot is typical of those constructed in the rural South during the railroad expansion period. (Courtesy of North Carolina Division of Archives and History.)

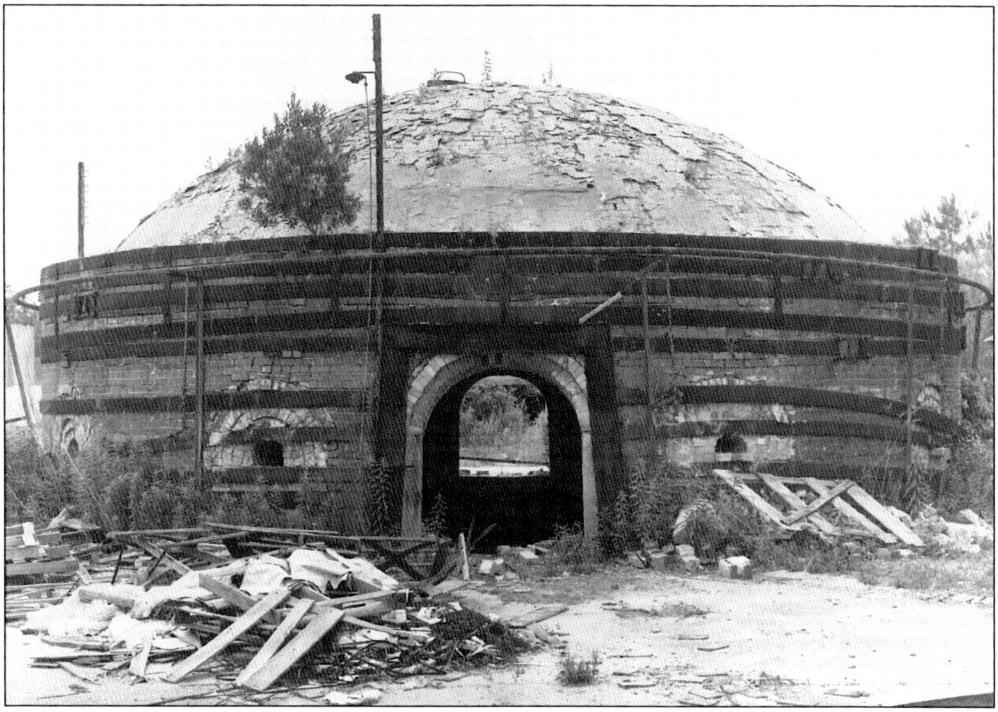

Roseboro Brick Making. This abandoned "beehive" brick kiln in the Roseboro vicinity is part of the remains of a once-extensive brickyard. Brick making was an early industry in the Roseboro area and continues to this day. (Courtesy of North Carolina Division of Archives and History.)

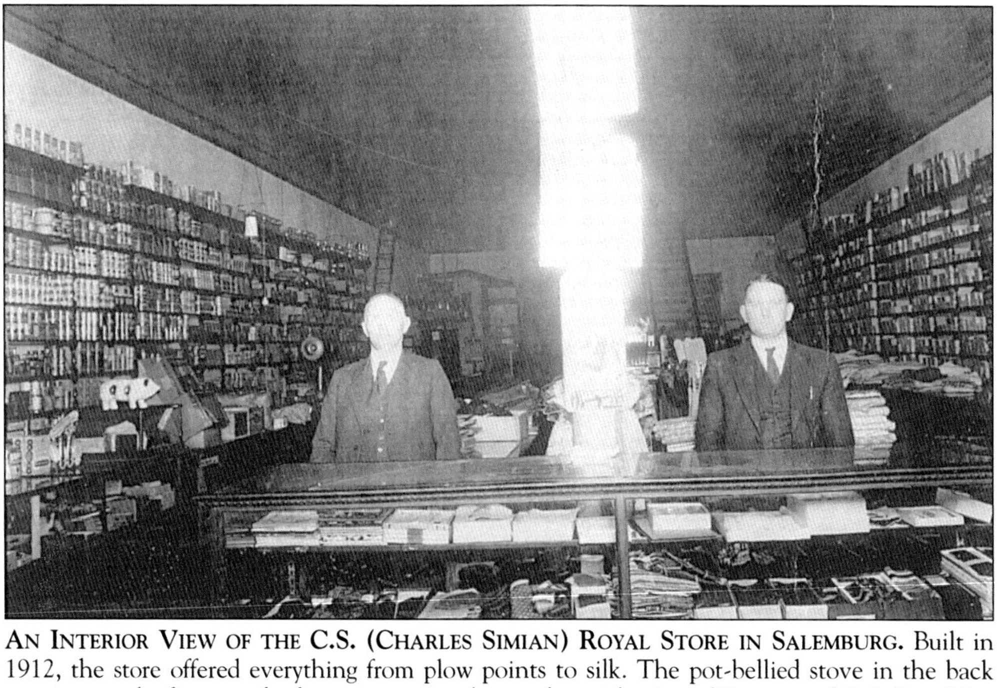

An Interior View of the C.S. (Charles Simian) Royal Store in Salemburg. Built in 1912, the store offered everything from plow points to silk. The pot-bellied stove in the back corner was a loafing spot for farmers on rainy days and at night time. (Courtesy of C.A. Royal.)

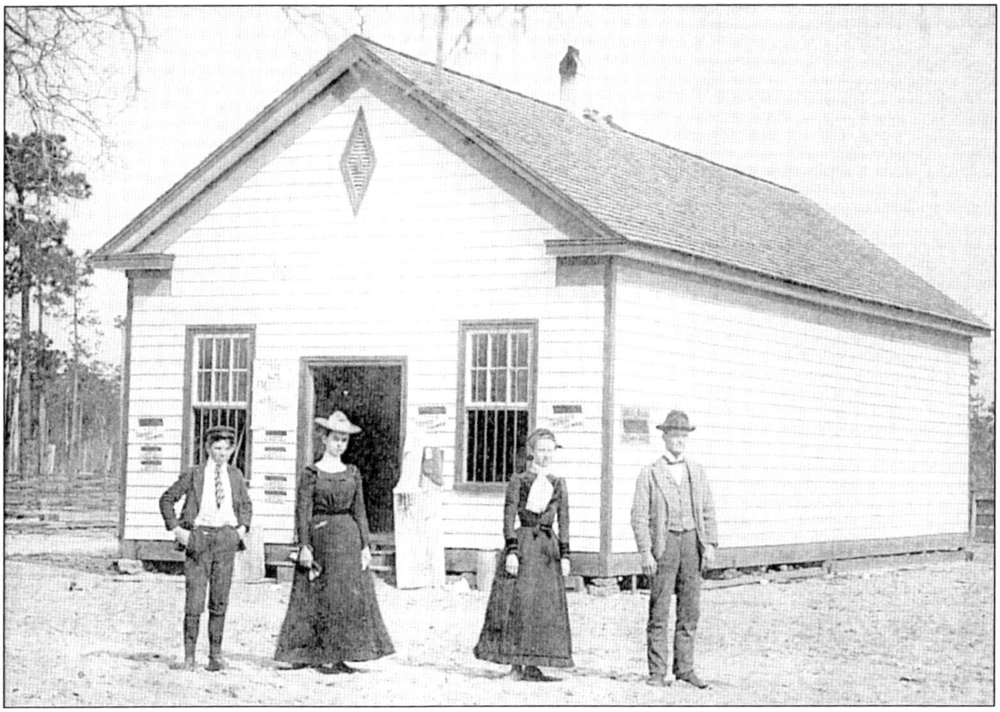

The C.S. Royal Store. The first C.S. Royal store was a small wooden structure built in Salem in 1890. Young Charles Simian Royal quit school in the seventh grade to become a shopkeeper. Later, he would add a turpentine still and a cotton gin to his business. (Courtesy of C.A. Royal.)

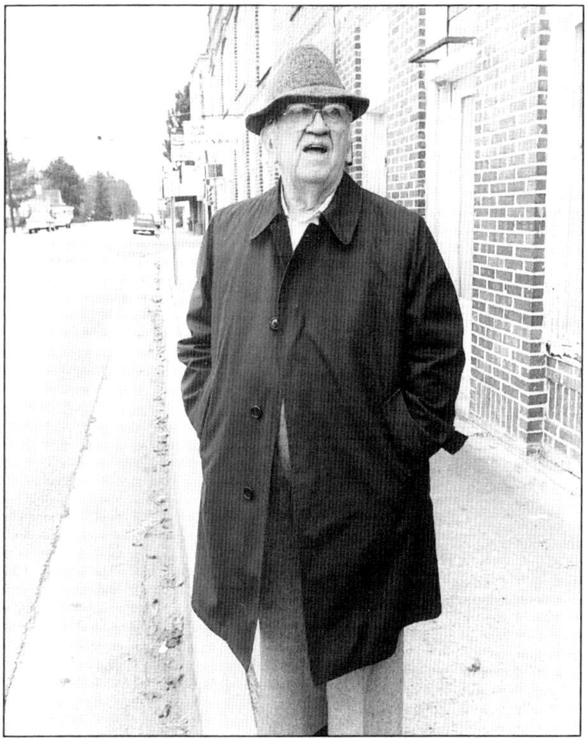

Dr. D.M. Royal, Standing by His Office on the Main Street of Salemburg. Dr. Royal was a country doctor who cared for many of Sampson's rural people. He braved mud-rutted roads and long, cold nights to deliver many of Sampson's babies. (Courtesy of Dorothy Royal.)

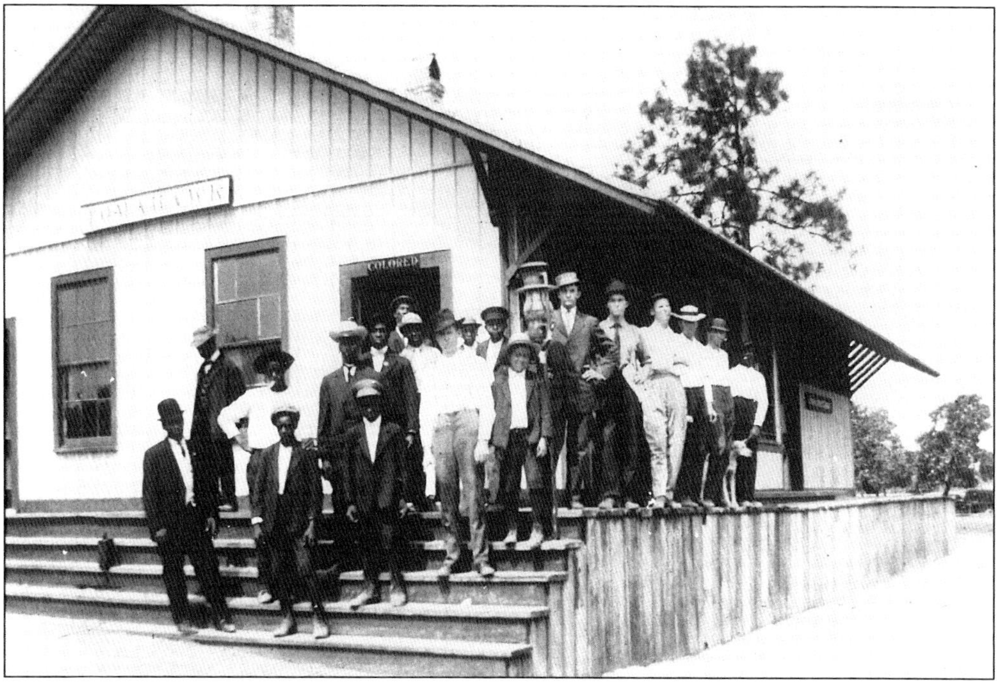

WAITING FOR THE TRAIN AT THE TOMAHAWK DEPOT, C. EARLY TWENTIETH CENTURY. Tomahawk was first called Arran by the Scottish settlers in remembrance of their beloved home, Arran Island, in the old country. (Courtesy of Sampson County History Museum, Inc.)

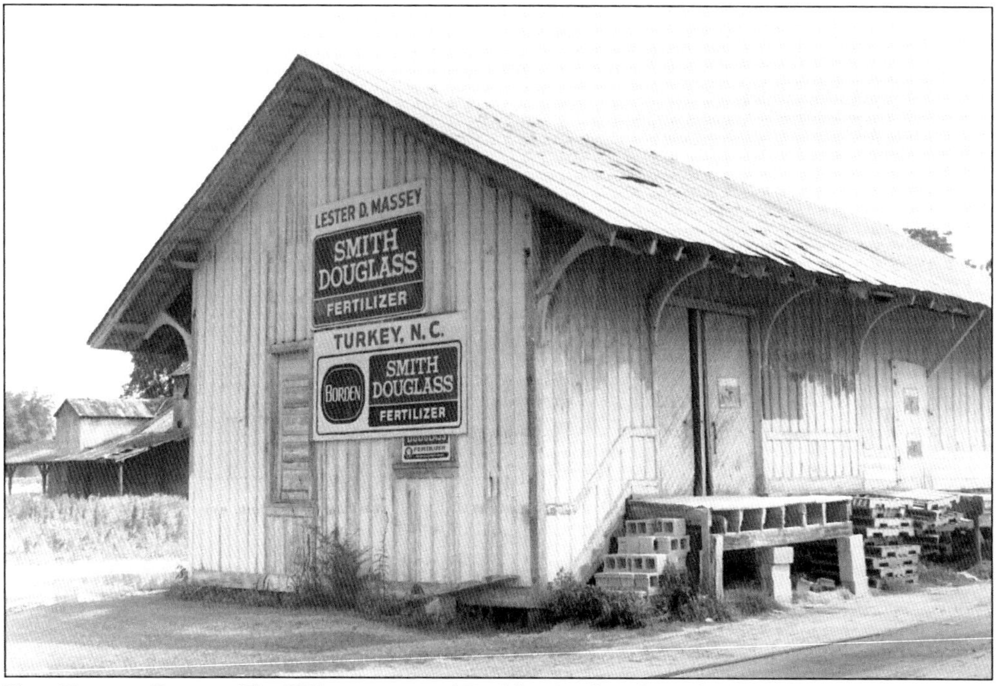

THE TURKEY DEPOT. The Wilmington and Weldon Railroad was built through Turkey around 1888 and followed the old Clinton-to-Warsaw plank road. This depot was built in 1912. (Courtesy of North Carolina Division of the Archives and History.)

Seven

Early Meetinghouses

In olden days, the meetinghouse was often the chief building in the community, and its primary purpose was to house the church. The meetinghouse often doubled as the schoolhouse, and it also served other community needs.

The circuit-riding preacher visited his assigned churches on a rotating schedule, and often preached on Saturday and Sunday while in a community. The hourglass might run through twice before the sermon concluded.

Men and women were separated in the old church. The men used the right-hand door and sat on the right side of the house. The women and children, meanwhile, used the left-hand door and sat on the left side of the house.

Before George Washington was president of the United States, the circuit-riding preachers had established churches in the backwoods of what became Sampson County. Sampson County's Rowan Baptist Church was the first Baptist church between the Neuse River and the South Carolina state line.

Many of our older citizens can vividly recall "hellfire and brimstone sermons" preached in the meetinghouse that frightened even the hard of heart. Those early meetinghouses were the beginning of the many religious groups we find in Sampson today, and did much to establish our collective values.

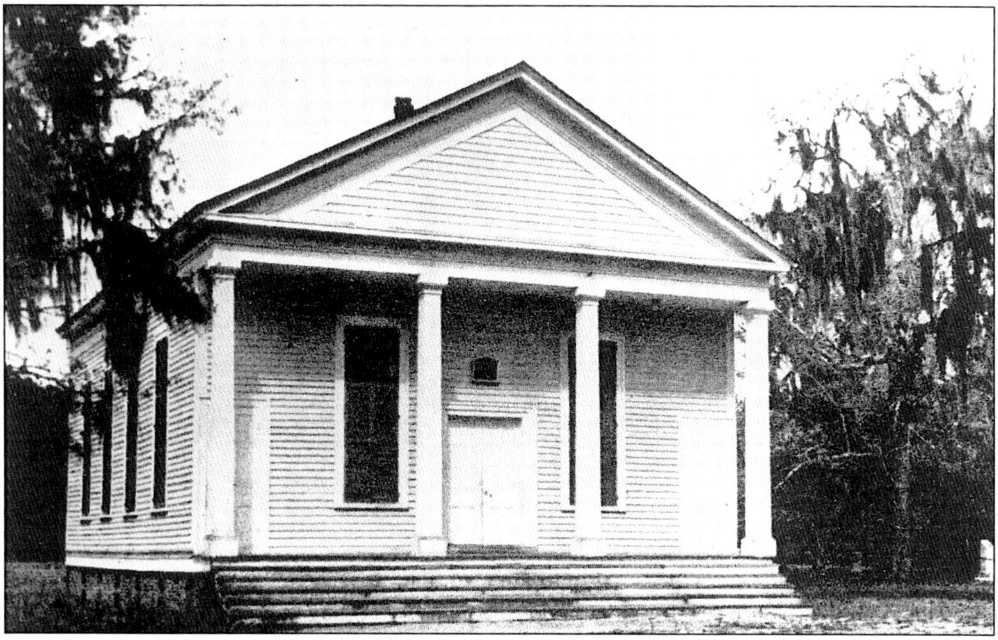

BLACK RIVER CHAPEL IN IVANHOE, 1920. Organized in 1740 as a Presbyterian church, the group's first meetinghouse was constructed of hewn logs. The third house, situated among live oaks hung with moss as seen in this 1920 photo, was built in 1859. Early sermons were preached in the Gaelic language. (Courtesy of North Carolina Division of Archives and History.)

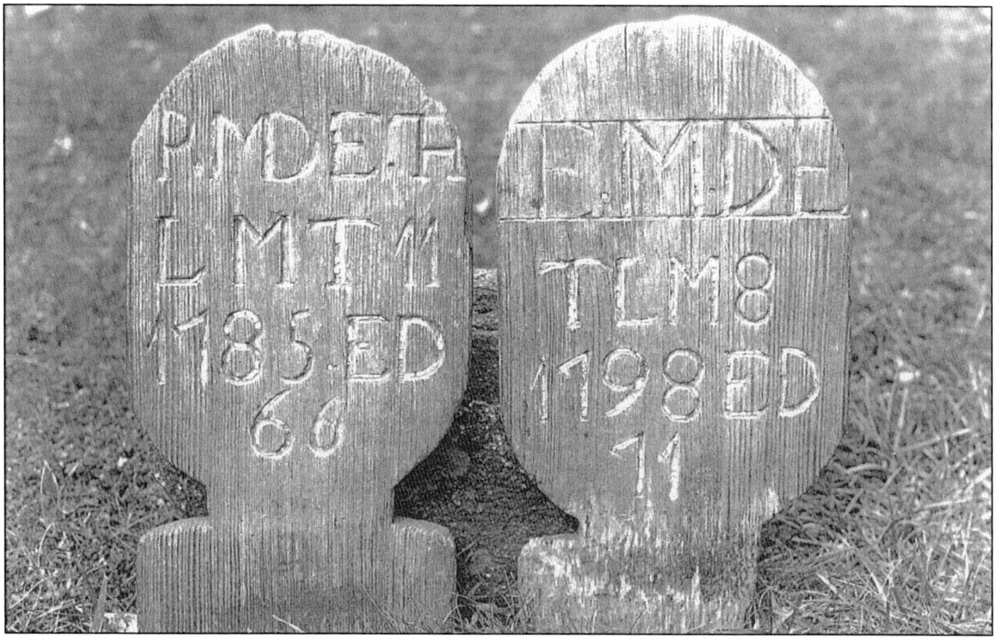

THE GRAVE MARKERS OF PATRICK AND ELIZABETH KELSO MURPHY. This pair were buried at Black River Church. The grave markers are carved from longleaf pine, and the following is the code to the markings: P(atrick) M(urphy) De(parted) H(is) L(ife) T(he) 11(th) 1785 (ag)ed 66; E(lizabeth) M(urphy) De(parted) T(his) L(ife) M(month) 8(th) 1798 (ag)ed 71. (Courtesy of Charles and Laura Murphy.)

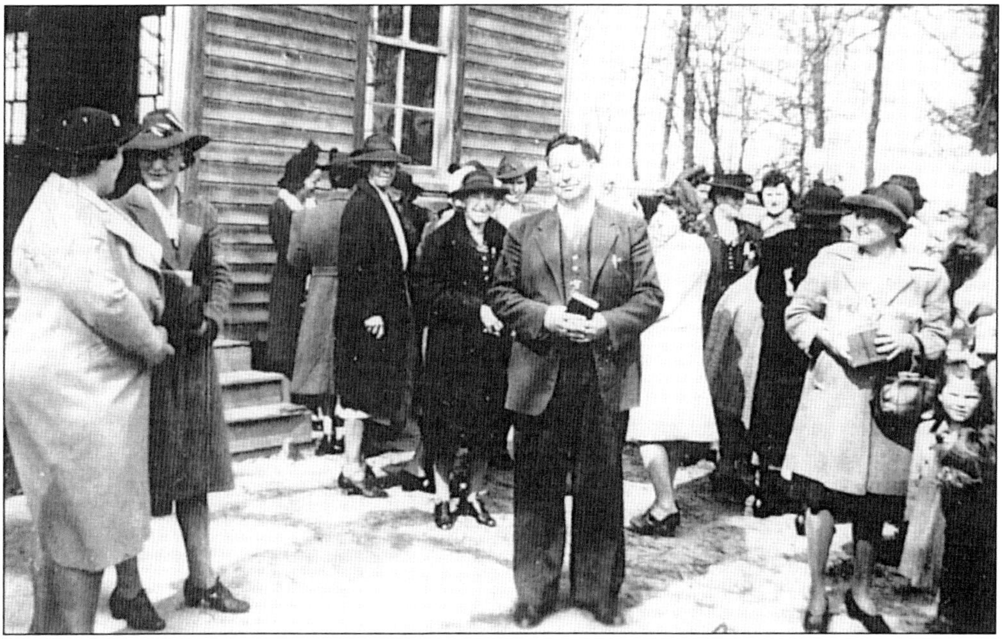

"Baptist Church at the Seven Mile Meetinghouse," Established c. 1760. The meetinghouse pictured is the group's third and was built in 1920. The preacher in the photo is Millard F. Westbrook, who, at the age of 12, was seen as a young "John the Baptist" preaching to his peers from a box pulpit. Older people spied him first, and then, as many as 500 adults flocked to hear him. The church disbanded in 1993, when only two members remained. (Courtesy of Callie Jones Hinson.)

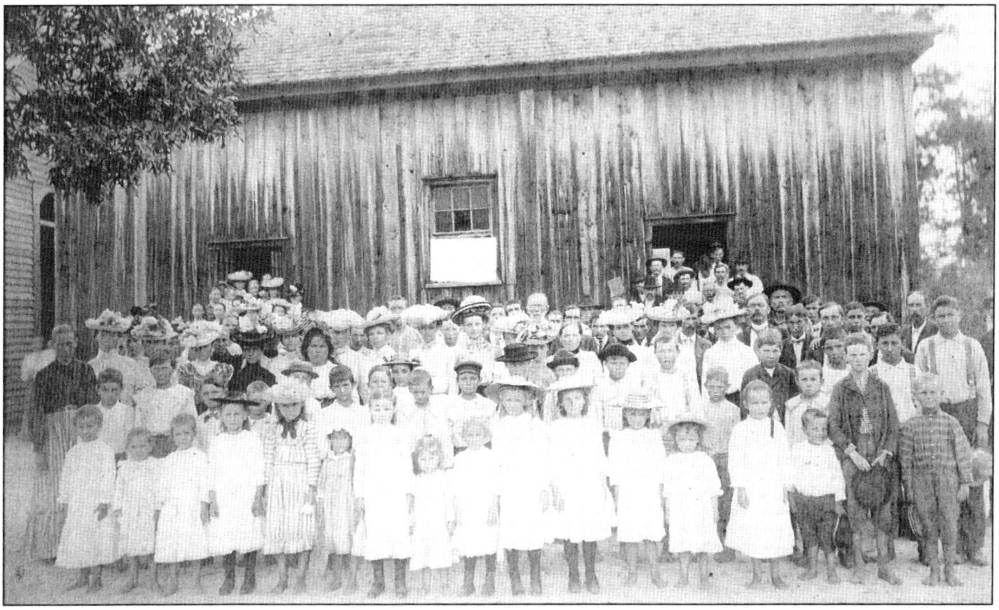

The Baptist Chapel Meetinghouse, 1901. This house was built c. 1846. Prior to the completion of this building, a log structure had served the community as the Taylor's Swamp Meetinghouse from c. 1786. Taylor Swamp Regular Baptist Church was reorganized as the Baptist Chapel Missionary Baptist Church around 1840. (Courtesy of Houston Wrench.)

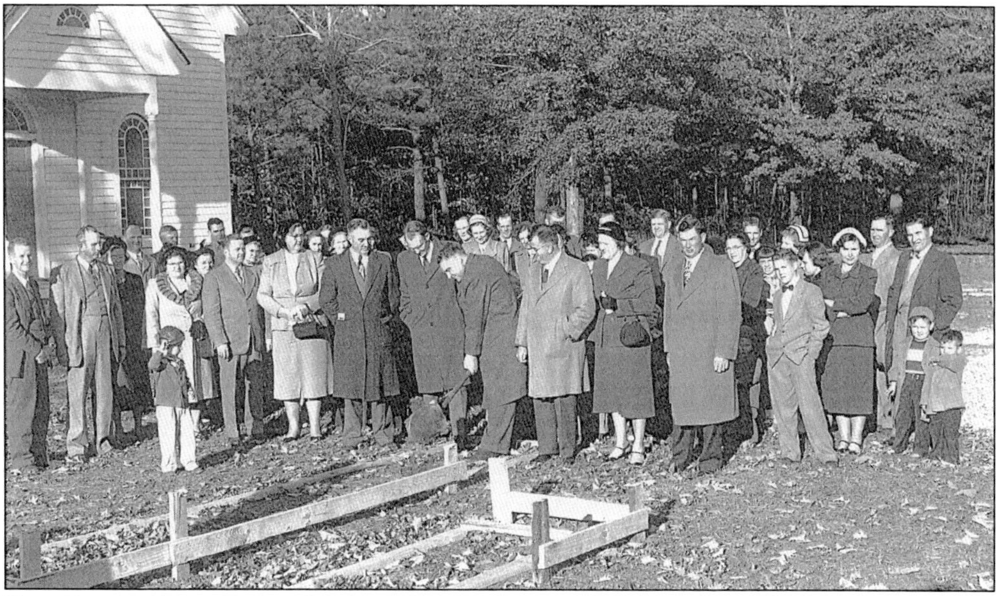

THE GOSHEN METHODIST CHURCH GROUNDBREAKING, 1952. From left to right are O.D. Parker, O.W. Darden, Mrs. C.A. Sutton, Mrs. Lillie Mae McLamb, J.G. Weeks, Mrs. H.M. Daughtry, N.L. Daughtry, Reverend Dennis Kinlaw, Reverend C.D. Barcliff, A.C. Lindsay, Mrs. I.R. Daughtry, Luby Boyette, and W.B. Sutton. (Courtesy of Janie Daughtry.)

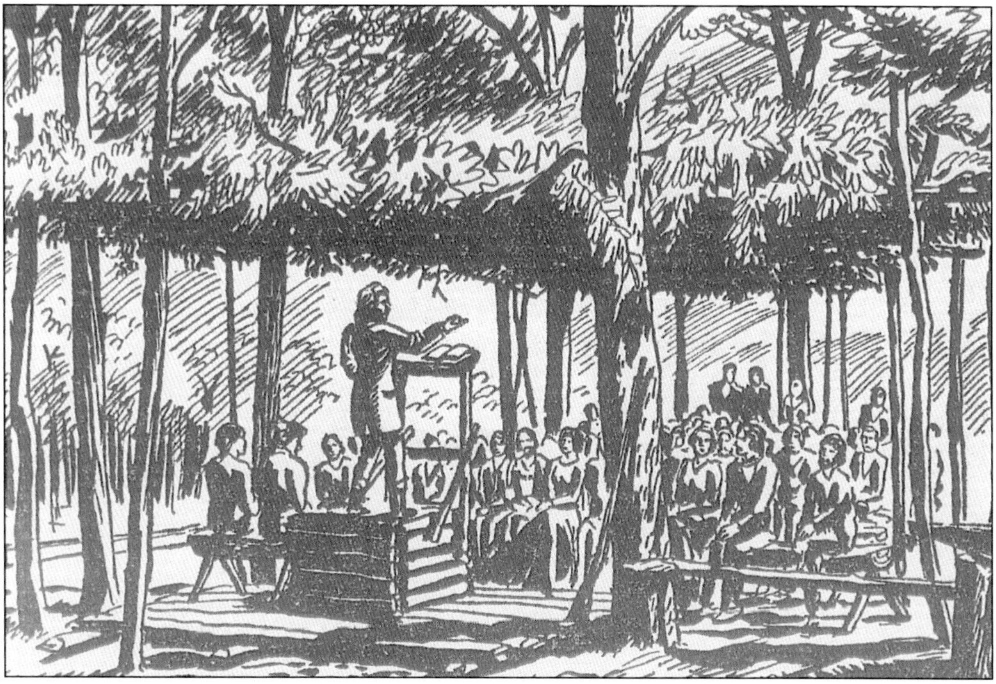

BRUSH ARBOR. A brush arbor served as a meeting place for the early Goshen Church until a log meetinghouse could be built. The concept of worshipping in a brush arbor may be rooted in scripture—(Leviticus 23:40, 42): "take the boughs of goodly trees . . . and the boughs of thick trees and willows of the brook . . . to make shelters or booths." The Goshen circuit dates from 1792. (Courtesy of Janie Daughtry.)

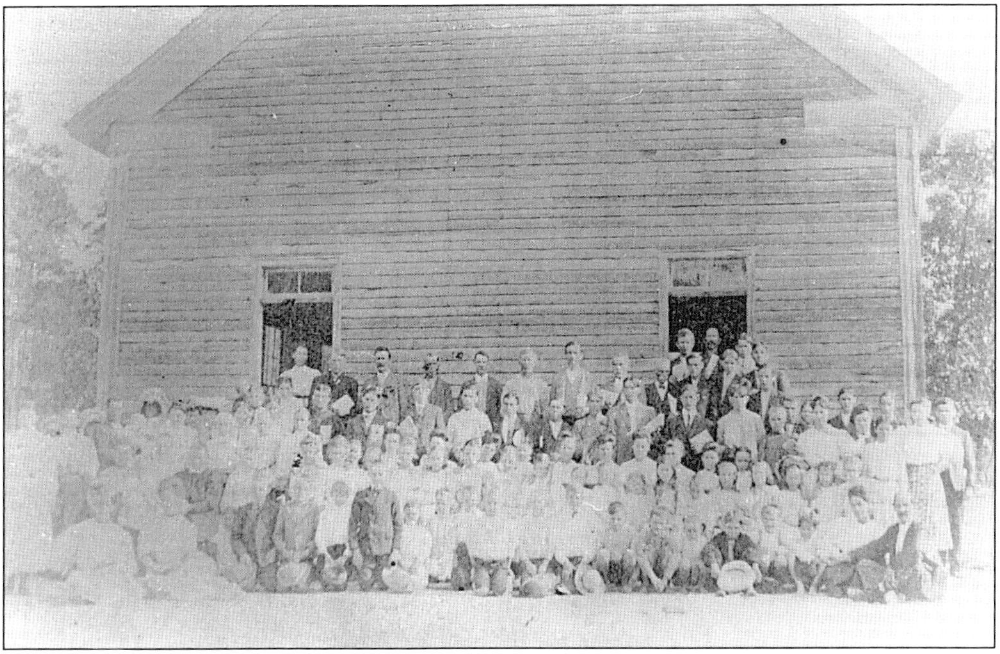

AN EARLY BAPTIST MEETINGHOUSE. Harnett was organized as a Regular Baptist Church in the late 1790s. The common school used the Harnett meetinghouse in its earliest history. (Courtesy of Clarence E. McLamb Jr.)

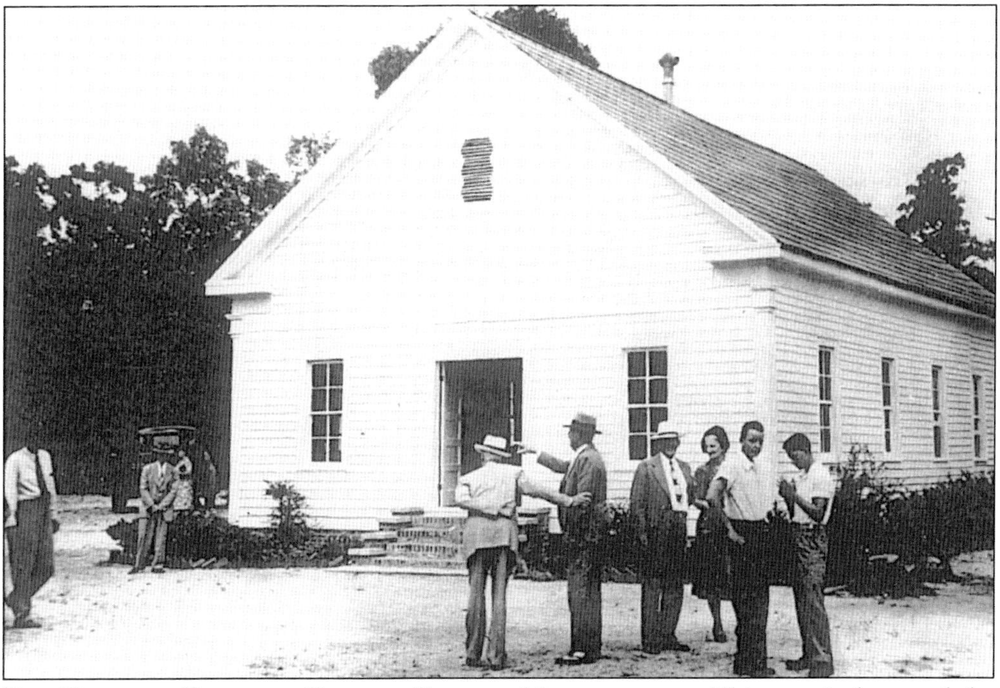

THE HARNETT PRIMITIVE BAPTIST CHURCH MEETINGHOUSE. This meetinghouse of the Harnett Primitive Church served its congregation into the 1950s. In the beginning, the members of the congregation belonged to the Regular Baptist Church, but after 1827, the order split to form the Primitive and Missionary Baptist. (Courtesy of Clarence E. McLamb Jr.)

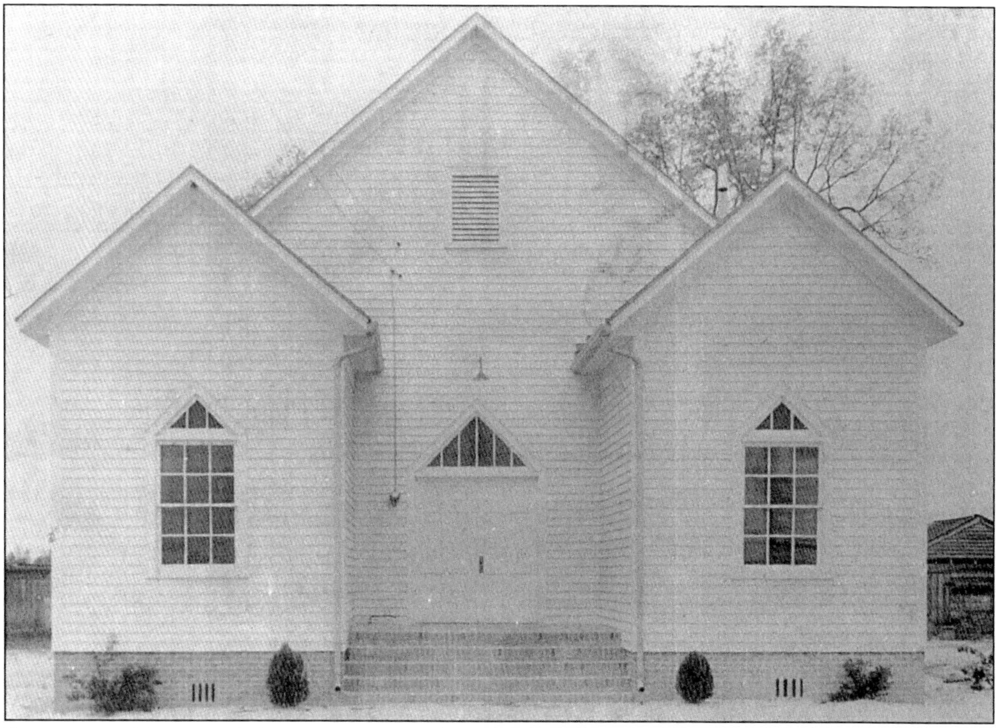

BETHESDA CHURCH MEETINGHOUSE. Bethesda is the only Quaker church in Sampson County. Pictured is the second meetinghouse, which replaced the first one built in 1880. The meetinghouse is located in the Plain View Township and was named Bethesda, meaning "place of worship." (Courtesy of Bethesda Church.)

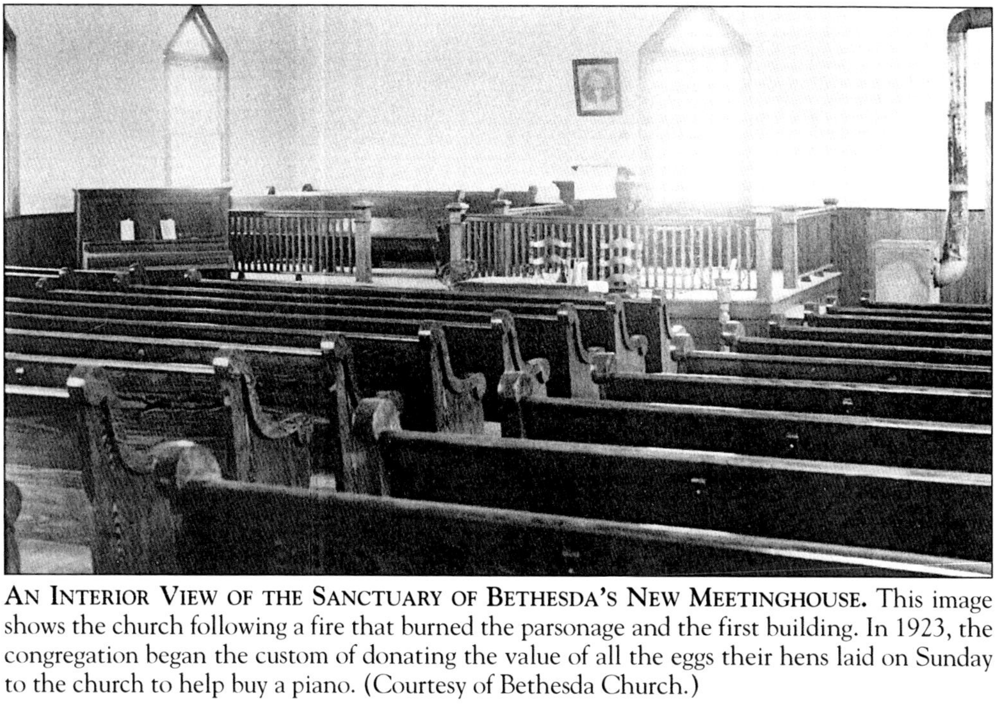

AN INTERIOR VIEW OF THE SANCTUARY OF BETHESDA'S NEW MEETINGHOUSE. This image shows the church following a fire that burned the parsonage and the first building. In 1923, the congregation began the custom of donating the value of all the eggs their hens laid on Sunday to the church to help buy a piano. (Courtesy of Bethesda Church.)

PREACHER ROB JACKSON. Jackson is credited with founding Robert's Grove Baptist Church. The Good Book he holds commanded the respect of our earlier citizens. (Courtesy of Clarence E. McLamb Jr.)

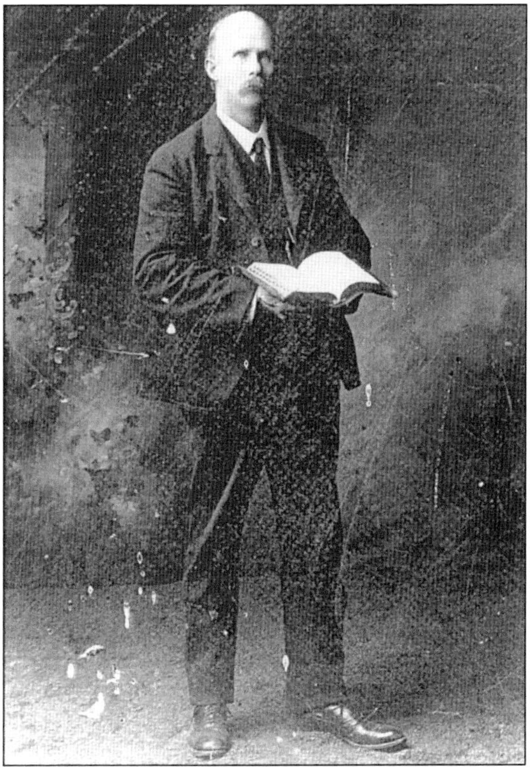

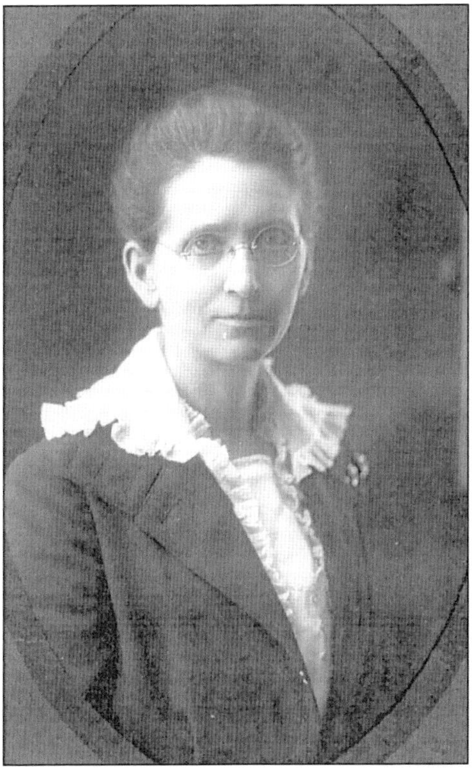

ELIA J. HOBBS. The following note was written to Elia J. Hobbs, pictured here, by her brother in Georgia on September 7, 1895: "Dear Elia, it is with much pleasure to me to be able to tender this good book. If you will read it, live it, act it and obey its teaching, God will give you a home eternal in heaven. [Signed] W.I. Hobbs." The church and the Bible had a powerful influence on early Sampson County citizens.

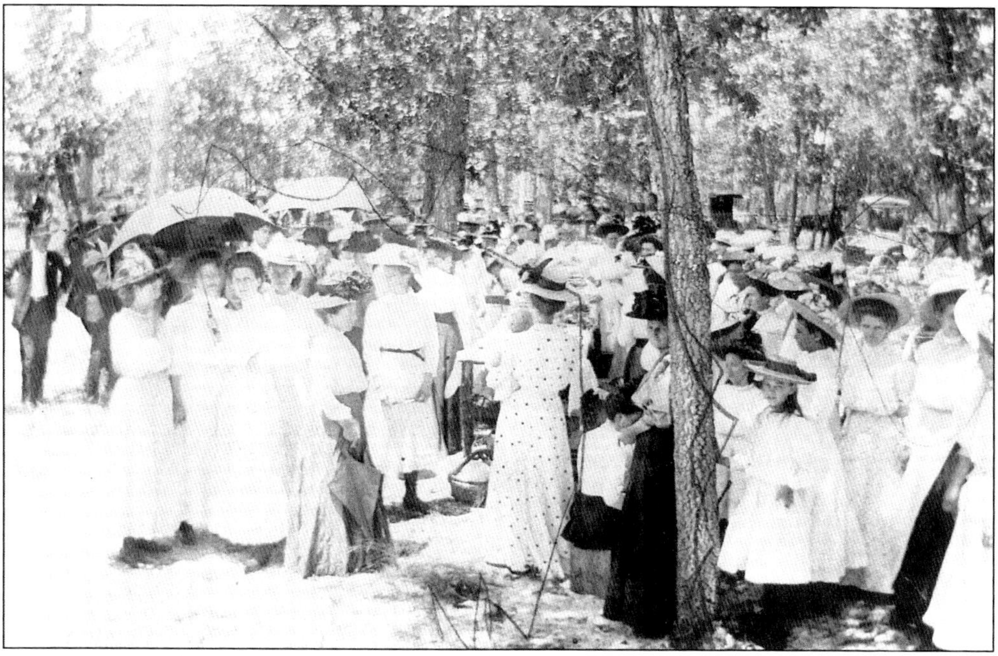

HOMECOMING. Dinner on the grounds gave little girls and ladies an opportunity to dress in their Sunday best. This scene is somewhere in lower Sampson County in the early twentieth century. (Courtesy of Sampson County History Museum, Inc.)

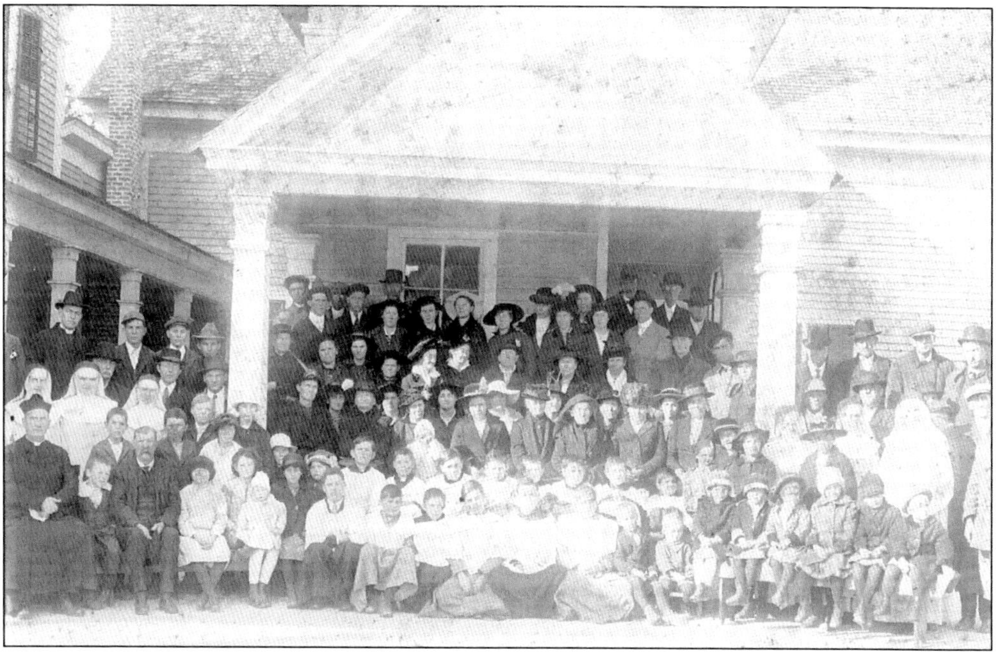

THE NEWTON GROVE CATHOLIC CHURCH, 1917. Father Irwin, seated on the extreme left in this picture, was serving St. Mark Church at this time in the history of the first Catholic church in Sampson. Dr. John Carr Monk, a Newton Grove physician, converted to Catholicism and founded the church as a result of reading a newspaper wrapper on a package. The article was titled "The True Church." (Courtesy of Albert and Ann Herring.)

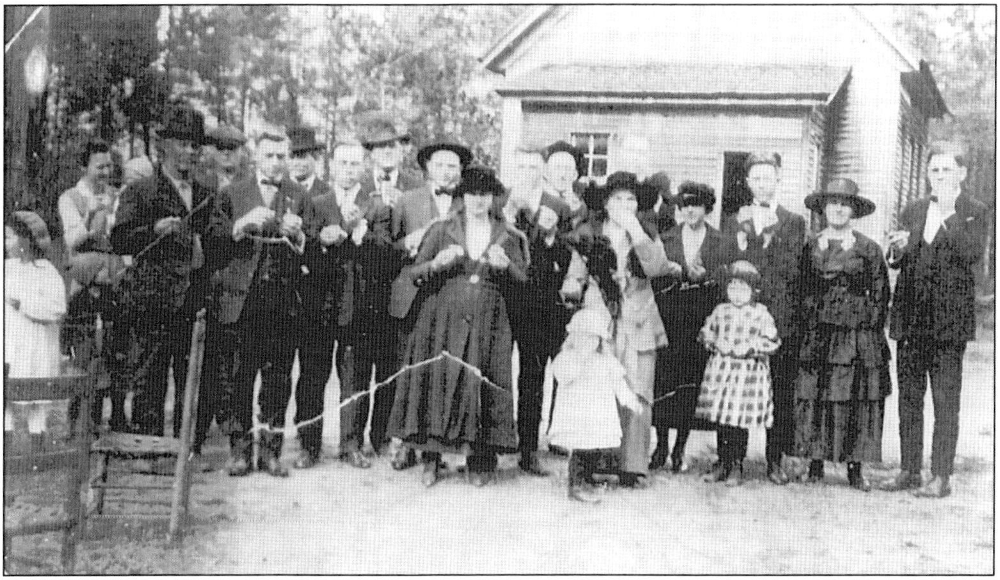

THE LATTER-DAY SAINTS (MORMON) CHAPEL, MAY 1920. This chapel was located 2 miles east of Piney Green, near the Huntley Post Office. The Crumpler Mill Pond was used by the congregation for baptismal services. (Courtesy of Jerome D. Tew.)

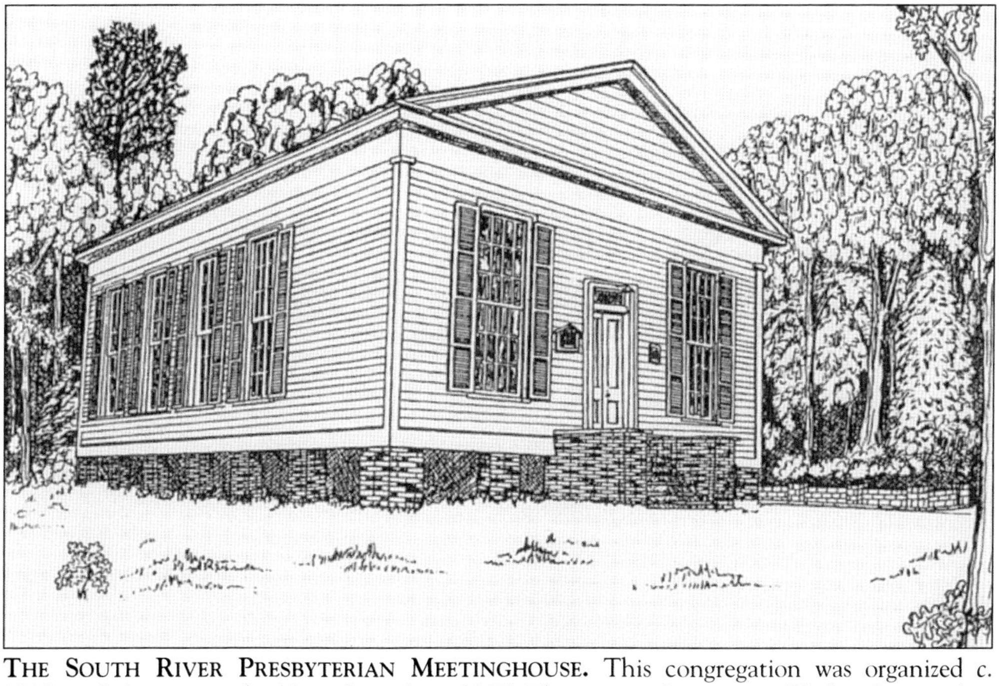

THE SOUTH RIVER PRESBYTERIAN MEETINGHOUSE. This congregation was organized c. 1795, and the present building dates from 1857. The meetinghouse is in Bladen County, but most of the churchgoers lived in the Garland vicinity of Sampson County. (Courtesy of Catherine Solan.)

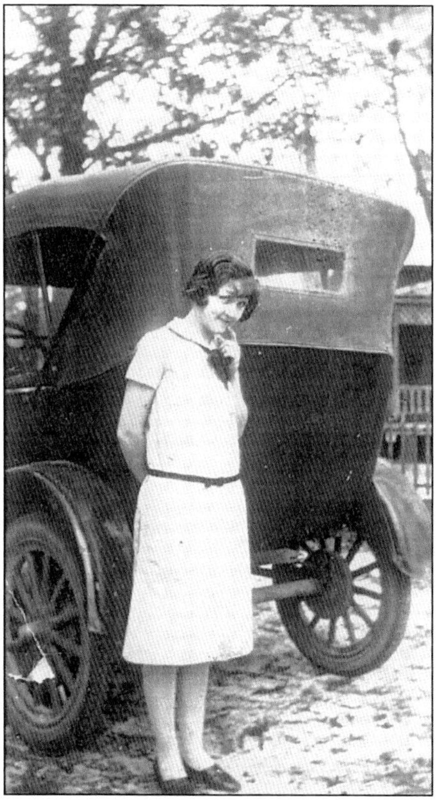

BETTY COLWELL AND HER FAMILY'S NEW CAR IN TURKEY ON A SUNDAY AFTERNOON, C. 1921. The horseless carriage began to show up at the meetinghouse in the 1920s. (Courtesy of Martha Coffield.)

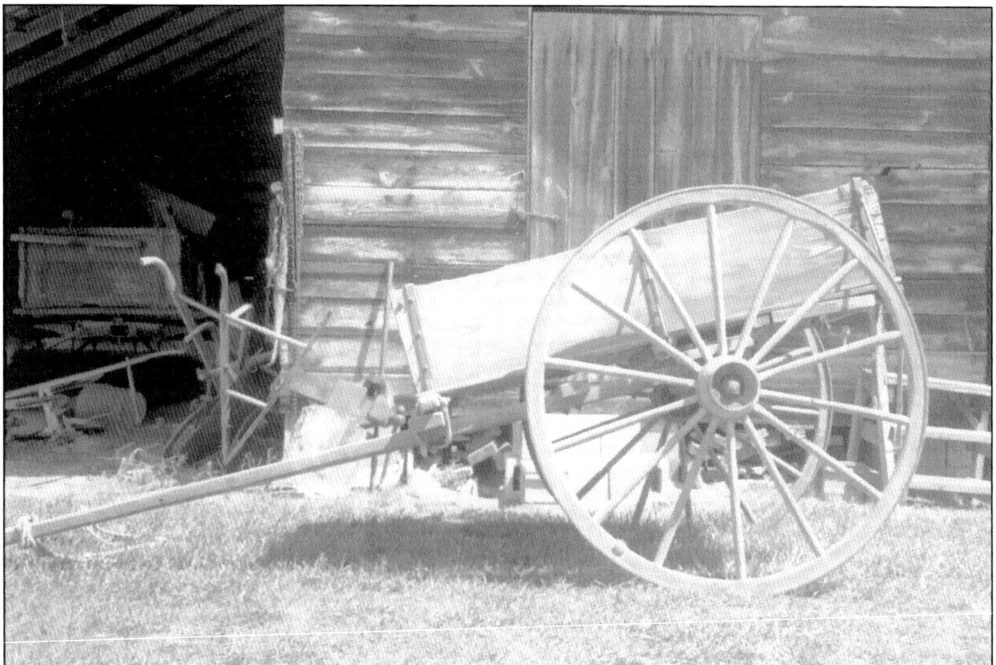

OX CART. The ox cart was one mode of transportation for our early citizens. This ox- or mule-drawn cart was a common sight at early rural worship services. (Courtesy of Houston Wrench.)

Eight

RURAL LIFE

The memories many have taken with them from the farm and their rural environment become relished mental treasures that only increase in value as the years slip by. The hardships seem to fade away and the joy and pleasures that are distilled from our memories are what remain. The ways of rural farm life have instilled special values deep into the souls of many of Sampson's children.

In 1860 Sampson's population was 16,624, and her agriculture population was estimated to be over 16,000. Rice was once a common crop in Sampson. The 1850 census listed 53 farmers as being rice farmers, and they grew 227 acres. Cotton was first grown for home use before the invention of the cotton gin. Cotton became a major crop after the cotton gin was introduced. Many farm families thought it more important for their children to pick cotton than to attend school.

Sampson County has been viewed as the huckleberry county by our neighboring counties. Earlier this century Sampson County huckleberries were shipped to our northern neighbors by rail. This enterprise sparked many humorous stories, such as Sampson folks have rings around their ankles (caused by standing in swamp water while picking huckleberries) or Sampson folks have hooks on their navels to hang the huckleberry bucket. Today we can laugh at these memories.

Most all of our citizens are closely tied to our rural beginnings and will readily identify with this chapter.

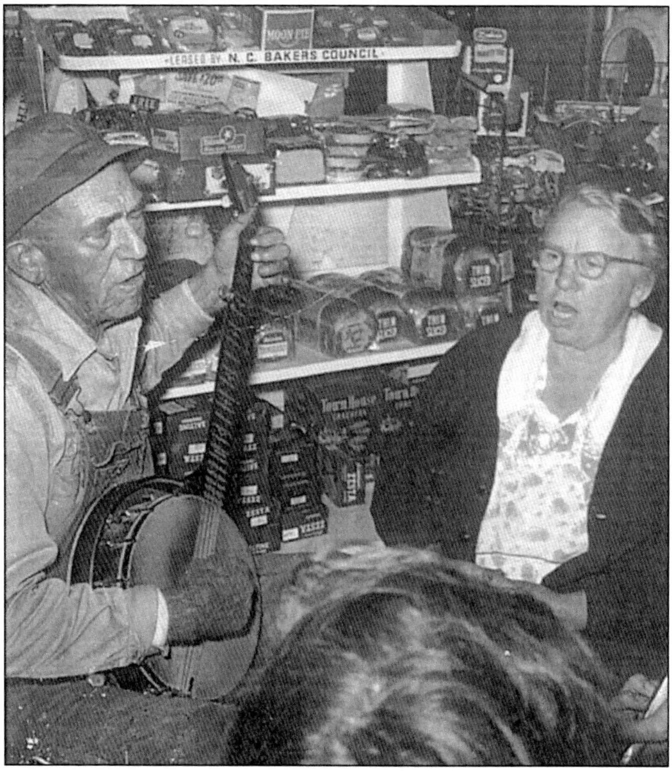

THE COUNTRY STORE. This was the gathering spot of many rural communities, the place where news and gossip were exchanged. Here, Ozzie and Nellie Carter entertain customers at the old Taylor's Bridge country store around mid-century. (Courtesy of George C. Burton.)

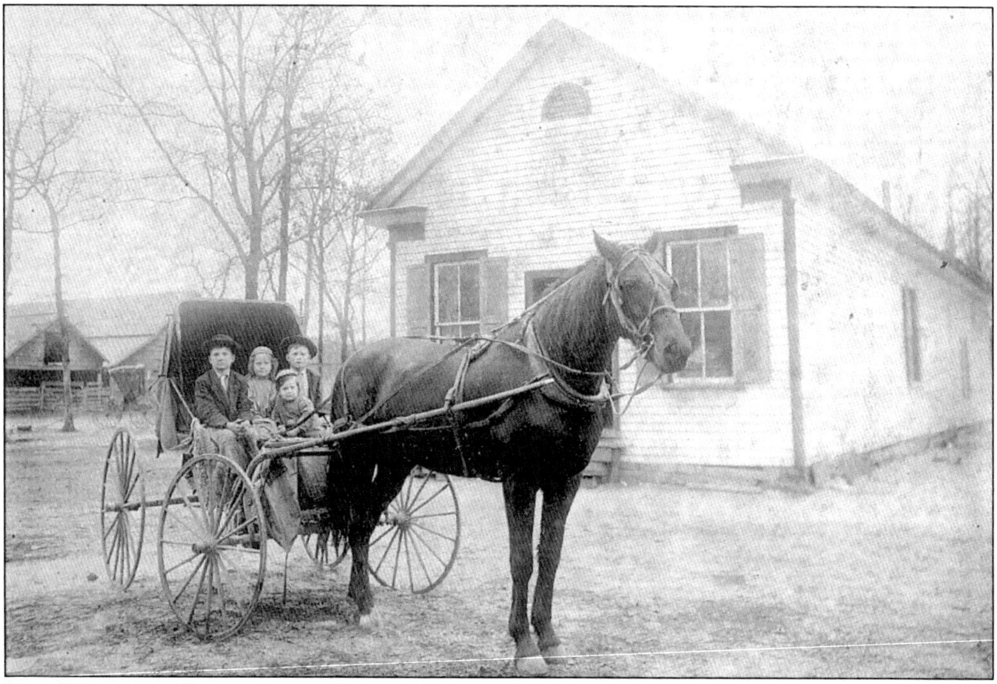

THE WILLIAMS CHILDREN IN FRONT OF THE RURAL STORE OF J.T. WILLIAMS IN MINGO TOWNSHIP. Williams was a dealer in general merchandise, country produce, cotton, standard fertilizers, and manufactured naval stores. (Courtesy of Tom Williams.)

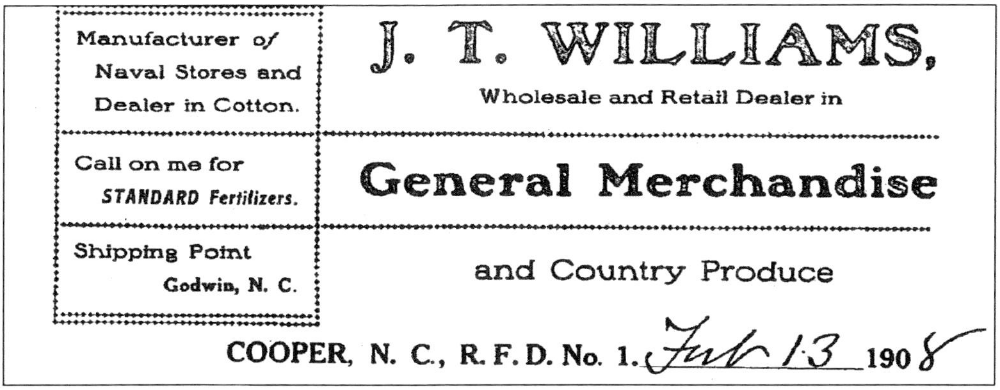

Manufacturer of Naval Stores and Dealer in Cotton.

Call on me for STANDARD Fertilizers.

Shipping Point Godwin, N. C.

J. T. WILLIAMS,

Wholesale and Retail Dealer in

General Merchandise

and Country Produce

COOPER, N. C., R. F. D. No. 1. Feb 13 1908

A 1908 LOGO. This logo demonstrates the importance of the country store to rural communities earlier in the twentieth century. Merchandise was shipped to Godwin Station by rail and was then hauled 8 miles by mule and wagon to the store. (Courtesy of Troy Wrench.)

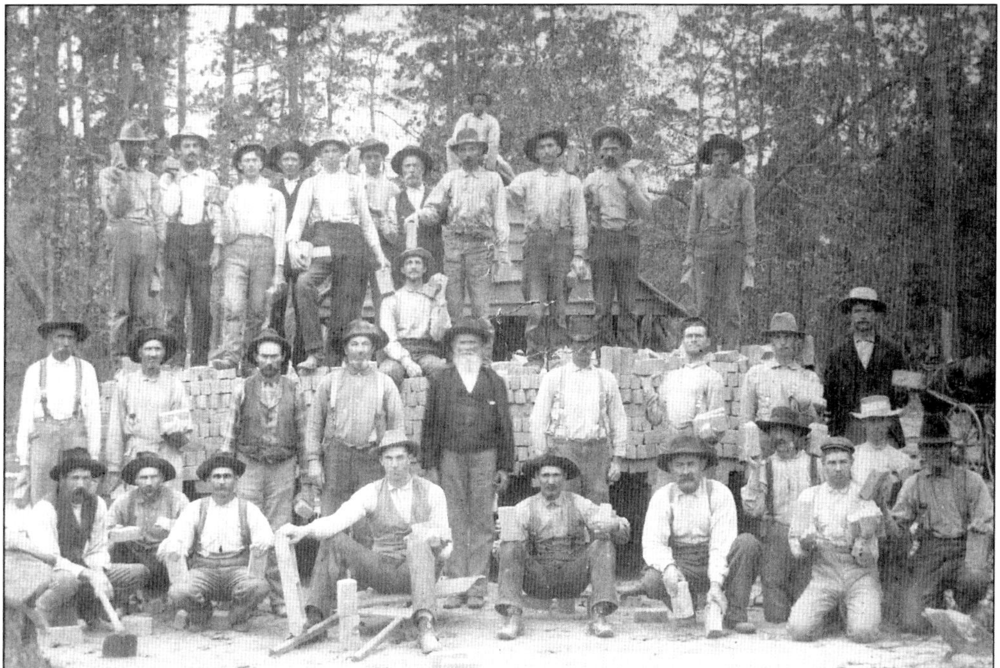

BRICK MAKERS AT THE OLD HERRING POST OFFICE (VANN'S CROSS ROADS). From left to right are the following: (front row) Henry Parsons, Budd McLamb, Jim Jones, Adam Butler, Walt Parsons, Joel Jones, Preston Murphy, Edgar McLamb, Albert Carter, and B. Parsons; (middle row) Robert W. Jones, George Keen, Elijah Bennett, George Jones, Henry Daughtry, Bob Carter, Bonnie Warwick, Foy Best, and Ammie Best; (back row) Monroe Parsons, Laudie Jones, Alpheus Warrick, Gardner Parsons, Gaston Butler, Atlas Carter, B. Best, Allie Parsons, Marion Keen, Daniel Keen, John Keen, and Jim Hairr. (Courtesy of Callie Jones Hinson.)

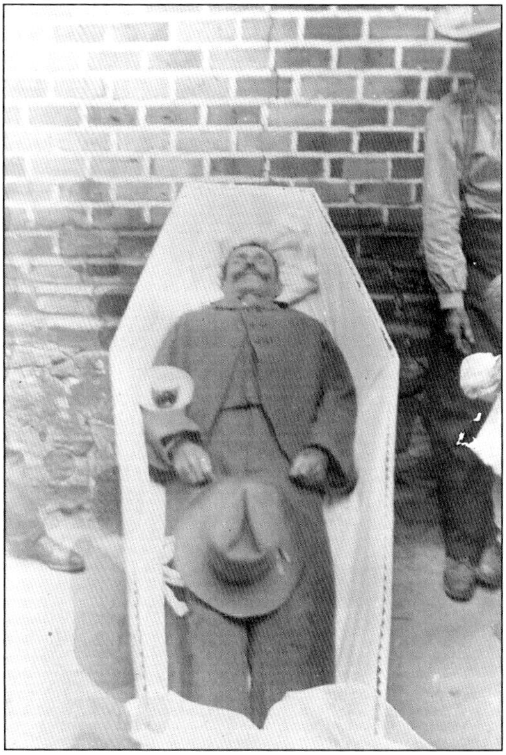

Joel William Wrench. A veteran of the War Between the States, Wrench died in 1915. Anner, his daughter-in-law, laid his body out on the porch and prepared it for burial. Wrench's sons Frank and Claude built the coffin. The funeral services were conducted at the home place, and the body was hauled by mule and wagon to the family burial plot. Wrench's coffee cup, resting on his arm, was buried with him. (Courtesy of Myrtle Honeycutt Page.)

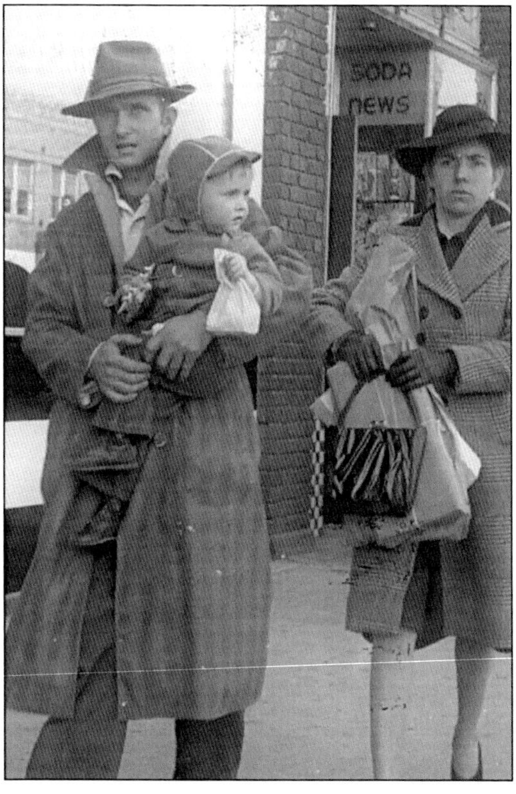

Alton, Mildred, and Ray Page on a Saturday Shopping Trip to Fayetteville, 1940. Many Sampson County farm families traded eggs, butter, a side of meat, or other items for supplies when they went into town. (Courtesy of Mildred Page.)

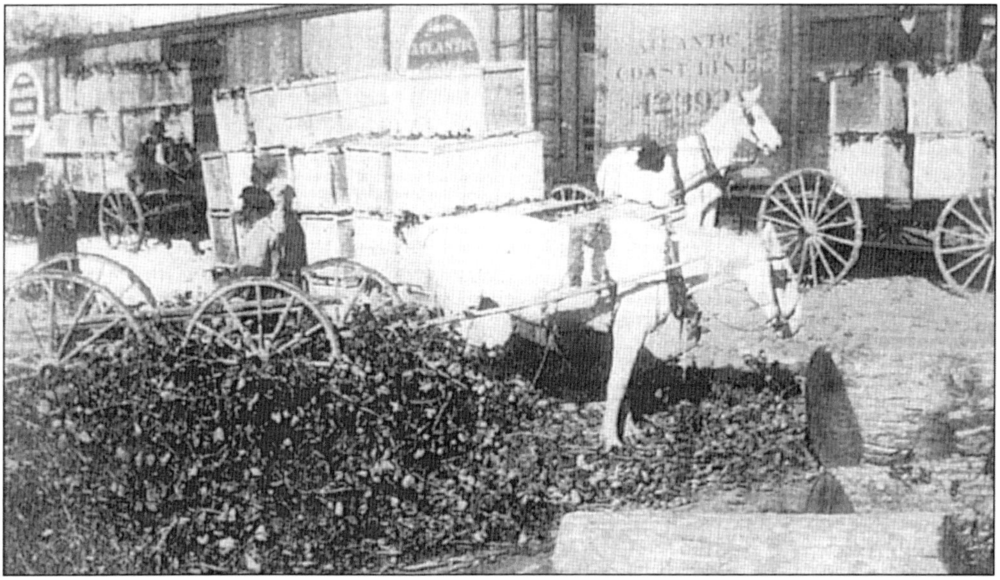

R.H. MELVIN BROTHERS. R.H. Melvin Brothers of Harrells Store expanded their horse- and mule-trading business to also deal in the holly business. Carloads of packaged holly were shipped to the J.H.G. Atkinson Co. of New York in the early days of the twentieth century. (Courtesy of Lela Harrell.)

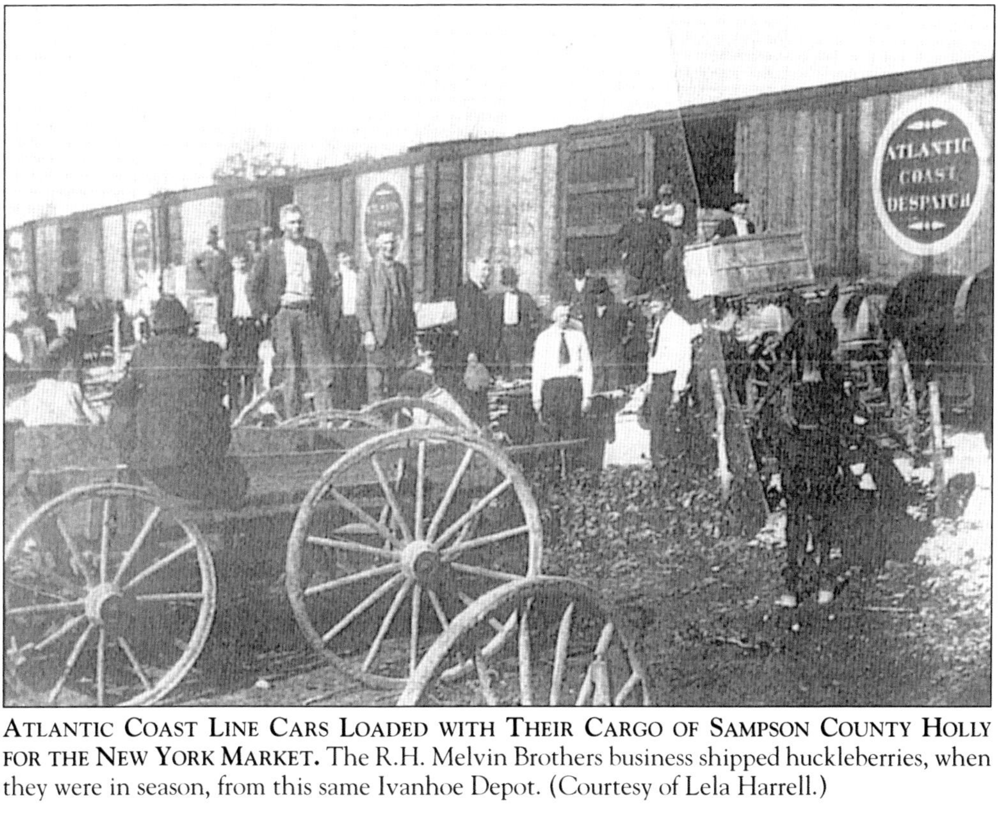

ATLANTIC COAST LINE CARS LOADED WITH THEIR CARGO OF SAMPSON COUNTY HOLLY FOR THE NEW YORK MARKET. The R.H. Melvin Brothers business shipped huckleberries, when they were in season, from this same Ivanhoe Depot. (Courtesy of Lela Harrell.)

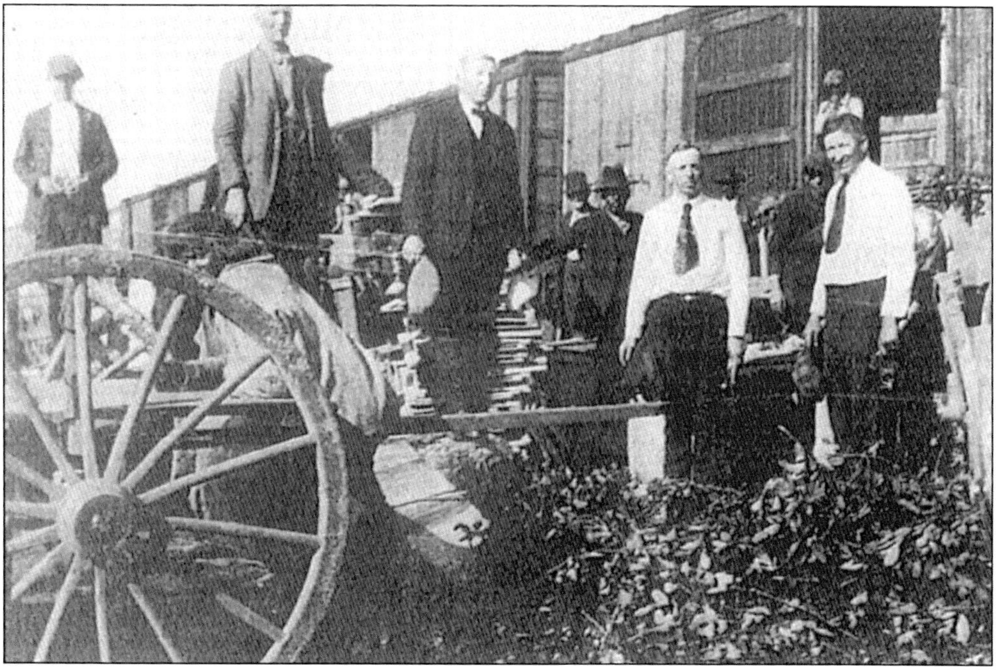

THE MELVIN BROS. Raymond Melvin is pictured here second from the right. The Melvin brothers survived the bank closing of 1929 and the Great Depression because their payment for the holly shipments had not been deposited in the bank before the crash. (Courtesy of Lela Harrell.)

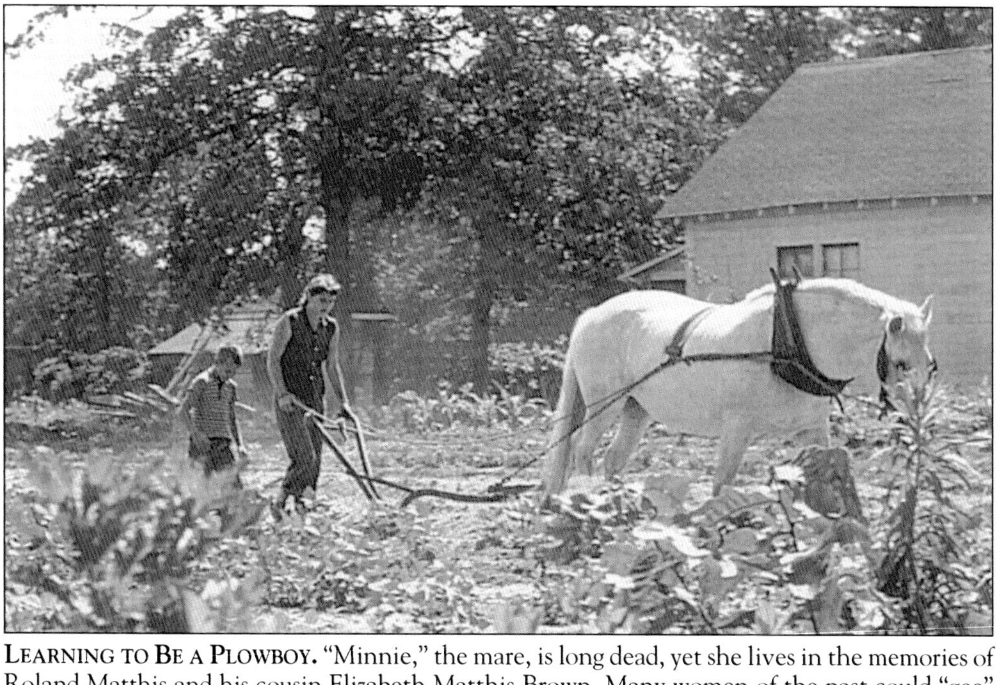

LEARNING TO BE A PLOWBOY. "Minnie," the mare, is long dead, yet she lives in the memories of Roland Matthis and his cousin Elizabeth Matthis Brown. Many women of the past could "gee" and "haw" the horse or mule as well as any man. This picture was taken in 1948. (Courtesy of George C. Burton.)

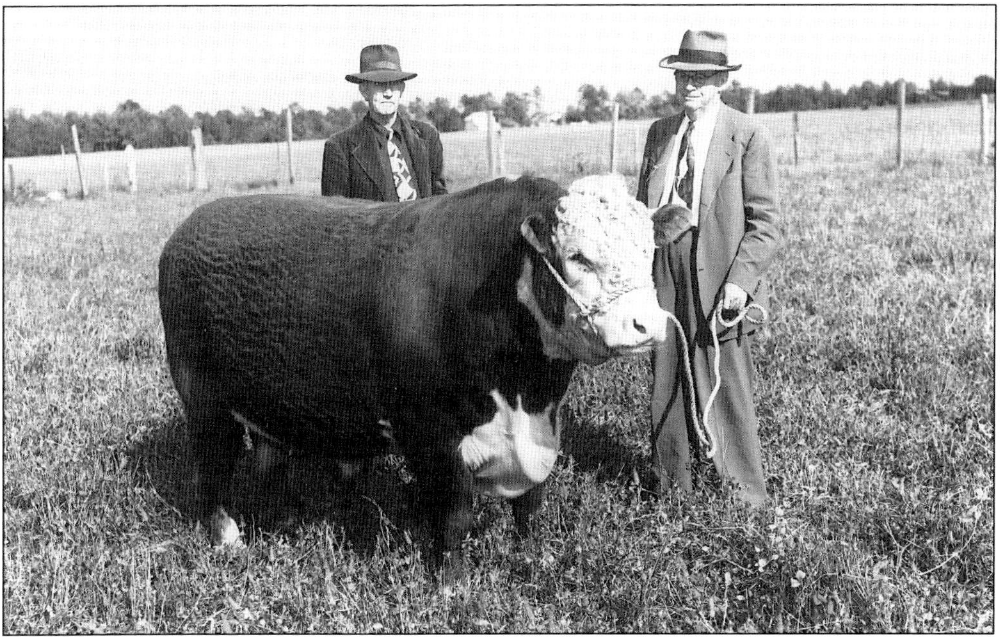

North Carolina State Senator Henry Vann (Right) on His Farm with County Agent E.J. Morgan, c. 1949. The Vann farm is located near the old Herring High School. (Courtesy of George Upton.)

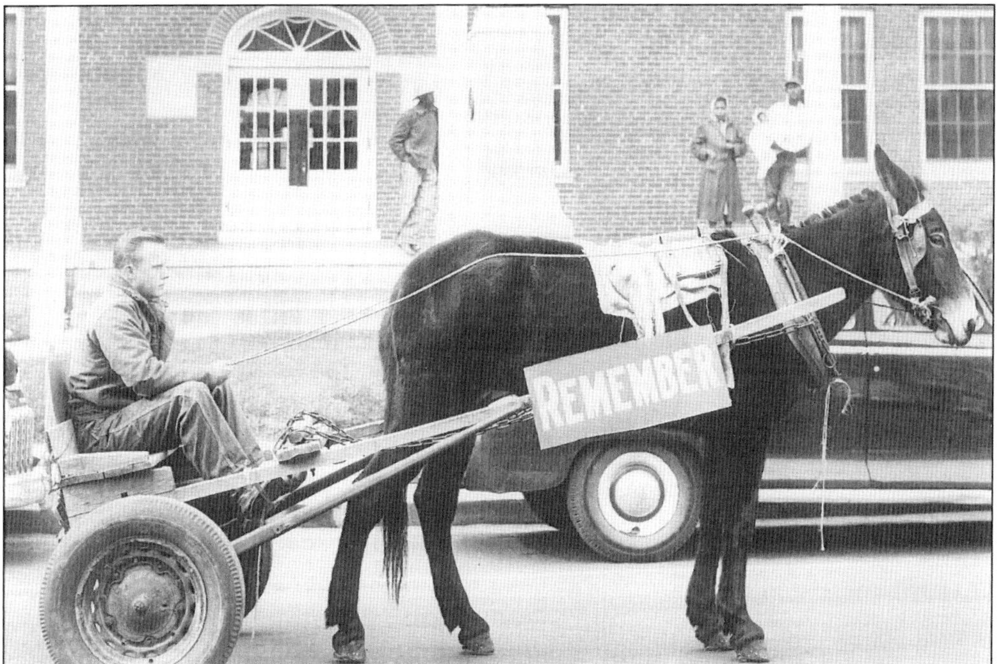

The Hoover Cart. In 1947, the mule plowed on the weekdays and pulled the Hoover Cart on Sundays. The cart was built from the rear end of the family car, which was parked during the Depression because of a shortage of money and gasoline. (Courtesy of Sampson County History Museum, Inc.)

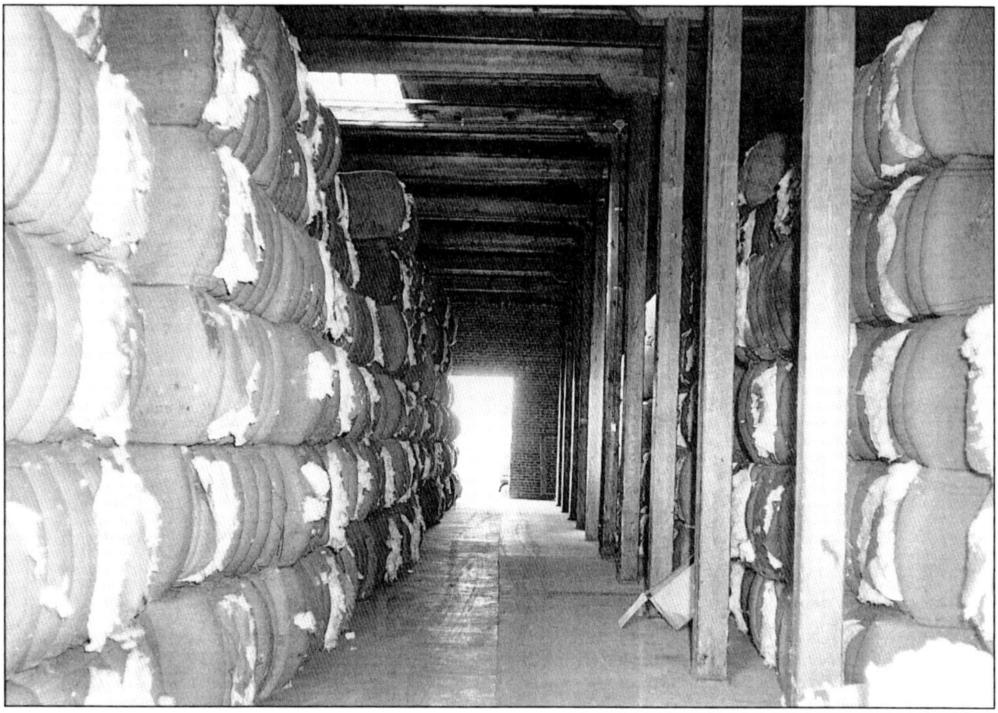

SAMPSON COUNTY COTTON STORED IN A CLINTON WAREHOUSE, 1950S. Cotton was once a major crop of lower Sampson County. (Courtesy of Clinton Area Chamber of Commerce.)

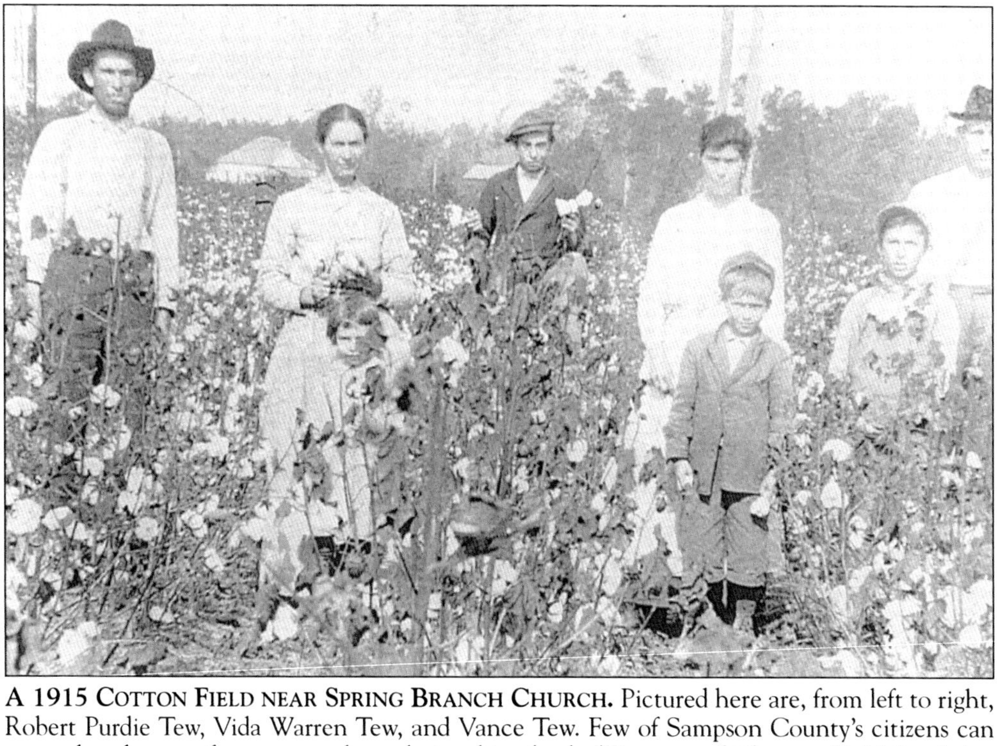

A 1915 COTTON FIELD NEAR SPRING BRANCH CHURCH. Pictured here are, from left to right, Robert Purdie Tew, Vida Warren Tew, and Vance Tew. Few of Sampson County's citizens can remember the tug of a cotton sack on their aching back. (Courtesy of Clarence E. McLamb.)

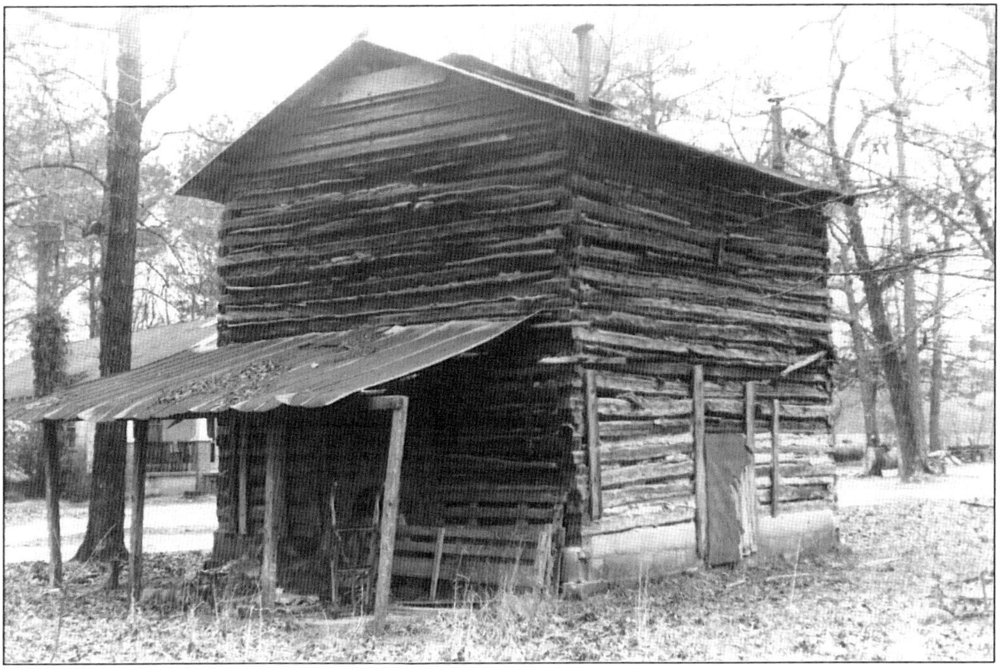

A Sampson Log Tobacco Barn. This barn is one of hundreds of tobacco barns that have dotted the rural landscape of Sampson County's vanishing past. The scene also hints at the role tobacco played in the past century. (Courtesy of North Carolina Division of Archives and History.)

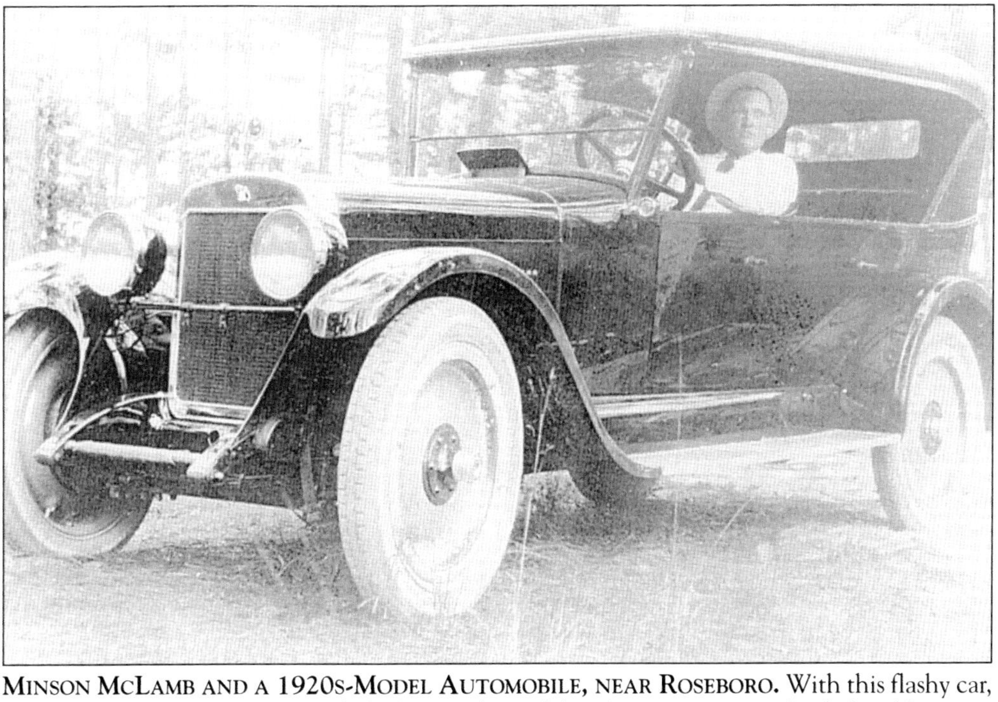

Minson McLamb and a 1920s-Model Automobile, near Roseboro. With this flashy car, McLamb courted many a young lady, but in the end, he chose to remain a bachelor. (Courtesy of Clarence E. McLamb Jr.)

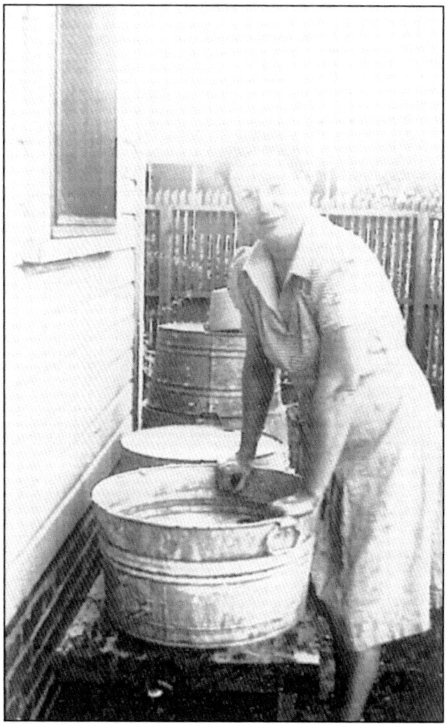

ELEMN WARWICK BASS BISHOP ON A WASH DAY, 1936. Before the age of washing machines, wash day started with a fire around the wash-pot to boil the hard-to-clean items. The scrub board and lye soap were close by. (Courtesy of Joyce Bass Binkley.)

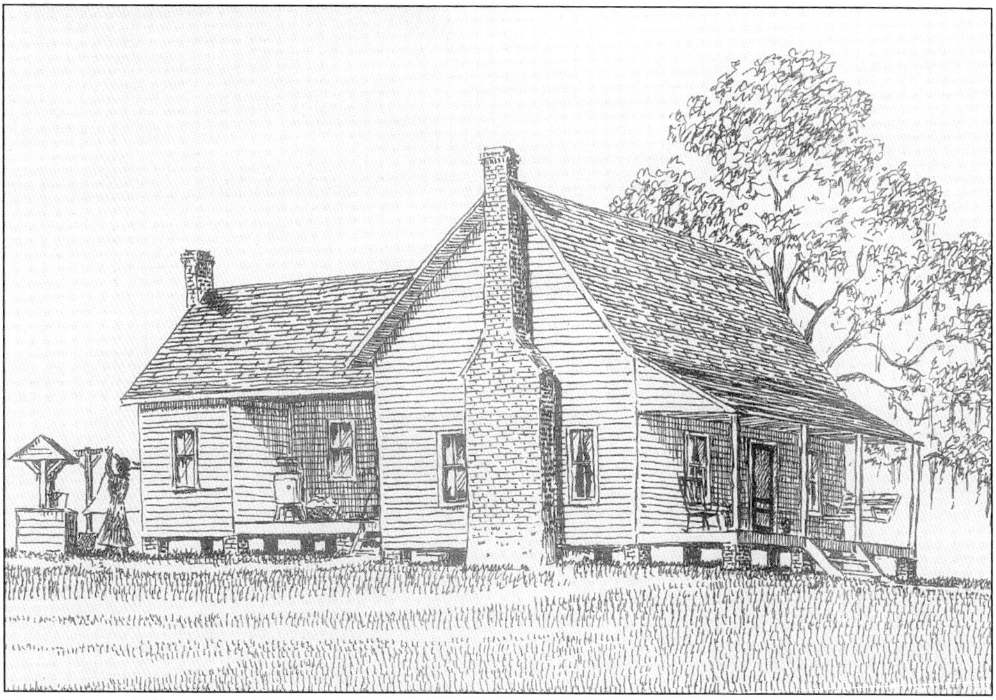

THE JAMES WARWICK HOUSE. Located in the Newton Grove vicinity, the Warwick house was built in the early 1800s and torn down around 1995. It was constructed with wooden pegs. Mondays were wash days on most farms in Sampson County back in the days of our grandmothers. (Courtesy of Joyce Bass Binkley.)

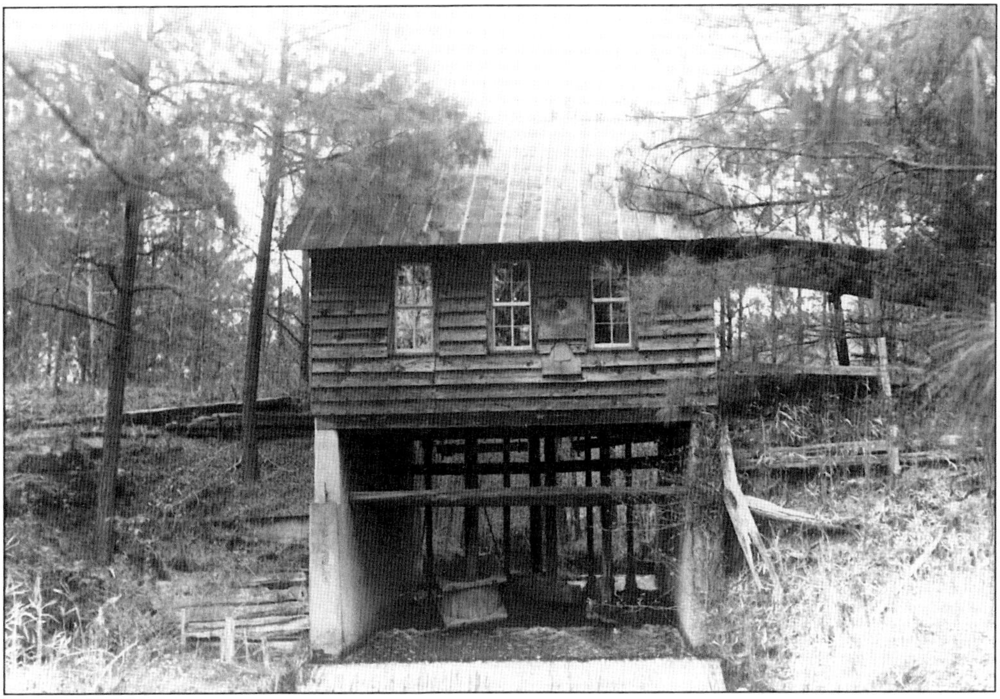

Vann-Boney Mill in the Taylors Bridge Vicinity. This mill was rebuilt in the early 1930s on the site of a previous mill, which dated to around 1800. The mill was last in operation in 1956 and had ground grain for five generations before the mill stones became silent. (Courtesy of North Carolina Division of Archives and History.)

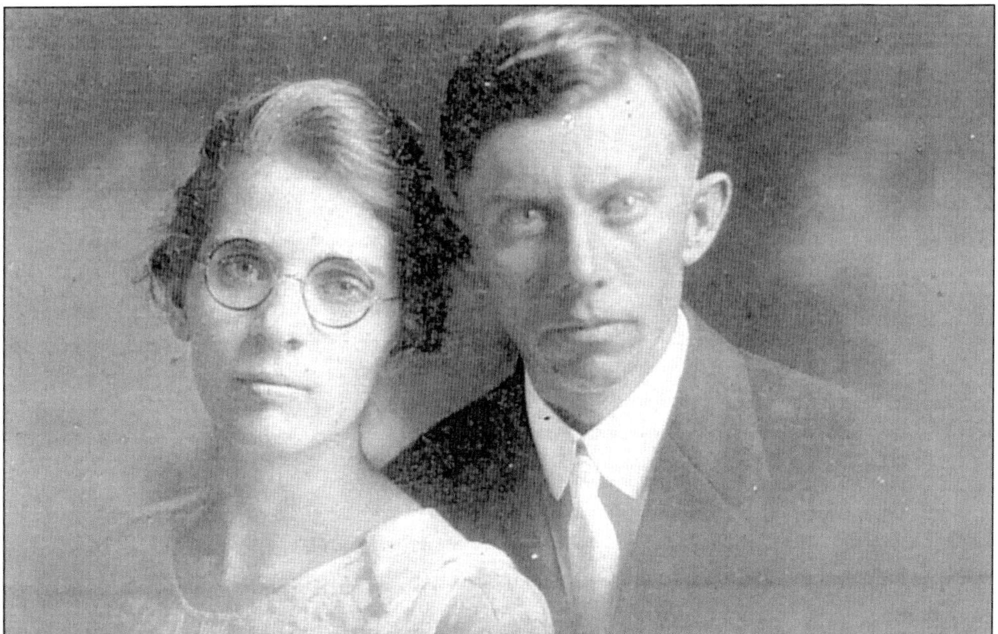

The Boneys. Matt and Elizabeth Boney purchased the Vann-Boney Mill from Hugh Vann in 1934 and operated it until 1956. (Courtesy of Roland E. Matthis.)

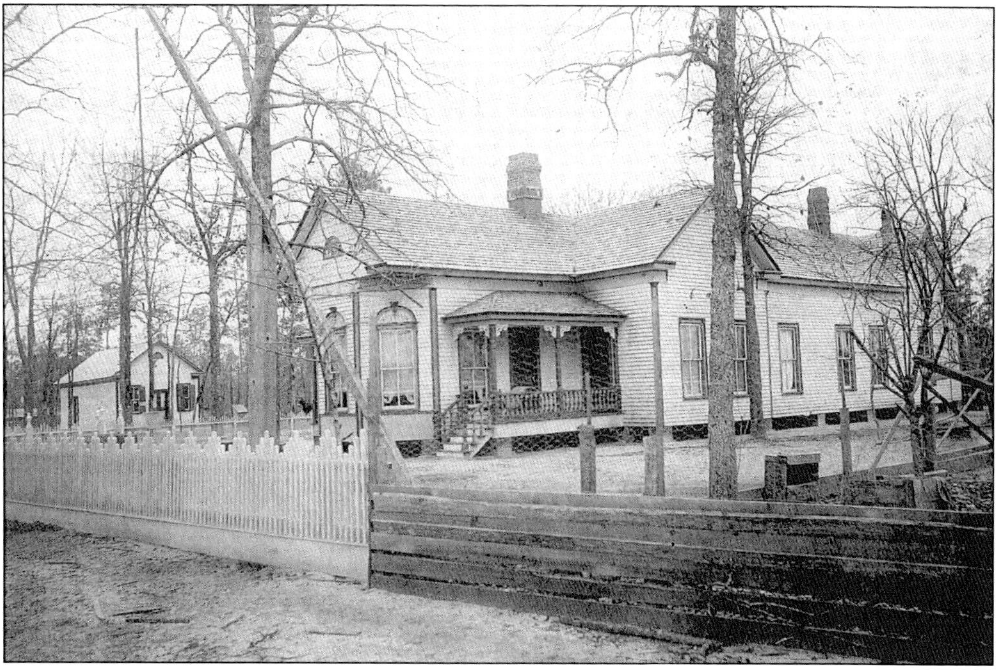

The J. Thomas Williams Place near Williams Lake, c. 1915. The Williams place had a view of a well sweep and the country store across the road. (Courtesy of Tom Williams.)

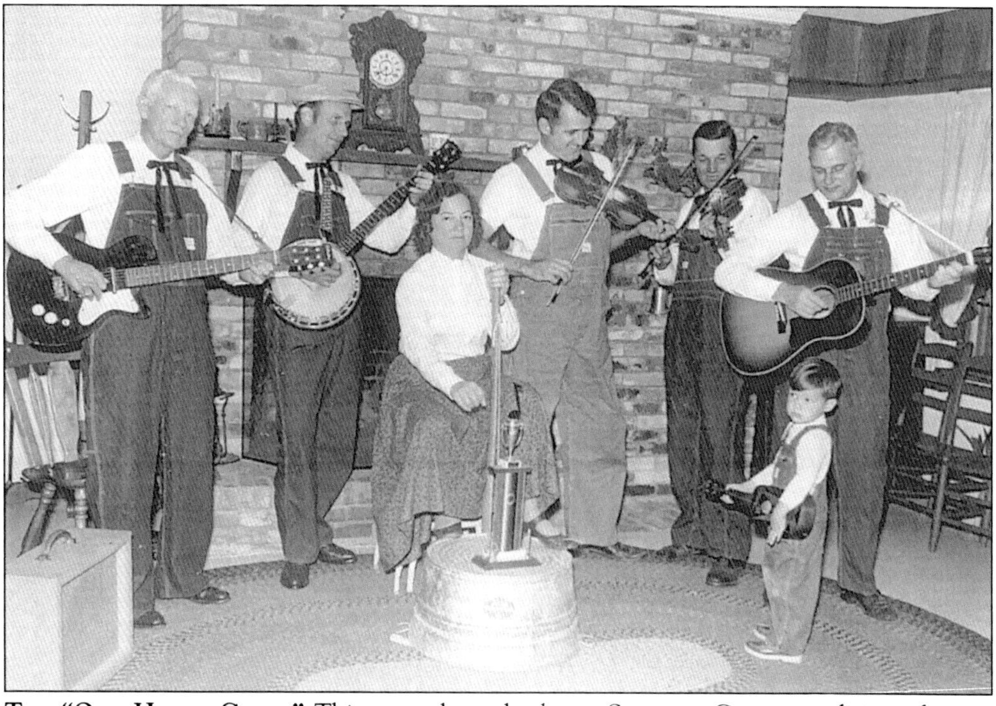

The "Out House Gang." This group kept the lower Sampson County tradition of string music alive well into the twentieth century. From left to right are Zeke Crumpler, Bill Lee, Fay Gaddy, Roland Matthis, Monk Matthis, Charles Gaddy, and Elliott Matthis. (Courtesy of George C. Burton.)

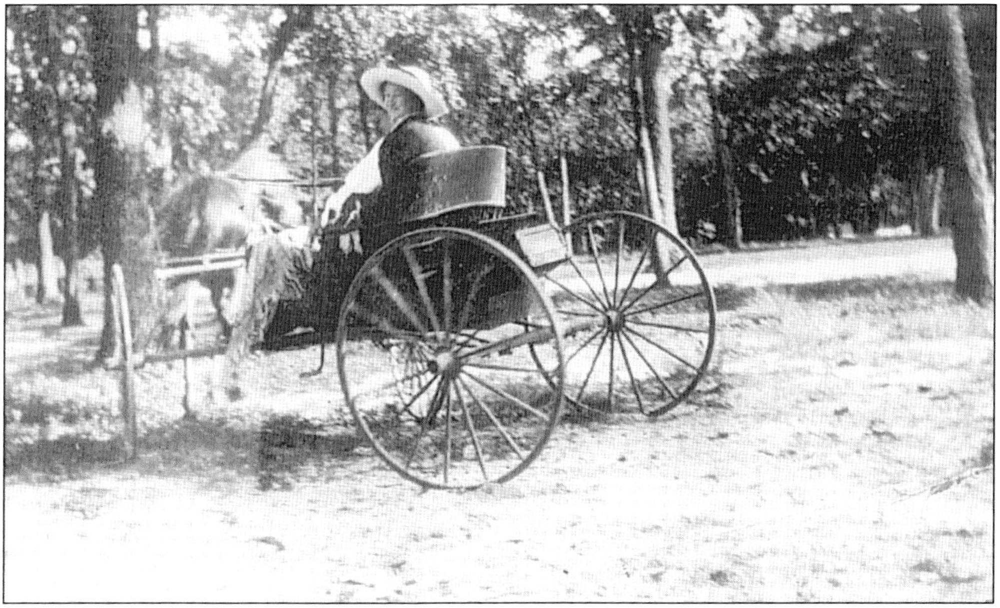

THE LEGENDARY EDNA ROBINSON, C. 1910. From the Ivanhoe vicinity, Robinson kept men in their place with a buggy whip, but she never married. She was one of the four daughters of John W. Scott Robinson; only one of her sisters married. (Courtesy of Catherine Solan.)

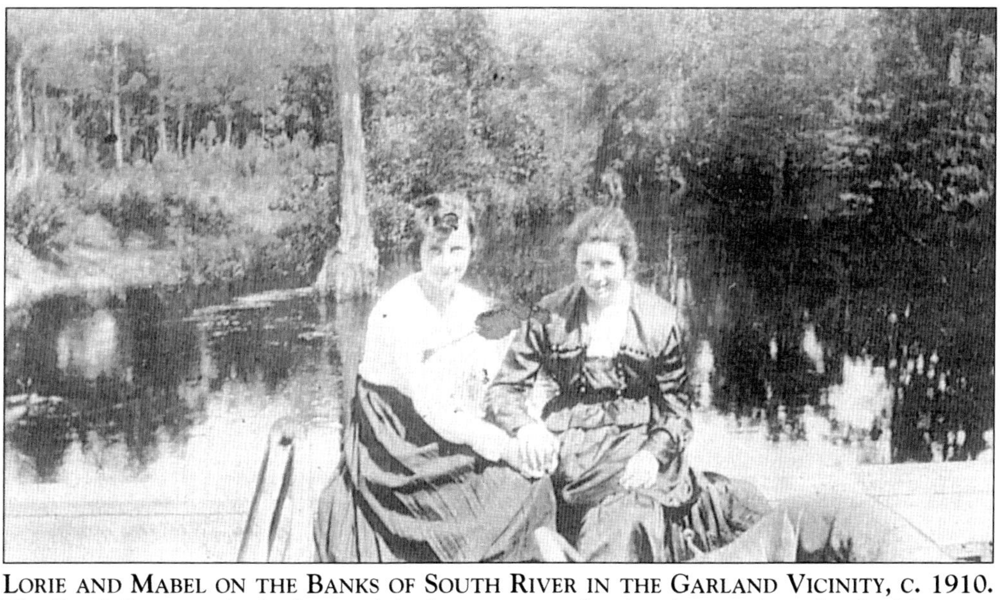

LORIE AND MABEL ON THE BANKS OF SOUTH RIVER IN THE GARLAND VICINITY, C. 1910. The South River, in the background, had seen many rafts of timber pass by its banks. (Courtesy of Catherine Solan.)

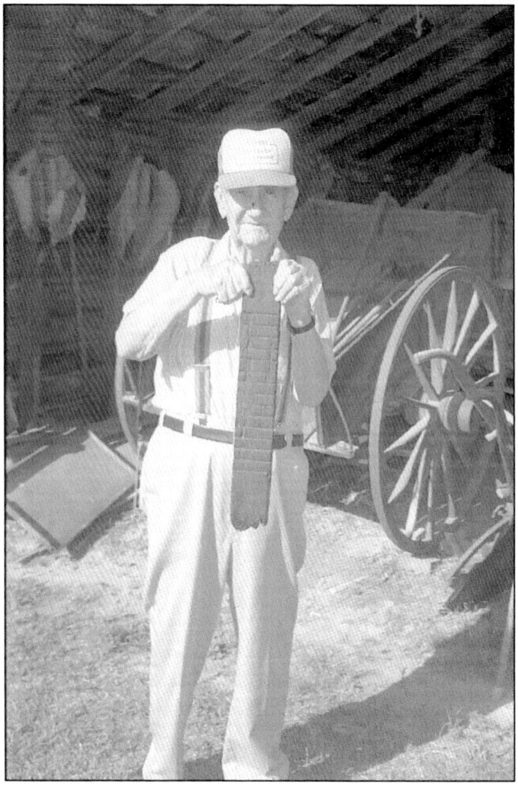

Mileage Marker. Held by Houston Wrench, this mile post with 15 notches in it marked the half-way point from Roseboro to Dunn. The mileage was measured by counting the revolutions of the buggy wheel. This marker was in the edge of Luther M. Wrench's farm yard and was preserved when the road was graded and widened earlier in the twentieth century. (Courtesy of Houston Wrench.)

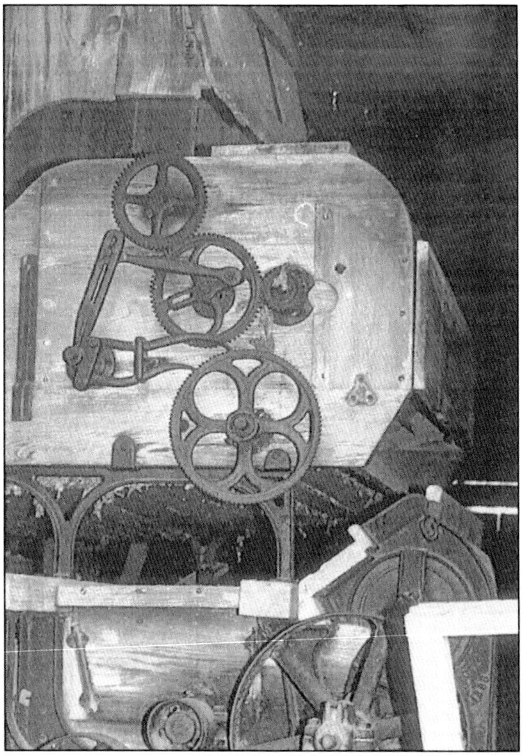

A Cotton Gin. This gin, built by A.J. Johnson in 1880, was powered by a 25-horsepower steam engine. Cotton was a major cash crop in the area of Clear Run in lower Sampson County, where markets were available because of river transportation. (Courtesy of Merrie and Amos Johnson.)

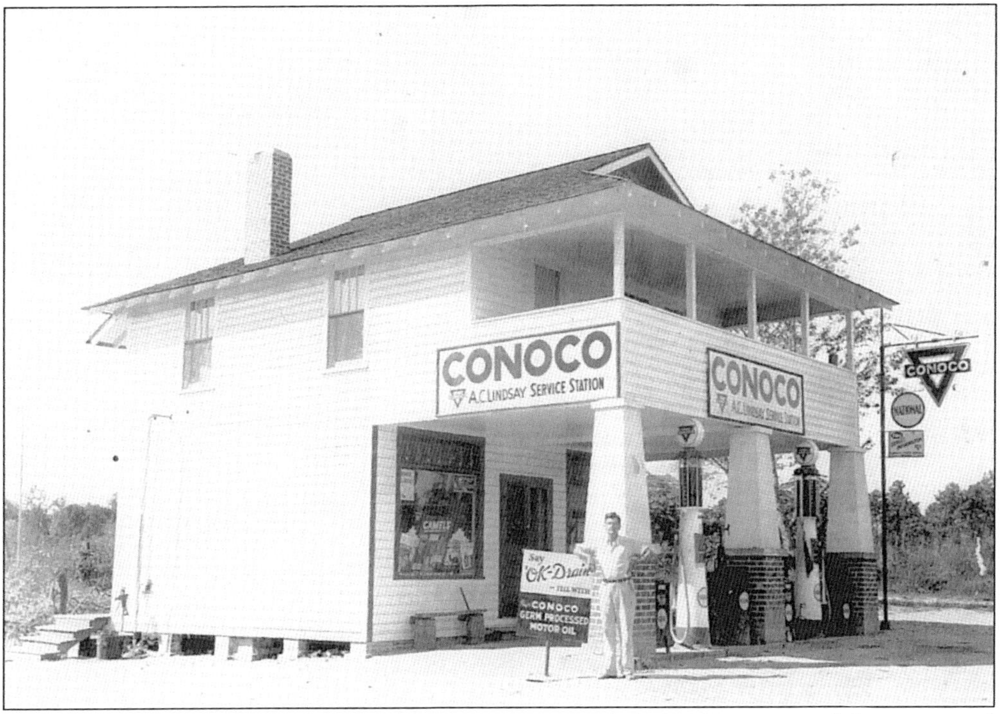

A COUNTRY STORE IN THE HOBBTON VICINITY, 1936. A.C. Lindsay operated this store until 1977, but he was not open on Sundays with the exception of a few Sunday afternoons during World War II. The Lindsay family lived above the store. Farmers spent many rainy days pushing soft drink caps across a cardboard checkerboard while tall tales were repeated and embellished. (Courtesy of Robert W. Lindsay.)

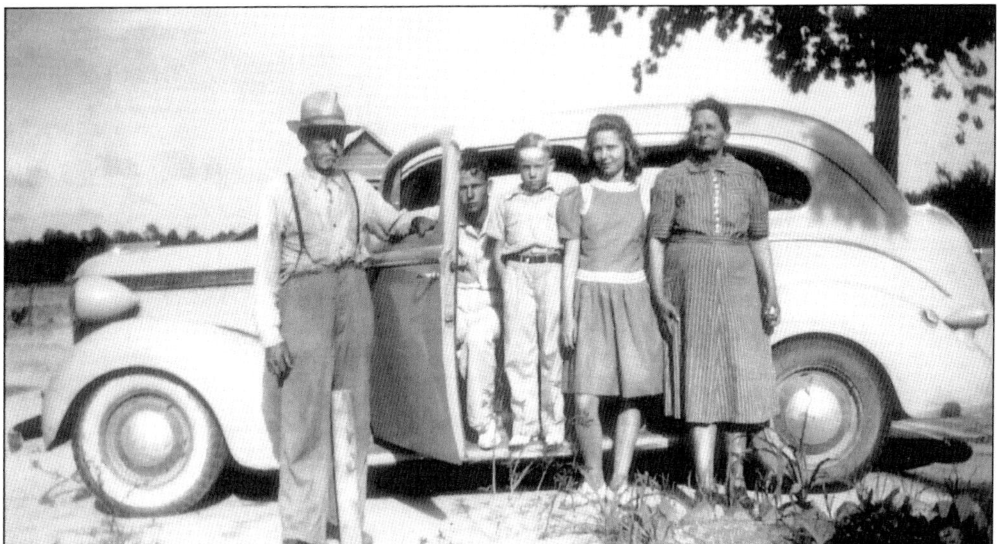

THE JOHN WRIGHT CARTER FAMILY OF THE INGOLD VICINITY, C. 1942. From left to right are John, Joe, Graham, Oleta, and Maggie Fryar Carter. Many farm families loaded up in the car and went to Clinton to shop on Saturday afternoons. (Courtesy of Don Carter.)

ACKNOWLEDGMENTS

This work is, first, a tribute to many of Sampson County's citizens and friends who were willing to share their treasured photographs with all who will enjoy and identify with the scenes presented in this book. These assorted images provide an invaluable glimpse into our past. Please take special note of the credits assigned to each image. The North Carolina Division of Archives and History, the Sampson County History Museum, Inc., the Sampson County Historical Society, and Mary John Parker all supplied either pictures or information for this project. Special thanks go to my wife, Margaret, for proofreading the text and to David F. King and Henry L. "Fes" Turlington, for their aid in collecting photos.